Aspen grove, Santa Catalina Mountains

SOUTHERN ARIZONA TRAILS

DAVID MAZEL
AND ROBERT BLAKE

WILDERNESS PRESS
BERKELEY

(formerly published as Arizona Trails)

First Edition June 1981
Second Edition August 1985
Third Edition March 1989
Second printing April 1991
Third printing December 1992
FOURTH EDITION January 1998

Photos by the authors except as noted
Front cover photo:
    Goosehead Rock, near Mt. Lemmon Highway, Santa Catalina
    Mountains—© 1998 by Randy A. Prentice
Back cover photo:
    Big Balanced Rock, Chiricahua National Monument
    —© 1998 by Robert Blake
Book design and production by Margaret Copeland
Map by Barbara Jackson
Drawings by Annie Mazel
Cover design by Larry B. Van Dyke

Library of Congress Card Catalog Number 97-42410
International Standard Book Number 0-89997-216-0

Manufactured in the United States of America

Published by   Wilderness Press
                2440 Bancroft Way
                Berkeley, CA 94704
                (800) 443-7227
                FAX (510) 548-1355
                wpress@ix.netcom.com
                www.wildernesspress.com
                Write, call, fax or email us for a free catalog

Library of Congress Cataloging-in-Publication Data

Mazel, David.
    Southern Arizona trails / David Mazel and Robert Blake. -- 4th ed.
        p.   cm.
    Rev. ed. of: Arizona trails. 3rd ed. 1989.
    Includes index.
    ISBN 0-89997-216-0
    1. Hiking--Arizona--Guidebooks. 2. Backpacking--Arizona-
-Guidebooks. 3. Arizona--Guidebooks. I. Blake, Robert, 1946-
II. Mazel, David. Arizona trails. III. Title.
GV199.42.A7M39 1998
917.9104'33--dc21   97-42410
                                                     CIP

Contents

Trailheads List

This is a list of the trailheads and the trips they are for (indicated by the numbers following the trailhead name). If (start) or (finish) come after the trip number, the trip is a shuttle trip.

1. **Canyon Lake**
   1, 5 (finish), 14 (finish)
2. **First Water**
   2, 3, 4, 5 (start), 6 (start), 7 (start)
3. **Tortilla & Tortilla Well**
   8, 20 (start), 21
4. **Peralta**
   6 (finish), 7 (finish), 9, 10, 11, 12, 13, 14 (start), 16 (finish), 20 (finish)
5. **JF and Woodbury**
   15, 16 (start), 17
6. **Rogers Trough** 18, 19
7. **Reavis** 22
8. **Romero Canyon** 23, 29 (finish)
9. **Magee Roadend**
   24, 25, 28 (finish)
10. **Cactus Picnic Ground**
    26, 27, 28 (start), 29 (start), 30 (start)
11. **Sabino Canyon Roadend**
    30 (finish), 31, 32 (start), 35 (finish), 36 (finish), 40 (finish)
12. **Lower Bear Canyon Picnic Ground** 32 (finish), 33
13. **Showers Point Campground**
    34, 35 (start)
14. **Mount Lemmon Highway**
    36 (start)
15. **Marshall Gulch Picnic Area**
    37, 38, 39, 40 (start)
16. **Douglas Spring Trailhead**
    41, 42, 46 (finish)

17. **Tanque Verde Trailhead** 43, 44
18. **Miller Creek** 45, 46 (start)
19. **Bog Springs Campground** 47
20. **Madera Canyon Roadend**
    48, 49, 50
21. **Florida Canyon Trailhead** 51, 52
22. **Rustler Park** 53, 54
23. **Turkey Creek Trailheads** 55, 56
24. **Rucker Camp** 57, 58
25. **South Fork Picnic Area** 59, 60
26. **Cave Creek** 61
27. **Echo Canyon Trailhead** 62
28. **Massai Point** 63
29. **Blue Lookout Roadend**
    64, 73 (finish)
30. **Lower Blue River** 65, 66
31. **Blue Camp** 67, 68, 69, 70
32. **Hanagan Meadow** 71 (start)
33. **Blue River** 74 (finish)
34. **Blue River South** 71 (finish)
35. **KP Cienega**
    72, 73 (start), 74 (start)
36. **Sheep Crossing** 75
37. **Phelps Cabin** 76
38. **Barnhardt Trailhead**
    77, 78, 79, 80, 82 (finish)
39. **City Creek Trailhead**
    81, 82 (start)
40. **Sheep Bridge** 83, 84

Foreword by the Co-author

Many hiking guidebooks cover one mountain range or the vicinity of one city in great detail. Such books are of enormous value to nearby residents and are listed in suggested reading lists within this book. But what of the casual visitor with only a few weeks in the area? Is this person to buy and lug around an entire library of hiking books?

This book, *Southern Arizona Trails*, is intended for such visitors, as well as nearby residents who just don't wish to visit each and every trail in each and every range. *Southern Arizona Trails* is a sampler guidebook of trails and routes in six wilderness areas, one national park, one national monument, and a primitive area. While not a comprehensive guide to the trails of any of these areas (except Mount Baldy Wilderness), trips described range the gamut from some of the most popular hikes in the areas to some of the most obscure and isolated.

Originally published as *Arizona Trails*, *Southern Arizona Trails* is of value to owners of the original book as it has been extensively updated and includes new hikes. The Grand Canyon hikes were removed for this new edition. All of the trailheads were visited in spring, 1997, trip descriptions have been updated, and many of the trails have been re-hiked in their entirety.

Future editions will allow time to re-visit every foot of trail. If readers should happen to see a hiker holding a copy of *Southern Arizona Trails* while taking notes, that may be your co-author getting the next edition ready.

—Robert Blake

Acknowledgments

David Mazel

Many people helped to create this book. My brother Mark Mazel drove me to and from innumerable backcountry trailheads. My wife Annie Mazel contributed her drawings and considerable moral support. Sanford and Jeannine Mazel supported me both morally and materially through much of the work. Janice Fryling, Christopher Nyerges and Joe Southern printed the photographs. My sincerest thanks to them all.

I was assisted by many others, and I would like to thank them as well.

Virginia L. McCardle of Mesa;

Ken Barnes of Pasadena City College;

Pat Sullivan of McCurdy Nature Center;

Paulette L. Claus of the National Geographic Society;

Clay Baxter, Dean L. Berkey, Bernard H. Brunner, Charles W. Denton, Charles A. Dexheimer, Bob Dyson, James L. Kimball, John McKelvey, William L. Russel Jr., Jerald D. Tower, Donald A. Van Driel, Johnny R. Wilson, Steve R. Plevel and Lee Redding of the United States Forest Service; and Harthon L. Bill, Vicki H. Black, Karen Brantley, Mark Engler, Richard W. Marks, John C. O'Brien and Bruce W. Shaw of the National Park Service.

Acknowledgments

Robert Blake

I am grateful to the following people for their assistance in updating this book:

Bill Barcus, Payson Ranger District

Greg Hansen, Mesa Ranger District

Kevin Hood, Douglas Ranger District

Introduction

To some people, the thought of hiking or backpacking in Southern Arizona might seem ludicrous. After all, isn't the entire state just a vast, barren desert, bone-dry and choked with dust? Then, upon reflection, images come to mind that shatter the illusion: the amazing rock formations in Chiricahua National Monument; the sparkling springs found in the Superstition Wilderness; the gleam of winter snow on the rugged peaks encircling Tucson. Suddenly it becomes obvious that, tucked away in the undeveloped recesses of the state, there must exist a wealth of beautiful hiking country.

And so there does. As of 1997, Arizona contained nearly six million acres of land officially classified as wilderness by either the state or the federal government. Closed to motor vehicles, forever spared the scourges of modern "development," and containing a wide range of ecosystems and landforms, these wildlands can provide the wilderness enthusiast with a variety of memorable hiking experiences. You can camp out beneath cool forests of pine and fir, where the wind sighs fretfully in the boughs, or on the sere desert flats, where the nights are warm and full of stars. You can scramble up twisting, forgotten canyons, where you might stumble across the remains of an ancient Indian dwelling or the fresh track of a cougar or a bear. Whatever you are looking for in the outdoors—rushing streams, jagged peaks, mountaintop vistas that stretch for a hundred miles, without a city in sight—you can find it in Arizona, along with plenty of peace and quiet, challenge and adventure, and that indefinable quality called wilderness.

The purpose of this guide is twofold: to introduce you to some of this magnificent country, and to ensure that your visits to it are as safe, comfortable, and informed as possible. Trails in nine separate wilderness areas are included, grouped according to geographical similarities into four regions.

The *Superstition Wilderness* chapter covers hikes in the extremely rugged, relatively low-elevation Superstition Mountains near Phoenix. The *Southeastern Ranges* include the pine-topped Santa Catalina,

Rincon and Santa Rita mountains, all near Tucson, as well as the Chiricahua Mountains (including Chiricahua National Monument) in the extreme southeast corner of the state. The *Eastern Highlands* region takes in the White Mountains and the Blue Range, in east-central Arizona near the New Mexico border. The *Mazatzal Wilderness* is a region of high peaks and rugged desert country northeast of Phoenix.

How to Use this Book

▲ Each trip description contains a heading, which provides certain basic information at a glance. On a *round trip,* you can hike to a specific backcountry destination, then return to the trailhead via the same route. The mileage given for such a trip represents the total distance you will have to hike, both going and returning. On a *loop trip* you do not have to retrace your steps to return to your vehicle; you enter and leave the wilderness by different trails. Some treks begin and end at different trailheads, necessitating a *shuttle.* Car shuttles can be handled in a variety of ways. You can talk a friend into dropping you off at your departure point, then have him or her pick you up at your destination at a prearranged hour (or day). With two cars, you can park one vehicle at the destination, then transport the entire party to the jumping-off point in the other car (which will have to be picked up on the drive home). This is a very time-consuming and energy-inefficient method of handling long shuttles, though it works well for shorter ones. A more innovative approach is to split the party into two groups, which then hike the route in opposite directions, each ending up where the other began and returning with the other's vehicle. Car keys can be exchanged when the groups pass each other, though it is good insurance to provide each party with extra keys beforehand.

▲ Each trip has been graded for overall difficulty. *Leisurely* routes are generally under 5 or 6 miles long, and entail an *elevation gain* of less than 1000 feet. (The elevation gain listed for each trip takes into account all climbs of more than 40 feet, along the entire length of the route.) *Moderate* treks can be up to 12 or 14 miles long, with up to 2500 feet of elevation gain; anything harder than that is listed as *strenuous.* Many trips can be done either as dayhikes or backpacks. For example, a strenuous dayhike, when spread out over two or more hiking days, can become a moderate backpack. These numerical guidelines are only approximate; in borderline cases we have taken into consideration overall trail conditions, availability of shade and water along the route, and other, more subjective factors before making a classification.

⚠ Most of the trips fall into either the moderate or the strenuous category, but that does not mean this guide is only for athletic hikers—*nowhere is it written that you must hike a particular trip's entire length in order to have an enjoyable outing.* On many trips a saddle, a hilltop, or a stream crossing partway along the route makes a natural turnaround point for the more leisure-oriented backcountry explorer.

⚠ Because weather patterns fluctuate widely from year to year, it is difficult to recommend an ideal hiking season for many of the trips. The seasons given should be considered only rough guidelines; before setting out on a trip in an unfamiliar area it is always a good idea to check the regional weather summaries that appear in the newspapers.

⚠ Each trip heading has a water summary, which lists places where water is likely to be available during the trip's recommended season. To help you determine how much water you will need to carry, the distances of these points from the trailhead are given in parentheses. In most areas, streams and springs rely heavily on winter and summer precipitation for replenishment; during drier-than-normal years, all water sources not listed as "year-round" should be considered suspect, and should be checked out with the appropriate government agency (listed at the end of each chapter's preface). During wetter-than-normal years, water will generally be available at places other than just those listed in the summary.

⚠ The figures in parentheses indicate distance (in miles) from the trailhead, and elevation (in feet) of the point in question. These are usually given at readily recognizable places along the route—at passes, stream crossings, trail junctions, and so on.

⚠ Campsites are listed as being poor, fair, good, or excellent, depending on such factors as the scenic value of the setting, availability of water and shade, and overall "feel." Most sites mentioned will have a small fire ring and cleared area, though in less frequently visited areas the term "campsite" or "tentsite" may be used simply to denote a good spot to bed down, even if it shows no evidence of previous use.

⚠ The topographic maps that cover each hike are listed at the beginning of each trip. A fold-out map in the back of the book shows all trailheads for the trips in this book, and which trips they are for.

⌃ Trails in this guide range in condition from carefully constructed, frequently maintained "highways," such as the Chiricahua National Monument's well maintained trails, to routes that are almost entirely cross-country. If a given trail might prove too difficult for beginners, this is noted in the short introduction which proceeds each trip description. On these fainter routes you will often find *ducks, cairns* and *blazes* to help guide you. A duck consists of one or two small stones placed conspicuously on top of a bigger rock. A cairn is a larger, more obvious pile of many stones. A blaze is a gash (usually in the shape of an "i") carved in the bark of a tree with an axe.

⌃ Junctions are listed as signed or unsigned, but bear in mind that trail signs are not fixed features of the landscape. (Unethical hikers sometimes use them for firewood, or cart them home as "souvenirs.") A "poorly signed" junction is one where a sign is in place, but is unreadable due to vandalism or weathering.

Life Zones

Plants tend to form distinct communities whose nature depends on elevation and exposure. Hence any particular community will be found wherever the elevation and exposure are right. The concept of "life zones"—the notion that most plant species can prosper only within limited elevation ranges—is useful for grouping plants that are commonly found together. The most common trees and shrubs in Arizona in each zone, called "indicators" for that zone, are shown in the table below.

Hikers who are familiar with Arizona's life zones can use the concept as a sort of crude "altimeter" when traveling in unfamiliar areas. When plants are mentioned in the text, it is not our intention to give an exhaustive account of the local flora, but merely to help you visualize the sort of country you will be hiking through. As for wildflowers, those mentioned in the text represent only those which we *saw* and *identified* during the particular *season* we did our field-checking. Other visitors, hiking in a different season, perhaps, or with sharper eyes, will likely see other flowers as well.

Equipment

Since even the easiest trips in this guide venture into fairly rugged country, every hiker will want to wear a pair of sturdy, well-broken-in boots. A wide-brimmed hat, sunscreen, and sunglasses are rarely amiss; even on cool winter days, the sun's glare can be uncomfortable.

During the summer and winter rainy seasons you will need a poncho or parka. In the cooler months, or when hiking in the high country, always carry a windbreaker and a warm sweater. In general, clothing should be sturdy and loose-fitting; wear cotton for warm weather, wool or synthetic fleece for cold weather. All hikers should carry an emergency kit (containing matches, money, and a whistle in addition to first-aid items), a compass, extra food, maps, and this book. On most trips you will have to carry water; make sure your containers are sturdy and leakproof.

Backpackers will find they need nothing unusual in the way of gear, aside from extra water containers. Those unfamiliar with the tasks and disciplines of backpacking may wish to consult *Backpacking Basics*, also published by Wilderness Press, an excellent guide for the novice.

Maps

One of the most useful articles that can be carried, whether on a dayhike or an extended backpacking trip, is an up-to-date map. The topographic quadrangle maps have contour lines, showing elevations. When the hiker has learned to interpret such maps it will be possible to see at a glance: where the trail enters a drainage or climbs a ridge; where the trail rises or falls in elevation; where the terrain is steep or fairly level. The map can also show the location of springs but cannot tell which springs are useful. The topographic maps also show great detail but can be very out of date. One, for the Superstition Wilderness, dates to 1948. Old maps often do not show all the trails and roads that access an area. Also, many hikes require several topo maps. A wilderness map is often not as detailed as the topographic map, but it has enough detail to follow a trail and is usually kept fairly up to date. These sell for $4-$5 at ranger stations or visitor centers (same maps, different prices—Roosevelt Lake Visitor Center, en route from the Mazatzals to the Superstitions has the $4 maps and a wide selection) or at the big map shops and outdoor suppliers of Tucson and Phoenix, where they cost a lot more. Recreation maps are potentially the most useful of all. For example, one recreation map uses both front and back to cover the same terrain as the corresponding wilderness map and gives a better scale. However recreation maps vary in quality. At least one such map was seen to have a recent year in large print, but smaller print showed that the map was a reprint from many years earlier. The largest hiking club in the state, based in Tucson, publishes excellent recreation maps. See the Appendix for a list of places to buy maps.

Hazards and Precautions

Dehydration

Anytime you are not sure of water availability along your route, carry *at least* ½ gallon of water per person per day—1 gallon or more during hot weather. It is better to store your water in several small containers than in a single large one—it is easier to handle, and a single leak will not endanger your whole supply.

Unfortunately, giardiasis contamination has become a problem in many areas. Many chemical water-treatment methods are ineffective against the giardia organism, so all water taken from streams and springs should be boiled or filtered before drinking. Consult the annual *Backpacker* magazine *GearGuide* issue in selecting a water filter.

If you entertain paranoid visions of dying of thirst on any of these hikes, remember that most of this book's trips are short enough that you could reach one trailhead or another in a forced march of less than a day. (Many of the trailheads, however, have no water supplies, so it is wise to keep a few gallons in your car.) If for some reason you find yourself out of water and more than a day's walk from help, the best thing to do is probably to walk *out* the same way you can *in*. To conserve your body's water, maintain a moderate, "no sweat" pace, and wear long-sleeved clothing. In moderate temperatures you will not die of thirst in two days' time, which is long enough to get out of any area reached by this book's hikes. In an extreme case, dehydration might begin to impair your judgment by that time; this is the reason for turning around and hiking out on a familiar trail (unless, of course, you are well past your trip's halfway point). Do *not* go off willy-nilly in search of water. You probably won't find any, and will only confuse the efforts of those who may eventually have to come looking for you. Always let someone back in town know your planned route and schedule, and then *stay on that route*.

Weather

In many areas of the state, between mid-June and early September, hardly a day goes by without a spectacular afternoon thunderstorm. If you see cumulus clouds building up nearby, avoid ridges, hilltops and flat, open area. Remember that thunder heard in the distance may be right on top of you in a matter of minutes, so move *quickly* to the nearest safe place.

Which spots are safest during an electrical storm? Best of all is the base of a steep slope or cliff. In open country, head for any sort of depression and squat down, after ditching any metal gear a safe distance away.

Summertime is also flash-flood season, and washes and canyon bottoms should be abandoned if a heavy storm appears to be brewing. Backpackers are similarly advised to resist the temptation to bed down in the luxuriously soft sand of dry streambeds. (Sand is very hard to sleep on anyway because it compacts.)

Though not the norm, heavy rain (and snow at higher altitudes) is possible throughout the winter months. Occasionally a low-pressure system will stray in from the Pacific coast and sit over the state for several days, causing thoroughly miserable hiking conditions (but also replenishing springs and streams, and preparing the land to explode with spring wildflowers). Such storms can sometimes mire access roads so badly that hikers may find themselves stranded for several days at their trailhead. Such occurrences can usually be avoided by checking the local weather forecast before leaving home.

Extreme heat and cold are best avoided by hiking a trip within its recommended season. Should you feel an irresistible urge to hike during hot weather, there are several ways to increase the safety and enjoyment of your trip:

1. Choose a hike that is both physically easy and easy to follow.

2. Carry at least 1 gallon of water per person per day, if none will be available en route.

3. Wear a hat, and light-colored, loose-fitting, long-sleeved cotton clothing. (This helps reduce water loss through sweating. Many hikers will prefer to wear little more than a pair of shorts; this is fine, but only if plenty of water is available for drinking and if you use a sunblock.)

4. Hike early in the morning or late in the afternoon. If the moon is near full, try hiking at night—the desert can be enchanting by moonlight.

5. Take it easy—rest and drink frequently, before you feel you need to.

Venomous Creatures

Rattlesnakes are found in nearly every corner of the state, but are not aggressive and will not strike unless they feel cornered. Should you be bitten, *remain calm*—adrenaline may compound the toxicity of the venom, and a quickened pulse only serves to spread it faster. Have a member of the party go for help immediately, unless it is only an hour or two to the trailhead, in which case the victim can be carried out by companions. In many cases, he or she will be able to walk out unassisted. Someone should still precede the main party, to arrange for help to be available at the trailhead.

Cut-and-suck snakebite kits are available at sporting-goods and some drug stores, and should be carried if you will be hiking alone or far from civilization. For short trips they are not necessarily recommended, as the do-it-yourself surgery required may be riskier than any rattler's venom. If you elect to carry one, know how to use it. Before cutting, remember that the victim's chance of survival is very high, even with no treatment at all.

Scorpions. Only two species of Arizona scorpions—each attaining a length of no more than 2"—are potentially fatal to humans, and these have so far killed only a few small children. The larger, more common species of scorpion can inflict a painful wound, but if stung you need hardly say your prayers.

Coral Snakes. This beautifully banded, venomous serpent is rarely seen, and has never been known to bite a human, much less kill one. It can be distinguished from the similar false coral snake by noting the arrangement of the colored bands: red adjoins black in the false coral, whereas red adjoins cream in the true.

The **Gila monster,** one of only two venomous lizards known to science, is a chubby, stub-nosed fellow who grows to be about a foot long. Gila monsters may be identified by their beaded, black-and-tan splotched skin. Although their venom is potentially fatal, they are too sluggish to be of concern to humans. (Only people who actually pick them up and handle them have been known to be bitten.)

Centipedes and **tarantulas** can also give a painful bite, but are never fatal.

Any bite, whether poisonous or not, carries with it the possibility of bacterial infection, and should be washed thoroughly, disinfected, and bandaged. The surest way to avoid these creeping and slithering hazards is to watch where you place your hands and feet. Be particularly careful when stepping over rocks and logs or when walking through brush. At night, zip your tent doorway up a few inches. If you have no tent, prop up the perimeter of your groundcloth with small branches or stones.

Killer bees have now reached Arizona, and several people have been attacked and several have died as a result of multiple stings. While an individual killer bee sting is no more dangerous than that of the honey bee, killer bees are more likely to attack in numbers. Give any bee respect and room.

Rules, Regulations and Backcountry Courtesy

The days are long past when one could go into the wilderness, cut down trees and branches to build shelters and feed roaring bonfires, and in general do as one pleased. Today's wilderness is too scarce and fragile a resource to be treated cavalierly; as backcountry use increases, it becomes increasingly crucial that all visitors heed the following common-sense rules and regulations:

1. Camp at least 100 feet from streams, farther from springs (to avoid spooking the shy wildlife which depends on them for water). Avoid sleeping in meadows or on soft vegetation; bedding down on pine duff is almost as comfortable and far less destructive.

2. Bury human waste under at least 6" of soft, biologically active soil, far from water sources, trails, and popular campsites.

3. Soap (including biodegradable soap) must be kept out of streams and springs. If you must use soap, carry a pot of water to your camp and do your washing there.

4. Anglers will need a valid Arizona state fishing license.

5. When fire and smoking restrictions are in effect on national forest lands, smoking is not permitted while traveling through designated areas. Campstoves may be used when most fire restrictions are in effect. Also, when there is no firewood available to boil water or prepare food, a lightweight backpacking stove can add a lot of comfort to the outdoor experience.

6. Cutting switchbacks eventually destroys trails, and is illegal in national forests and parks.

7. In any wilderness area, you are required to pack out what you pack in.

8. Pack and saddle stock have the right-of-way on trails; hikers should move a few feet off the trail and stand quietly until the animals pass.

9. Cutting plants and trees (including dead but standing snags), tormenting wild animals, chopping down signs, and painting rocks are all prohibited.

10. In national forests, group size is limited to 15 persons; the stay limit is 14 days.

11. As of this writing, wilderness permits are not needed to enter Arizona's national forest wildernesses, but they may be in the future. In Saguaro National Park backpackers must obtain a

permit to camp within the park (available at the park visitor centers). Chiricahua National Monument allows camping only in the established campground.

Ultimately, the only protection which our wildlands enjoy lies not in rules such as those above, but in the attitudes of people who visit them. All of us who love this magnificent wilderness country would do well to remember that we have not inherited it from our parents, but have only borrowed it from our children. Let's return as much of it as we can to them.

Further Reading

Flowers of the Southwest Mountains (5th edition), by Leslie P. Arnberger and Carolyn Dodson (Southwest Parks and Monuments Association, Tucson, Arizona, 1983)

Flowers of the Southwest Deserts (9th edition), by Natt N. Dodge and Carolyn Dodson (Southwest Parks and Monuments Association, Tucson, Arizona, 1983)

Desert Hiking (3rd edition), by Dave Ganci (Wilderness Press, Berkeley, California, 1993)

Desert Wildlife, by Edmund C. Jaeger (Stanford University Press, Stanford, California, 1961)

The Desert Year, by Joseph Wood Krutch (University of Arizona Press, Tucson, Arizona, 1985)

Voice of the Desert: A Naturalist's Interpretation, by Joseph Wood Krutch (William Morrow and Co., New York, New York, 1955)

Woody Plants of the Southwest, by Samuel H. Lamb (Sunstone Press, Santa Fe, New Mexico, 1977)

Desert Tree Finder: A Pocket Manual for Identifying Desert Trees, by May Theilgaard Watts and Tom Watts (Nature Study Guild, Berkeley, California, 1974)

Rocky Mountain Tree Finder: A Pocket Manual for Identifying Rocky Mountain Trees, by Tom Watts (Nature Study Guild, Berkeley, California, 1972)

Backpacking Basics, by Thomas Winnett and Melanie Findling (Wilderness Press, Berkeley, California, 1994)

Arizona Atlas & Gazeteer, by DeLorme Mapping (DeLorme Mapping, Freeport, Maine, 1993)

Area 1—The Superstition Wilderness

Comparatively low in elevation, arid, and exceptionally rugged and beautiful, the 160,000+ acre Superstition Wilderness affords some of the finest desert hiking to be found anywhere. Elevations range from under 2000 feet, in the canyons of the west end, to over 6000 feet in the eastern uplands. This is less vertical relief than is found in the other regions covered by this guide, but don't be fooled—this is extremely rugged country, ringed with cliffs, studded with thorny cacti, and shot through the steep-walled, deeply eroded canyons. The fact that these mountains have survived as wilderness, in spite of their proximity to the sprawling Phoenix metropolitan area, is a testament to their harshness and inaccessibility. The periphery of the wilderness area is in fact visible from within the city limits, but once one enters the more remote parts of the backcountry, the city could just as well be a thousand miles away.

The highest point in the western part of the wilderness is 5077-foot Superstition Mountain. A number of narrow canyons drain north-westward from here, slicing through a once-rolling landscape of mesas and hills before emptying into the Salt River. To the south, the land falls abruptly away along a steep escarpment to the floor of the Arizona desert. The vegetation in this western area consists primarily of a typical Lower Sonoran mixture of paloverde, saguaro, prickly pear and hedgehog cactus, jojoba and creosote bush, with some Upper Sonoran plants such as agave, mountain mahogany, and shrub live oak showing up at higher elevations. A smattering of single-leaf pinyon pines are found in the Pinyon Camp area near Fremont Saddle, and small copses of cottonwood, sycamore, netleaf hackberry, sugar sumac, velvet ash, and Arizona walnut grow near springs and along canyon bottoms. Except for the fairly common collared peccary, or javelina, the local mammalian life is mostly nocturnal; the largest animal you are likely to see (by moonlight, probably) is a striped or spotted skunk, a raccoon, a woodrat or a ringtail cat. In the daytime you will almost surely be able to spot a Cooper's or a red-tailed hawk, possibly a golden eagle as well. In the spring, a host of smaller birds can be identified in forested, well-watered areas.

The eastern half of the wilderness is considerably higher than the western, with dense chaparral cloaking its sunnier slopes, and pockets of pinyon pine, one-seed juniper, alligator juniper and ponderosa pine growing in shadier, more sheltered places. Stream-courses are more likely to have water here than in the west, and their serene, oak- and sycamore-shaded banks can provide delightful camping. Being harder to reach from Phoenix, this area is also less frequently visited; hence hikers here have a greater chance of finding genuine solitude, and of glimpsing such shy animal residents as the cougar, the desert mule deer, and the black bear.

Both halves of the Superstitions are uncomfortably hot between May and October, but summer hiking can be feasible in the eastern area *if* you begin your trip very early in the morning, early enough to reach your destination before the hottest part of the day. Violent thunderstorms are quite common in July and August, and often provide a measure of relief from the midday heat. Winter temperatures are generally pleasant, but visitors should be prepared for an occasional downpour. In the higher elevations, be equipped for cold weather and the possibility of light-to-moderate snowfall.

The Superstitions contain no perennial streams, and even the most reliable springs have been known to become unpotable during drought years. For dayhikes and short backpacking trips, it is advisable to carry all the water you need; this is not only the safest policy, but it also frees you of the necessity of camping near springs. (Please remember that many wildlife species depend on these springs for their water, too, but will not use them if they see humans nearby—try to make your camp at least a few hundred yards away.) Lengthy backpacking trips should be attempted only after it rains, when springs and streams are likely to have water.

Under provisions of the Wilderness Act of 1964, some cattle grazing is currently allowed within the wilderness area. This grazing does not cause *too* much of a disturbance ecologically, we are assured by the Forest Service, but the sight of a decidedly tame heifer in otherwise wild country detracts mightily from the area's wilderness aura. Cows can also foul springs, leave their droppings in otherwise attractive campsites, and in myriad other small ways make nuisances of themselves. One can only hope that existing grazing allotments will be gradually phased out over the next several years.

The geological history of the Superstition Mountains is complex. During the mid-Cenozoic era, about 30 million years ago, this was gently sloping, open country, located between the geologically stable Colorado Plateau region and the far more active Basin and Range province. About 29 million years ago, in response to forces not yet fully understood, hot lava bubbled up from deep within the earth, forming a cluster of mountains rising 2-3000 feet above the surrounding level. This activity was later followed by a series of more violent eruptions, which spread a thick carpet of volcanic ash over a wide area. As this layer thickened, the hot ash was compressed by its own weight and welded together to form the rock known as "tuff." So much magma was ejected in these tremendous eruptions that the surface rocks caved in for lack of support, forming a gigantic pit, or "collapse caldera," about 9 miles in diameter. Another siege of volcanic activity pushed up the center of this caldera to form the present steep-walled Superstition Mountain area. The debris from these explosions was not hot enough to fuse into tuff; instead it formed the pale yellow rock which is now exposed at Palomino Mountain and on top of Battleship Mountain and Geronimo Head. Some 18-15 million years ago, black lava oozed out of the caldera, hardening into the dark basalt layer which presently caps Black Mesa and Black Top Mesa. The current rugged relief of the Superstition Mountains' interior is due mainly to water erosion, particularly the scouring action of repeated flash floods. Weaver's Needle, the single most dominant landmark in the wilderness, is a tall spire of dark lava that apparently hardened in the neck of a volcano and was subsequently exposed by erosion. (The Needle, by the way, was named for Pauline Weaver, a (male) frontier scout. The local Indians are said to have referred to it with a far more graphic name—the word that meant, in their language, "stallion's penis.")

The human history of the region goes back at least 700 years; ruins of the Hohokam and Salado Indian cultures have been found and dated at 1200-1300 AD. (Trips 17, 19, and 21 visit the site of one Salado dwelling.) After the abandonment of these sites (an unexplained event, presumably related to the wholesale abandonment of hundreds of similar dwellings across the Southwest), Apache raiders found the rugged range to be a secure base from which to conduct forays against Tohono O'odham and Pima Indians, and later against white settlers.

Many readers will recognize the Superstition Mountains as the (alleged) home of the (equally alleged) Lost Dutchman Gold Mine. In all probability this mine never existed, but the legends concerning it are interesting enough to be touched on lightly here. Many variations exist, the most commonly told story being that, in the early 1800's, one Don Miguel Peralta discovered a fabulously rich vein of gold somewhere in the inaccessible reaches of what was then northern Mexico, on land that had been awarded to the Peralta clan by the Spanish Crown. The lode was named "El Sombrero," after a distinctive, hat-shaped peak which loomed within sight of the mine. (The yarn-spinners invariably equate this peak with Weaver's Needle.) Following the Mexican-American War, the Peraltas hurried northward to milk their mine one last time, before the land surrounding it would be ceded to the United States. In its haste, the party purportedly left itself open to Indian attack, and was almost completely wiped out by a band of Apaches.

Some 30 years later, the legend goes on, a man named Jacob Waltz—the Dutchman—saved the life of one of the survivors of the Peralta massacre, who divulged the mine's location out the gratitude. Waltz furtively worked the mine for years; those who tried to follow him to his treasure either got lost in the Superstitions' labyrinthine canyons or were ambushed and killed outright by the wily Waltz. The Dutchman died in 1891, without ever revealing the location of the mine—though he left behind enough "hints" that a small army of rainbow riders has been searching for it to this day.

Hikers should be aware that this legend has absolutely no basis in verifiable fact. The "Peralta Grant" never existed, but was merely a fabrication perpetrated as part of James Addison Reavis' infamous land fraud scheme of the late 1800's. Contemporary newspapers never mentioned a man named Waltz as having a mine of any value; if the Dutchman did show up in Phoenix from time to time, loaded down with gold about which he kept rather quiet, he may have simply been acting as a fence for dishonest laborers, who were "high grading" (filching) ore from nearby mines. To the professional geologist, the idea that there could be gold in these mountains is ludicrous on its face, a volcanic field being the last place one would expect to find precious metals. The Superstition region has in fact been investigated by the U.S. Bureau of Mines, whose report states flatly that it is a "non-mineralized area."

Unfortunately, so powerful is the Lost Dutchman legend that such disclaimers have failed to prevent the aforementioned self-styled "prospectors" from digging around in search of the mythical treasure; several of the hikes in this chapter lead past the ugly scars they have left behind. And they are still looking! Wilderness enthusiasts will be glad to know that mining activity within the wilderness area has been put on hold until the validity of existing claims can be determined. Unfortunately, illegal activities remain a serious problem. Eventually, one hopes, the legend will no longer be taken seriously, and visitors to this beautiful, wild region will be more prone to appreciate its fabulous scenery, curious wildlife and challenging trails. It is these things, after all, which constitutes the *real* treasure of the Superstition Mountains.

Managing Agencies

Forest Supervisor's Office
Tonto National Forest
2324 E. McDowell
P.O. Box 5348
Phoenix, AZ 85010
(602) 225-5200

Mesa Ranger District
26 N. MacDonald Street
P.O. Box 5800
Mesa, AZ 85201-5800
(602) 379-6446

Further Reading

Hiker's Guide to the Superstition Wilderness, by Jack Carlson and Elizabeth Stewart (Clear Creek Publishing, Tempe, Arizona, 1995)

Tales of the Superstitions, by Robert Blair (Arizona Historical Foundations, Tempe, Arizona, 1975)

The Treasure of the Superstition Mountains, by Gary Jennings (W.W. Norton and Company, New York, New York, 1973)

Superstition Wilderness Management Plan (1972). Available for inspection at local Forest Service offices.

TRIP 1
CANYON LAKE TRAILHEAD TO INDIAN PAINT MINE

- ▲ **9.0 miles round trip; 1640' elevation gain**
- ▲ **Moderate dayhike or backpack (2 hiking days)**
- ▲ **Trailhead 1, Canyon Lake**
- ▲ **Maps**
  Superstition Wilderness or *Mormon Flat Dam quadrangle*
- ▲ **Season: November to April**
  *No permanent water along route; La Barge Creek (mile 3.9) and
  Boulder Creek (near mile 4.5) have water during rainy periods only*

Features

Indian Paint Mine is the primary destination of this fine trip, but
hardly its sole *raison d'etre*. For enroute to the mine the hiker encoun-
ters magnificent vistas at almost every turn—views of rocky,
saguaro-studded hillsides, of the rugged Mazatzal Range rising
above Salt River Canyon, and of the famous landmark of Weaver's
Needle embedded deep in the Superstition backcountry. An added
bonus is the opportunity to linger or camp in La Barge Canyon or
Boulder Canyon, either of which is a good bet to contain a clear, running stream during the rainy season.

Canyon Lake

Trailhead Route/Camping

From Apache Junction drive about 14 miles northeast on State Highway 88 to Canyon Lake. As the highway skirts the south side of this reservoir it crosses two narrow bridges; the trailhead is on the right-hand side of the highway just past the second bridge, 15.4 miles from Apache Junction. This approach is paved all the way. The trailhead can also be reached by driving 28.9 miles southwest on Highway 88 from Roosevelt Dam; 21.4 miles of this route are well-graded dirt road. Parking and/or camping is available across the street from the trailhead at the Canyon Lake Marina. Be sure to use the trailhead parking area to the right of the gate.

Description

The trailhead is located at the bridge adjacent to the Canyon Lake Marina entrance gate (0.0; 1680). Ignore the trail that leads along the lake; take the Boulder Canyon Trail which parallels the highway and a low fence, but then swings right and goes uphill steeply. As soon as we gain a little elevation a nice view opens up across the placid waters of Canyon Lake, backgrounded by the swelling foothills of the Mazatzal Mountains. The ground cover along this first part of the trail is rather sparse, consisting chiefly of yellow paloverde, buckhorn cholla, jojoba, brittlebush, pale green prickly pear, some medium-sized saguaros and a smattering of agave. A few faint side trails branch off here and there but the main trail is very well used and easy to follow.

After climbing several hundred feet we arrive at the top of a small hill (0.8; 2160) and the Superstition Wilderness Boundary sign. Behind the sign a short trail leads to a nice viewpoint. This is a good place to get acquainted with some of the more prominent landmarks of the western Superstitions, such as Geronimo Head (the high, rugged line of cliffs to the southeast), Battleship Mountain (the square-cut formation sitting atop the ridge which divides Boulder and La Barge canyons), and the obvious, slender pinnacle of Weaver's Needle. As we rise higher we will soon be able to see Superstition Mountain, the high point of the dark, massive ridges far to the south.

From this hilltop the trail continues to rise up a rocky hillside then follows the crest of a ridge. Soon we reach another hilltop (1.6, 2360) with an even better view. From here the trail follows the ridge while circling left of two small hilltops. At a small saddle beyond the first of these hills it is possible to look down into Boulder Canyon and La Barge Canyon and see whether there will be water available on the route ahead. From the second saddle the trail winds away to the right around some high hills. Eventually a ¾-mile long, switchbacking descent brings us to an unsigned fork at the bottom of the canyon. The right-hand path (blocked by a line of small stones to keep hikers from straying) leads down to La Barge Creek, which usually has running water from the beginning of the winter rainy season until April or so. (As with all streams in these arid mountains, the "live" season of this creek varies greatly from year to year, depending on weather conditions. Hikers who will not be packing in all of their water should contact the Forest Service and get an up-to-date report on the water situation before starting their trip).

The trail that goes straight here, paralleling the creek, is the continuation of our route, which leads upcanyon then crosses the stream (3.9, 1870). Hikers with time on their hands can make a worth-while sidetrip from this point: leave the trail at the crossing, and boulder-hop 1.3 miles directly up La Barge Creek to a fabulously spooky "box," or narrows, in the canyon. At its narrowest point this bottle-neck is only a few dozen yards across, with walls that rise almost vertically some 500' on either side. (Caution: do not enter this area if a heavy storm seems imminent.)

Beyond this crossing the trail leads gradually away from the creekbed into an area of red rocks stained with blotches of bright green lichens. Some nice saguaros and teddy-bear chollas grow along this section, as well as a few doughty scrub oaks. After a short, gentle climb we reach Paint Mine Saddle (4.5; 1960), just beyond which, on the left, is Indian Paint Mine. Here you will find a vertical mine-shaft and a few ruins. (Use caution if you approach the shaft closely.) Apparently nothing of any value was ever taken from the ground at this old site; like all the other "mines" which dot the Superstitions, this working was almost certainly a will-o'-the-wisp, a dead-end for some diehard prospector who felt sure he'd at long fast ferreted out the legendary Lost Dutchman lode. At least the deluded fellow was able to do his digging in a spectacular setting—the saddle affords magnificent view of Battleship Mountain, looming almost directly above, and of the cliffs of Geronimo Head, rising a sheer 1500' above La Barge Creek.

Backpackers looking for campsites would do well to continue downhill from Paint Mine Saddle about 200 yards to Boulder Creek, which has more water and more comfortable tentsites than La Barge. If for some reason you find yourself without water, and both Boulder and La Barge creeks are dry, water *may* be available at Second Water Canyon (see Trip 5).

Return the way you came.

TRIP 2
FIRST WATER TRAILHEAD TO GARDEN VALLEY AND BLACK MESA

- **6.6 miles round trip; 670′ elevation gain**
- **Leisurely dayhike**
- **Trailhead 2, First Water**
- **Maps**
  Superstition Wilderness or *Goldfield quadrangle*
- **Season: November to April**
  No reliable water available along route

Features

Black Mesa affords a superb view of Weaver's Needle, in addition to many other, less famous landmarks which it behooves the hiker to learn to recognize before venturing further into this rugged back-country. Along the way the route passes through dense fields of mesquite and paloverde, thickets of spiny cholla, and a "forest" of tall saguaros. All in all, this trip is an excellent introduction to the magnificent desert country of the western Superstitions.

Trailhead Route/Camping

From Apache Junction drive 5.7 miles northeast on State Highway 88, then turn right onto First Water Road (Forest Road 78). This point can also be reached by driving southwest 38.6 miles from Roosevelt Dam; the first 21.4 miles are well-graded dirt road. Follow First Water Road (OK for passenger cars) 2.6 miles to the parking area at its end, and pay the $4 trailhead parking fee. The Dutchman's Trail begins just beyond the Superstition Wilderness boundary sign. Dispersed camping is not permitted in this area. However, Lost Dutchman's State Park is adjacent to Forest Road 78 and offers campsites at $9/night. Trail connections from the state park day use area to Forest Road 78 permit hiking to the trailhead from the campsites and avoid the $4 trailhead parking. This will add 5-6 miles to the round trip hiking depending on campsite location.

Description

From the parking area at the end of the First Water Road (0.0; 2240) walk southeast along a heavily used trail a few hundred yards to a signed junction. Turn left and follow the path as it crosses First Water wash, then proceeds via a well defined path. Until recently, there were many confusing use-trails leading hikers astray but trail maintenance personnel have done a lot of work to eliminate confusion. At

Saguaros, paloverdes, and teddy-bear chollas above Garden Valley

a low saddle (0.8; 2280) a faint spur trail branches left; ignore this and
walk gently downhill to the right. After crossing a small drainage the
trail swings left and begins climbing north up the canyon of a tributary. About 0.5 mile later this rocky ascent tops out at the brink of
Garden Valley, a large flat between Hackberry and Black mesas. The
trail strikes off northward across this pretty area, threading dense
stands of foothill paloverde, honey mesquite and jumping cholla.
Doves, cactus wrens, curve-billed thrashers and Gambel's quail are
all common here, and observant hikers might also spot some
woodrat nests tucked away in the impenetrable cholla thickets, safely beyond the reach of inquisitive predators.

Soon the trail reaches the signed turnoff to Black Mesa (1.9; 2410),
where we turn right and resume climbing, almost imperceptibly at
first, then moderately. The dark, basaltic cap of Black Mesa is a remnant of the lava flows which bubbled out of the Superstition volcanic
field between 15 and 18 million years ago. Before huge parts of it
were breached and carried away by stream erosion, this basalt layer
covered a much larger area; today only portions of it remain, such as
at nearby Hackberry Mesa and at Blacktop Mesa, near Palomino
Mountain on the far side of Boulder Creek.

The gradient continues to steepen as we exit some nice stands of
teddy-bear cholla and work our way up a rocky draw planted with
stout saguaros. A mile later the route levels off again, this time at
Black Mesa. The view of Weaver's Needle rising up from far beyond

the flat expanse of this cholla-thicketed plateau is unforgettable. This vista can be especially enchanting on winter mornings, when the sun, hanging low in the southeastern sky, suffuses a fuzzy yellow glow across the foreground of spiny chollas.

About ¼ mile beyond the edge of the mesa, where the trail begins to descend gently toward the far side, there is a small clearing in the cholla. From here it is possible to work one's way left a few hundred yards, out of the cacti and up to a high point of the low ridge (3.3; 2850) north of the trail. With its fine views of Battleship Mountain, Geronimo Head, and high, swelling Superstition Mountain, this spot makes a good destination for today's trek.

Return the way you came, or continue on to Boulder Basin and return via the Dutchman's Trail (9.1 miles total; see Trip 4).

TRIP 3
FIRST WATER TRAILHEAD TO PARKER PASS, BOULDER BASIN, AND BLACK TOP MESA

▲ **11.2 miles round trip; 1870' elevation gain**
▲ **Moderate dayhike; leisurely to moderate backpack (2-3 hiking days)**
▲ **Trailhead 2, First Water**
▲ **Maps**
  Superstition Wilderness or *Goldfield quadrangle*
▲ **Season: November to April**
  Water available at West and East Boulder creeks (miles 3.6 and 4.4) during rainy periods only

Features
The Dutchman's Trail over Parker Pass offers the quickest access to the Superstition backcountry in the vicinity of Boulder Basin. Hikers can use this relatively easy entry route to save energy for greater endeavors—such as the stiff, 1,000-foot climb up to Black Top Mesa. This ascent is steep and laborious, but the fabulous view from Black Top's strategically located summit fully justifies the effort.

Trailhead Route
Follow the trailhead route for Trip 2.

Description
From First Water Trailhead (0.0; 2240), walk southeast along a heavily used trail a few hundred yards to the signed junction with the left-branching Second Water Trail. Turn right here, following the Dutchman's Trail (still a wide, heavily used trail at this point) as it

proceeds gently uphill, crosses First Water wash a few times, and then climbs more steeply toward a saddle on the left. The trail narrows to a bit as we drop slightly and then pass through another gap. Several faint spur trails branch off to either side through here; stay on the most worn pathway, which presently brings us to Parker Pass (2.5; 2630). Here there are good views back across the Goldfield Mountains, and forward to Palomino Mountain, Black Top Mesa and Weaver's Needle. Just to the north are the basalt cliffs of Black Mesa, and it is not hard to mentally extend this layer of solidified lava through space to meet the similar dark cap atop Black Top Mesa. These two formations were indeed once connected, part of the same lava flow; in the millennia since the Superstition volcanoes ceased erupting, erosion has carried away all but a few fragments of this once-extensive basalt layer.

From Parker Pass the trail winds gently downhill toward Boulder Basin, the flat at the base of Palomino Mountain. During this descent hikers may notice faint remains of use-trails that once confused hikers. After the trail levels off on the basin floor, it crosses the wash of West Boulder Creek (which does not generally flow until after a few good winter rains have replenished the water table), and then proceeds left (ignore the route to the right) to a signed junction with the left-branching Black Mesa Trail (4.1; 2280). (*Black* Mesa, the destination of Trip 2, should not be confused with *Black Top* Mesa, the goal of this trek.) There are some nice, but unshaded, campsites in this area, amid a smattering of mesquites and paloverdes. At the junction we continue straight ahead, climb up to a low ridge, and drop a short distance to the floor of East Boulder Canyon. Beyond here the trail leads past several faint, left-branching spurs (variants of the Boulder Canyon Trail), bringing us in less than ¼ mile to a junction marked by a signpost (4.4; 2300). Here, at the mouth of the deep gorge from which East Boulder Creek issues, the Bull Pass Trail branches left. This route begins faintly, but its continuation is plainly visible cutting up a hillside to the north.

Turning onto the latter, we cross East Boulder Creek (about as likely to have running water as its twin, West Boulder Creek), then climb steeply through a jumble of gigantic boulders which have spalled off the cliffs looming directly above. Beyond here the very rough trail veers to the right, then makes two switchbacks before arriving at Bull Pass (5.0; 2750). To reach Black Top Mesa from this sometimes windy gap, turn onto the faint pathway that can be seen branching off to the right. This climbs quite steeply at first, but the gradient eases as we gain the surprisingly grassy shoulder of the mesa. Soon the path grows very obscure, then peters out completely, leaving us to scramble the remaining few hundred feet to the top (5.6; 3354). From this centrally located summit one can pick out virtually every prominent landmark of the western Superstitions. Most obvious of these is Weaver's Needle, standing off to the southeast. Turning counterclockwise from this spire one next sees Needle Canyon, with Bluff Spring Mountain rising beyond it; then comes La Barge Canyon, backgrounded by the cliffs of Black and Malapais mountains, followed by Battleship Mountain, capping the divide between La Barge and Boulder canyons. Black Mesa rises beyond Boulder Basin; just to the left, and considerably closer, are the buff-colored cliffs of Palomino Mountain. To the southwest, in the distance, lie the massive, swelling ridges which culminate in 5057-foot Superstition Mountain.

The "Spanish Hieroglyphics" indicated on the topo as being nearby are neither Spanish nor hieroglyphics, but apparently just some nonsense associated with one of the many fruitless searches for the legendary Lost Dutchman treasure. These old graffiti are not easy to locate, and not particularly worth the trouble.

After soaking up the vista, return the way you came. Or return via the Black Mesa and Second Water Trails (12.0 miles total; reverse the steps of the first half of Trip 4.)

TRIP 4
FIRST WATER LOOP (FIRST WATER TRAILHEAD TO BLACK MESA, BOULDER BASIN, AND PARKER PASS)

- ▲ **9.1 mile loop trip; 920' elevation gain**
- ▲ **Moderate dayhike or leisurely backpack (2 hiking days)**
- ▲ **Trailhead 2, First Water**
- ▲ **Maps**
  Superstition Wilderness or *Goldfield quadrangle*
- ▲ **Season: November to April**
  Water available at West Boulder creeks (mile 4.7) during rainy periods only

Features

After sampling the interesting desert-plant communities of Garden Valley, and the spectacular views to be had from atop Black Mesa, this route drops down to Boulder Basin, where backpackers will find good campsites and ample sidetrip opportunities. The Dutchman's Trail provides for a change of scenery on the return route; this is, in fact, one of the few Superstition loop trips which is both highly scenic and short enough to appeal to most dayhikers.

Weaver's Needle from near Terrapin Pass

Trailhead Route

Follow the trailhead route for Trip 2.

Description

From First Water Trailhead (0.0; 2240), follow the route of Trip 2 to the cholla clearing atop Black Mesa (3.0; 2750), then continue along the Black Mesa Trail as it leads gently downhill in the general direction of Weaver's Needle. About 0.5 mile later the gradient steepens abruptly, and the trail soon swings left into a well-defined canyon. After we cross back and forth across a small wash, this canyon bends to the left; here our route veers right and climbs gently a short distance to a minor saddle (4.4; 2590). As the trail leaves this gap and works its way downhill, we are treated to some fine views of buff-colored Palomino Mountain, a heavily eroded remnant of the tuff layers laid down by the primordial Superstition volcanoes. Behind Palomino Mountain rises the graceful volcanic plug of Weaver's Needle.

The occasionally steep and rocky descent from Black Mesa soon ends, and the trail eases out onto the floor of Boulder Basin. At West Boulder Creek (dry except for periods following heavy rains) a spur path branches left; here our route continues straight ahead and crosses the streambed where the Black Mesa Trail is very indistinct and washed out. To reach the Dutchman's Trail, our return route, walk cross-country (or follow any of a number of faint use trails) toward the cliffs of Palomino Mountain. In 0.2 mile you will intersect the relatively obvious Dutchman's Trail within a few hundred feet of a sign (4.9; 2280) indicating the "official" terminus of the Black Mesa Trail. This sign is just west of the low saddle which would have to be crossed if one were to keep walking toward Palomino Mountain. There are many good campsites in the vicinity, but little shade (except for that provided by an occasional large mesquite or paloverde) and no water (except when West Boulder Creek is running). A variety of interesting explorations can be made from this central location—up East and West Boulder canyons, down Boulder Creek to Needle Canyon, or up to Black Top Mesa (see Trip 3).

When ready to return to the trailhead, turn right, onto the Dutchman's Trail, and follow it over Parker Pass (6.6; 2630) and on to First Water Trailhead (9.1; 2240) (reverse the steps of the first 4.1 miles of Trip 3).

TRIP 5
FIRST WATER TRAILHEAD TO CANYON LAKE VIA GARDEN VALLEY AND INDIAN PAINT MINE

- ▲ **8.7 miles one-way (13-mile car shuttle required); 820′ elevation gain**
- ▲ **Moderate dayhike or leisurely backpack (2 hiking days)**
- ▲ **Trailhead 2, First Water (start)**
- ▲ **Trailhead 1, Canyon Lake (finish)**
- ▲ **Maps**
  Superstition Wilderness or *Goldfield and Mormon Flat Dam quadrangles*
- ▲ **Season: November to April**
  Water is usually available at Second Water Spring (near mile 3.4) from the beginning of the winter rainy season until April or May; Boulder Creek (mile 4.2) and La Barge Creek (mile 4.8) have water only during rainy periods

Features
In spite of its moderate length, this trek traverses a surprisingly varied stretch of terrain, and affords a veritable kaleidoscope of fine vistas. Overnighters will find the itinerary just right for filling a

leisurely winter or spring weekend, and backpacker and dayhiker alike will appreciate the relatively short car shuttle involved.

Trailhead Route

Start: follow the trailhead route for Trip 2. Finish: follow the trailhead route for Trip 1 (Canyon Lake Trailhead).

Description

From First Water Trailhead (0.0; 2240), follow the route of Trip 2 to the signed trail junction in Garden Valley (1.9; 2410). Continue straight ahead here, and proceed along the Second Water Trail north, then northeast, past a cattle tank off to the left. Soon the trail begins dropping, almost imperceptibly at first, into the canyon that separates Black Mesa from Hackberry Mesa. As we begin to drop more steeply, through an area of angular, black basalt boulders (remnants of the lava flow which once covered much of this area), a nice view opens up to the northeast, across Boulder Canyon to Battleship Mountain, Geronimo Head, and, in the far distance, the Four Peaks of the Mazatzal Range. One can also catch an occasional glimpse of Weaver's Needle, just poking over the shoulder of Black Mesa.

Shortly after passing an unsigned, left-branching spur trail, the Second Water Trail cuts to the right, across a low ridge, and then drops into another drainage. A second spurious path branches to the right here; we ignore it and descend steeply past an impressive stand of saguaros to a nice campsite with a good view. Just below here, Second Water Canyon comes down from the right and joins our drainage. Second Water Spring, a short scramble up this side canyon, generally flows throughout the rainy season (but check it out with the Forest Service if you will be depending on it for water).

Below the confluence of Second Water Canyon, we pass a few more campsites, then descend more and more gently to a signed junction (4.0; 1940) just above Boulder Creek. Here we turn left onto the Boulder Canyon Trail, which promptly disappears among the sand and rocks of the wash. The next section of our route can be tricky: rockhop ¼–mile downstream, to a point where a small drainage drops directly down from the gap (Paint Mine Saddle) between Battleship Mountain and the next peak to the north. Scramble up this drainage a few yards, until you spot the continuation of the Boulder Canyon Trail leading uphill to the left. A short climb up the newfound trail now brings us to Indian Paint Mine and Paint Mine Saddle (4.2; 1970). To complete your trek from here, reverse the steps of Trip 1 the remaining 4.5 miles to Canyon Lake (8.7; 1680).

TRIP 6
FIRST WATER TRAILHEAD TO PERALTA TRAILHEAD VIA PARKER PASS, BULL PASS, LA BARGE CANYON, AND BLUFF SPRING

▲ **15.0 miles one-way (24-mile car shuttle required); 1790′ elevation gain**

▲ **Moderate dayhike; leisurely to moderate backpack (2-3 hiking days)**

▲ **Trailhead 2, First Water (start)**

▲ **Trailhead 4, Peralta (finish)**

▲ **Maps**
 Superstition Wilderness or *Goldfield and Weaver's Needle quadrangles*

▲ **Season: November to April**
 Water is usually available at Charlebois Spring (mile 8.0), La Barge Spring (mile 9.2), and Bluff Spring (mile 11.4) (check with Forest Service during dry periods); West and East Boulder creeks (miles 3.6 and 4.4) have water during rainy periods only

Features
La Barge Canyon, with its almost-always-reliable springs and its small, rainy-season-only creek, is the chief attraction of this route. The springs support small islands of vegetation that stand in sharp contrast to the stark aspect of the surrounding country; these oases are as attractive to the native wildlife as they are to the human visitor, making this trip a good choice for one who would observe the many birds and mammals which manage to eke out a living in these severe mountains.

Trailhead Route
Start: follow the trailhead route for Trip 2. Finish: follow the trailhead route for Trip 9.

Description
From the trailhead at the end of First Water Road (0.0; 2240), follow the route of Trip 3 to Bull Pass (5.0; 2750). Those who wish to make the strenuous but worthwhile sidetrip to Black Top Mesa should turn right here and follow the rudimentary pathway that leads steeply up to the top (see Trip 3). Otherwise, continue straight ahead, and descend moderately across a series of grassy hillsides to a minor saddle. Passing through this, the route next drops steeply into Needle Canyon, crosses a wash, and climbs gently to a signed

junction (6.1; 2480) in an open area offering a beautiful view of Weaver's Needle. Here we turn left, rejoining the Dutchman's Trail (which we abandoned back in East Boulder Canyon, in order to take the scenic "short cut" over Bull Pass), and then proceed across a sparsely vegetated flat before dropping into La Barge Canyon. In the canyon bottom is a signed junction with the Cavalry Trail (6.5; 2370), where we turn right, staying on Dutchman's, and ascend gently along the right-hand side of La Barge Creek. A few hardy cottonwood trees grow in this area, and the creek generally has running water after the first few winter rains.

A mile or so upcanyon from the last junction, the trail crosses a tributary wash, then swings left and climbs north a short distance to meet the spur path (8.0; 2500) to Charlesbois Spring. The spring, 0.2 miles up the spur, *almost* always has water; check it out with the Forest Service during spells of dry weather. This is one of the nicest springs in the western Superstitions, all the more so to those who arrive with parched throats and empty canteens. There are several good campsites in the area, beneath a comparatively lush overstory of cottonwoods and sycamores. The Forest Service asks that you not camp right on top of this spring. Black phoebes, bright red cardinals, Scott's orioles and robins are among the many birds you may hear singing in the trees here. Most of the larger mammals which frequent this oasis are nocturnal; venture out of your sleeping bag on a moon-lit night and you might come upon a family of skunks, a raccoon, or possibly a rare kit fox.

From the junction with the Charlebois Spring spur, the Dutchman's Trail cuts back to the right, climbs moderately a short distance to a low ridgetop, and then meets the Peters Trail at a signed fork. Here our route stays right, drops back into La Barge Canyon, and proceeds gently upstream, crossing the bouldery wash from side to side on occasion. After about a mile we enter a small copse of trees near the signed terminus of the Red Tanks Trail (9.2; 2610). La Barge Spring, which is nearly as reliable as Charlebois Spring and has a few nice campsites, is a short distance upcanyon from here.

To complete your trek, turn right at this junction and follow the Dutchman's and Bluff Spring trails the remaining 5.8 miles to Peralta Trailhead (15.0; 2420) (see Trips 12 and 10).

TRIP 7
FIRST WATER TRAILHEAD TO PERALTA TRAILHEAD VIA BLACK MESA, BOULDER BASIN, NEEDLE CANYON, AND BLUFF SADDLE

- ▲ 12.3 miles one-way (24-mile car shuttle required); 2240' elevation gain
- ▲ Moderate dayhike; leisurely to moderate backpack (2-3 hiking days)
- ▲ Trailhead 2, First Water (start)
- ▲ Trailhead 4, Peralta (finish)
- ▲ Maps
  Superstition Wilderness or *Goldfield and Weaver's Needle quadrangles*
- ▲ Season: November to April
  Water is usually available at West Boulder Creek (mile 4.7) and East Boulder Creek (miles 5.2 to 6.0) during rainy periods only

Features

Piercing the heart of the rugged western Superstitions, this route offers a succession of vistas which are among the finest in the range. Particularly impressive are the many views of spectacular Weaver's Needle. With several nice campsites located at about the halfway point, this trip is a natural for an overnighter.

Trailhead Route

Start: follow the trailhead route for Trip 2. Finish: follow the trailhead route for Trip 9.

Description

From the First Water Trailhead (0.0; 2240), follow the route of Trips 2 and 4 across Black Mesa to the end of the Black Mesa Trail in Boulder Basin (4.9; 2280). (One can also follow the slightly shorter, slightly less scenic Dutchman's Trail to this point; see Trip 3.) Backpackers will find plenty of level tentsites in this mesquite-and-paloverde-dotted valley, but shade is scarce, and water is generally available only following heavy rains. Somewhat more sheltered campsites can be found in nearby East Boulder Canyon.

At the Black Mesa Trail/Dutchman's Trail junction we turn left onto the Dutchman's Trail, climb eastward over a low ridge separating West and East Boulder creeks, then drop a short distance to a sign which indicates the start of the left-branching Boulder Canyon Trail. We continue on the Dutchman's Trail at this fork, as we do at the junction with the Bull Pass Trail a few hundred feet beyond, and climb gently past an outcropping of dark, graffiti-scarred rocks in the lower end of East Boulder Canyon. High cliffs loom to either side of us as we threat our way through this deep cleft—those of Palomino Mountain to the right, Black Top Mesa's to the left. After passing beneath a natural "hole in the wall" high up on the Palomino massif, the gradient steepens a bit, and presently we arrive at a signed junction with the right-branching Peralta Canyon Trail (5.9; 2470). Here we turn left, and follow the route of the second half of Trip 10 the remaining 6.4 miles to Peralta Trailhead (12.3; 2420). (It is also possible to turn *right* at this fork, and reverse the steps of the *first* half of Trip 10 to the same trailhead—12.2 miles total. Because Pinyon Camp makes such a nice overnight stop, backpackers may prefer this routing.)

TRIP 8
TORTILLA WELL TRAILHEAD TO PETERS MESA

▲ **10.6 miles round trip; 1880′ elevation gain**
▲ **Moderate dayhike or backpack (2 hiking days)**
▲ **Trailhead 3, Tortilla Well**
▲ **Maps**
   Superstition Wilderness or *Weaver's Needle quadrangle —*
   Horse Mesa Dam quadrangle shows the trailhead approach
▲ **Season: November to April**
   No permanent water along route; during rainy periods water may
   be available at Indian Spring No. 1 (mile 1.7), at Kane Spring (mile
   2.3), and in Peters Canyon (miles 3.7 to 5.0)

Features

This enjoyable excursion passes through a peaceful, comparatively unfrequented area of the Superstitions en route to a fine viewpoint atop Peters Mesa. The terrain is pleasantly varied, with an open, inviting feel not to be found in other, more rugged parts of the wilderness.

Trailhead Route/Camping

From Apache Junction drive northeast on State Highway 88 to the end of the pavement, about 23 miles. Continue along the unpaved highway for a little over a mile, then turn right onto Forest Road 213. This point can also be reached by driving 20.3 miles on Highway 88 southwest from Roosevelt Dam. The entire route is well-graded dirt road. The first several hundred yards of Forest Road 213 look like they were designed to torture-test 4-wheel-drive vehicles. There are plans to improve Forest Road 213 but they seem to be on the back burner. For current road status, call the Roosevelt Lake Visitor Center, open daily 7:45 A.M.-4:30 P.M. (except holidays); (520) 467-3200. Consider parking at the turnoff and walking 3.4 miles to the trailhead. On the way in you will see an old windmill and a faint turnoff. Keep to the most used road. The right-hand branch at a well traveled fork leads in 0.1 mile to a second windmill which marks *Tortilla Well*, the trailhead for Trips 8 and 20. The left fork goes several hundred feet to the end of the road at *Tortilla Trailhead*. Car camping is available at pulloffs along Forest Road 213, at the trailhead, or at the parking area at the junction of Forest Road 213 and Highway 88—though traffic on the dirt road would make this a dusty option. Consider camping at the Tortilla Flat Campground (U.S.F.S.) 7 miles west on Highway 88.

Description

From the Tortilla Well Trailhead (0.0; 3080) walk around the windmill and tank and pass through an open gate. In a few feet you will pass a sign for the Peters Trail. The trail continues southwestward from here and crosses the wash of Tortilla Creek, which supports a sparse riparian growth of cottonwoods and sycamores. The creek may have to be waded during rainy periods (you can tell beforehand

Outskirts of the Superstition Wilderness

by observing the creek where Highway 88 crosses it at Tortilla Flat). If the water is extremely high this hike is hazardous and not recommended, as there are as many as seven unavoidable creek crossings in the next half mile, as the trail follows the wash upstream through a cliffbound stretch of Tortilla Canyon.

After the final crossing (1.2; 3170), the trail veers to the right (southwest) and climbs gently alongside a tributary wash. The terrain soon opens up into a spacious, flat-bottomed valley which contains Indian Spring No. 1 (1.7; 3280), numerous spur trails (stay on the most visible trail) and some rather uninviting campsites. The spring may be dry—check with the Forest Service if you will be depending on this or any of the other water sources mentioned below.

Beyond here the trail continues to ascend gently and then more moderately up a ravine to Kane Spring (2.3; 3460). Here there are a few Fremont cottonwoods, a nice campsite, and possibly some water. From the spring, the pathway climbs more and more steeply, disdaining switchbacks for the most part, until it reaches the head of the ravine at an unnamed saddle (2.7; 3860). There is a poor, exposed, and frequently windy campsite here. Views are good to the southeast, across the hilly divide of Horse Ridge and a good part of the central Superstitions.

The trail next descends slightly southward, crosses a second saddle, and then drops farther to a junction. Here we turn right and climb in 0.3 mile to a third saddle (3.5; 3790). The trail is quite steep and rutted in places as it descends westward from here to the wash of Peters Canyon. Once on the canyon floor we proceed downstream, crossing the wash several times. There are a few nice campsites in this saguaro-studded area, and the creekbed often has water following heavy rains.

After the final crossing of the wash (5.0; 3280), the trail swings left and enters the ravine that can be seen opening up to the west. A short, stiff climb then brings us to a saddle atop Peters Mesa (5.3; 3580), which affords an excellent vista across La Barge Canyon to Bluff Spring Mountain and the famous landmark of Weaver's Needle.

The Peters Trail continues on from here to Charlebois Spring in the heart of the Superstition Wilderness (see Trip 20), but this mesa-top viewpoint marks the end of today's excursion.

TRIP 9
Peralta Trailhead to Fremont Saddle and Pinyon Camp

⌃ **4.6-6.6 miles round trip; 1350-1800′ elevation gain**
⌃ **Moderate dayhike or backpack (2 hiking days)**
⌃ **Trailhead 4, Peralta**
⌃ **Maps**
  Superstition Wilderness or *Weaver's Needle quadrangle*
⌃ **Season: November to April**
  No water available along route except after heavy rains

Features
The short, steep watercourse of Peralta Canyon provides one of the quickest and most scenic routes into the backcountry of the central Superstitions. This trip takes the hiker to the threshold of that country at lofty Fremont Saddle, which offers magnificent views over a large portion of the range. Backpackers have the option of continuing on to Pinyon Camp, a delightful campsite near the base of spectacular Weaver's Needle.

Trailhead Route
From Apache Junction drive southeast along U.S. 60 approximately 9 miles, then turn left onto Peralta Road (Forest Road 77). Follow this northeast for 5.4 miles to a fork, turn left, and continue 2.0 miles farther to the parking area at road's end. The route to this very popular trailhead is well signed. At the gate to Peralta Road a sign proclaims the land to be state trust land, no trespassing. However, many people use the land for dispersed camping and are not bothered. The trailhead area has not yet been posted "no camping" but the U.S.F.S. says that camping may be prohibited in the future. There are two main trailhead parking areas separated by a few hundred yards of narrow dirt road; each requires a $4 parking fee.

This popular trailhead can be a zoo during weekends. Don't even try for the upper trailhead parking if the area is packed.

Description
From the parking area at the end of the Peralta Road (0.0; 2420) follow the wide Peralta Trail north through a dense and varied vegetative cover of jojoba, scraggly mesquite trees, yellow-blossoming creosote bush, teddy-bear cholla, and some foothill paloverde. During the spring months this area is brightened by a number of wildflowers, including brittlebush, delicate yellow paperflower, tiny white eriophyllum, orangish globe mallow, fleabane and narrow-leaf aster.

The path quickly grows narrower as it enters Peralta Canyon, and we pass occasional patches of shade provided by sugar sumacs and shrub live oaks. The trail stays near the canyon bottom for the first 1.5 miles or so, climbing gently to moderately and crossing usually dry Peralta Creek a few times. Beyond here we abandon the creekside for the shadeless canyonsides above it, gaining good views down the throat of Peralta Canyon and of the many short pinnacles (reminiscent of the mysterious stone sculptures found on Easter Island) which seem to grow out of the slopes nearby.

Above here the trail returns briefly to the wash, crosses it, and then switchbacks steeply uphill. In the past these switchbacks have been shortcutted in many places, and the resulting erosion has made it difficult in spots to distinguish the real trail from the spurious ones. Please try to stay on the "official" pathway as best you can, because the only way to eliminate these destructive—and confusing—shortcuts is to concentrate use onto a single trail.

At length the switchbacks cease and we arrive at Fremont Saddle (2.3; 3766). This is the highest point reached by trail in the western Superstitions, and the views it affords are correspondingly extensive. To the north and northwest, parts of the Goldfield and Mazatzal mountains are visible far beyond the nearby, double-peaked crest of Weaver's Needle, while to the southeast the vista stretches across parts of the eastern Superstitions and the rows and rows of low desert ranges that wrinkle the earth between the 'Stitions and the Santa Catalinas. You may see a Cooper's hawk or a golden eagle soaring high above the canyons which fall away to either side of the saddle.

This spot is a good destination for dayhikers. Backpackers who wish to continue on to Pinyon Camp should follow the Peralta Canyon Trail as it drops down the slope north of the saddle, makes a few well-graded switchbacks, and then swings out onto the left-hand wall of East Boulder Canyon. A mile later, where the trail approaches East Boulder Creek, there is a nice flat with some fair-sized sugar sumacs and a few single-leaf pinyons. This is Pinyon Camp (3.3; 3320). There are good campsites here, as well as a superb, close-up view of Weaver's Needle, but no water except after a heavy rain.

Return the way you came, or continue on to Black Top Pass and return via Bluff Saddle (see Trip 10).

TRIP 10
WEAVER'S NEEDLE LOOP (PERALTA TRAILHEAD TO FREMONT SADDLE, BLACKTOP PASS, NEEDLE CANYON, AND BLUFF SADDLE)

- ▲ **12.7 mile loop trip; 2850' elevation gain**
- ▲ **Strenuous dayhike or moderate backpack (2-3 hiking days)**
- ▲ **Trailhead 4, Peralta**
- ▲ **Maps**
  Superstition Wilderness or *Weaver's Needle and Goldfield quadrangles*
- ▲ **Season: November to April**
  No permanent water along route; during rainy periods water is generally available at Pinyon Camp (mile 3.3), East Boulder Creek (mile 6.3), and possibly in other drainages

Features

This fine trip makes a complete circuit of Weaver's Needle, allowing the hiker to view this most famous of all Superstition landmarks from virtually every angle. The four passes crossed enroute command a variety of far-reaching vistas, making this one of the most scenic, if strenuous, routes in the entire range.

Trailhead Route

Follow the trailhead route for Trip 9.

Description

Follow the directions for Trip 9 to Pinyon Camp (3.3; 3320). From there continue gently down East Boulder Canyon, past some excellent campsites right in the shadow of Weaver's Needle. About a mile beyond Pinyon Camp, East Boulder Canyon falls off to the right, while the trail stays high on the canyonside and soon cuts left through a minor saddle (5.0; 3050). After dropping a short distance from here we meander across a small flat, then descend a few rocky switchbacks and swing across a hillside to another saddle, where we have a good view across East Boulder Canyon to distinctive-looking Black Top Mesa. The dark basalt layer atop this mesa is a solidified remnant of the lavas that oozed out of the Superstition volcanoes some 15-18 million years ago. It is most likely a part of the same formation found on nearby Black Mesa, though the intervening portion of the frozen lava flow has long since been carried away by erosion.

The trail does not pass through this saddle, but cuts back to the left and crosses the ridge ¼ mile farther along. Once we are on the Boulder Canyon side of this ridge a few unsigned spur trails branch off to the left and right; the correct path is for the most part visible below as it descends to the bottom of East Boulder Canyon via two long switchbacks. The fork at the bottom of the lower switchback can be confusing—be sure to go left here.

At a sign in East Boulder Canyon we meet the Dutchman's Trail (6.3; 2480). Backpackers will find a few fair campsites here, where there is generally running water during rainy periods. To continue on our loop back to Peralta Roadend, we turn right onto the Dutchman's Trail. In about 200 yards, after crossing East Boulder Creek, the trail passes a steep shortcut trail branching right, then turns sharply left and climbs one long switchback up to Blacktop Pass (7.0; 2790)("Upper Black Top Mesa Pass" on the topo map). Bluff Spring Mountain, Weaver's Needle, Palomino Mountain and Black Top Mesa are all visible from this point.

From Blacktop Pass we drop a short distance into a basin with comparatively gentle contours. Where a small drainage comes down from the right is an unsigned trail junction (7.4; 2640); here our route turns right, onto the Terrapin Trail (which may be incorrectly signed "Needle Canyon Trail"), and begins climbing again. The view of Weaver's needle from this area is exceptionally fine. Following a short, steep rise, the trail drops suddenly to a good campsite in a comparatively lush copse of netleaf hackberry and shrub live oak. Shortly beyond here, at a spot marked by a metal post, a use-trail branches left and proceeds up the bottom of Needle Canyon; our route swings right and makes a few very steep climbs up to the crest of a low ridge. Fortunately for the hiker, the remainder of the ascent

Weaver's Needle from Pinyon Camp

to Terrapin Pass (8.3; 3180) is considerably easier than the preceding passages. The pass offers nice, long vistas to the north and west; Superstition Mountain, Black Top Mesa and Palomino Mountain are visible, as are parts of the distant Mazatzal and Goldfield mountains. Weaver's Needle, of course, continues to dominate the view to the south.

Beyond Terrapin Pass the trail makes a few steep ups and downs as it works its way past the base of the Needle. After passing a brushy, overgrown section (and an inviting campsite beneath a large sugar sumac off to the right of the trail) the route reunites with Needle Canyon wash, whose gentle course is then followed to its head at Bluff Saddle (9.7; 3420). This is a picturesque area, with a complex array of rhyolite bluffs and pinnacles framing vistas of the distant mountains to the east and south. (To get the best views it is necessary to scramble up a short distance among the rocks on either side of the saddle.)

From Bluff Saddle we walk gradually downhill, winding between rock outcroppings and passing a couple of fair campsites among mesquite, agave, some medium-sized saguaros and lots of prickly pear. The trail grows rather obscure as it negotiates a low gap and begins dropping into a canyon—look for ducks to stay on the right track. At the bottom of this descent we cross a wash and meet the Bluff Spring Trail at a signed junction (10.4; 3160), where we turn right and proceed down-canyon, staying a little above the creekbed at first, then dropping down to the bottom. About ¾ mile later the trail disappears temporarily in the wash. Here we rockhop directly down the streambed, passing through a sort of narrows and ignoring a side trail which can be seen leading up a ravine on the right, until the Bluff Spring Trail reappears and begins climbing up the right-hand canyonside. About 0.3 mile later we reach a small saddle (11.6; 3000), where we catch one last glimpse of Weaver's Needle before beginning the descent back to Peralta Trailhead.

At the saddle, the trail swings to the right, then crosses a small drainage, and proceeds gently downhill to the south. After rounding a ridge, our route drops steeply toward the flatlands, passing a side trail to an old prospect hole on the right, until it intercepts the Dutchman's Trail coming in from the left. The combined Bluff Spring/Dutchman's Trail continues southwest a short distance to a crossing of Peralta Creek; the trailhead (12.7; 2420) is just beyond.

TRIP 11
Peralta Trailhead to Crystal Spring

▲ **9.3 mile loop trip; 1260′ elevation gain**
▲ **Moderate dayhike or backpack (2 hiking days)**
▲ **Trailhead 4, Peralta**
▲ **Maps**
   Superstition Wilderness or *Weaver's Needle quadrangle*
▲ **Season: November to April**
   *Water usually available at Crystal Spring (mile 5.8); check with
   Forest Service first*

Features
This loop route skirts the base of the Superstition Mountains, passing a variety of pleasant vistas across open desert country, then
climbs over Miners Summit and drops into the backcountry. With
nice campsites located just beyond the halfway mark, backpackers
will find this trip ideal for an overnighter.

Trail Route
Follow the trailhead route for Trip 9.

Description
From the end of Peralta Road (0.0; 2420) follow the combined Bluff
Spring/Dutchman's Trail across Peralta Creek, then to a signed junction just beyond. Here the two trails part; we turn right, onto
Dutchman's/Miners, and climb moderately across a hillside planted
with foothill paloverde, ocotillo, yellow-blossoming brittlebush,
canyon ragweed, jojoba, creosote bush and some tall saguaros. The
trail, rather wide up to this point, narrows as it swings across a
drainage and contours into a low saddle (0.5; 2540). After 0.4 mile of
gentle descending we reach and cross Barks Wash twice—the drainage
here is separated by an island. Our route swings left here and winds
along the fringe of Barkley Basin, gradually climbing up onto the
"bajada," or debris-slope, at the foot of the Superstition Mountains.
After passing beneath craggy Miners Needle we drop slightly into
the shallow wash which drains Miners Canyon (2.6; 2550), then begin
a moderate-to-steep, switchbacking ascent of the hillside beyond. As
we gain elevation a good view opens up across Barkley Basin to
Buzzard's Roost, standing guard over the Coffee Flat area to the east-
southeast, and an unnamed, oddly sculptured pinnacle just east of
the trail. Presently the switchbacks cease and the route climbs steadily northwest. The old Miners Trail is visible far below. After circling

around the head of Miners Canyon we meander up through a rocky area to Miners Summit (4.4; 3260), where the trail splits into three branches. The right-hand fork goes to Whiskey Spring, the middle path is the continuation of the Dutchman's Trail, and the left-hand branch is an unmaintained spur that should be avoided. We take the central fork and descend moderately via a single long switchback into the open basin to the north. After crossing a small drainage the trail climbs back up a bit, then drops into a tributary of Bluff Spring Canyon. In a comparatively lush area, featuring a nice stand of scrub oak, sugar sumac and netleaf hackberry, we cross a wash and meet the Bluff Spring Trail at a signed junction (5.8; 3020). Crystal Spring, off in the trees near this junction, usually has water; if not, try nearby Bluff Spring, located a few hundred feet left of an old corral which will be found just north of here. Neither of these springs is completely reliable, and during dry periods backpackers should check them out with the Forest Service before planning to spend the night here.

To return to Peralta Trailhead, turn left onto the Bluff Spring Trail and follow it west gently uphill. Shortly after you pass through a narrow section of Bluff Spring Canyon a spur branches off to the left; ignore it and continue gradually uphill to a low saddle, beyond which the route swings south to meet the signed, right-branching Terrapin Trail (7.0; 3160). Here we go left and follow the Bluff Spring Trail the remaining 2.3 miles to Peralta Trailhead (9.3; 2420) (see Trip 10).

TRIP 12
PERALTA TRAILHEAD TO WHISKEY SPRING, LA BARGE CANYON, AND CRYSTAL SPRING

- ▲ **14.4 mile loop trip; 1980' elevation gain**
- ▲ **Strenuous dayhike or moderate backpack (2-3 hiking days)**
- ▲ **Trailhead 4, Peralta**
- ▲ **Maps**
  Superstition Wilderness or *Weaver's Needle quadrangle*
- ▲ **Season: November to April**
  Water usually available at Whiskey Spring (mile 5.8), La Barge Spring (mile 8.6), and Bluff Spring (mile 10.8); check with Forest Service first

Features
The highlight of this trip is La Barge Canyon, a major drainage which slices across the heart of the western Superstition backcountry,

and which is a good bet to contain a clear, running stream during winter and early spring. With water and good campsites generally available at convenient intervals, backpackers who like to take their time and really *see* the country through which they pass can draw this excursion out over 3 or 4 hiking days—just right for a holiday weekend.

Trailhead Route

Follow the trailhead route for Trip 9.

Description

Follow the directions for Trip 11 to Miners Summit (4.4; 3260). Here we turn right, onto the Whiskey Spring Trail, and make a rough, steep climb to an unnamed saddle (4.9; 3380). The trail now drops quickly down a minor drainage, then swings left into Whiskey Spring Canyon and descends more gradually to the cement tank which catches the effluent of Whiskey Spring (5.8; 2940) (reliable except during dry seasons). There are a few nice campsites in this area, scattered beneath a spotty forest cover of medium-sized cottonwoods and netleaf hackberries.

At an unsigned trail fork 0.5 mile below Whiskey Spring we stay right, then climb a short distance and drop down to La Barge Creek, which generally contains at least a trickle of water during the winter rainy season. Immediately after crossing the creek to its north side we meet the Red Tanks Trail at a signed junction (6.6; 2800). If the creek is running high and the day is warm, you may wish to make a side-trip to some sparkling swimming holes in Upper La Barge Box, approximately 1 mile up-canyon. If not, turn left here and proceed down-canyon.

After climbing over a low ridge in order to "straighten out a bend" in the canyon, the trail tends to stay close to the streambed, disappearing now and then in the rather barren, bouldery floodplain and crossing from side to side frequently. After about a mile, a faint, unsigned spur trail branches right to Trap Canyon Spring (situated at the mouth of the narrow cleft that disappears between the steep bluffs to the north; water during rainy periods only). Continuing straight down canyon here, we presently arrive at La Barge Spring (8.6; 2610), just off to the right of the trail in a lovely grove of tall cottonwoods and sycamores. Backpackers will find delightful camping here, and reliable water (except possibly during very dry years—check with the Forest Service first). A variety of birds congregate in this area of La Barge Canyon during the spring months, including kinglets, black phoebes and bright red cardinals. The spring and the creek attract a number of mammals as well, most of them nocturnal;

Pine Creek, Superstition Wilderness

overnighters may be awakened in the dead of night by the noise of a raccoon, a ringtail cat or a woodrat investigating their foodstores.

A short distance beyond La Barge Spring the Red Tanks Trail ends at a signed junction with the Dutchman's Trail. To complete our loop to Peralta Trailhead we now turn left and begin climbing moderately up the right-hand side of Bluff Spring Canyon. A mile later, after dropping steeply back down to the canyon bottom, the trail swings right at a split in the drainage, then climbs gently to an open flat containing an old corral (10.8; 2980). Just beyond this enclosure a side trail branches right to Bluff Spring (there is generally water here, and at nearby Crystal Spring, except during very dry periods). A few hundred yards past this turnoff, at Crystal Spring (where there is a nice campsite shaded by comparatively large scrub oaks and netleaf hackberries), the Dutchman's Trail forks left at a signed junction. (The sign is located across the wash—you have to look for it.) Here we continue straight ahead, following the Bluff Spring Trail up-canyon past a spurious, left-branching sidepath. After tracing Bluff Spring Canyon to its head, the route tops out at a low saddle, then drops gently a short distance to a signed junction with the Terrapin Trail (12.1; 3160). Go left at this fork and follow the Bluff Spring Trail the remaining 2.3 miles to Peralta Trailhead (14.4; 2420) (see Trip 10).

TRIP 13
PERALTA TRAILHEAD TO MINERS SUMMIT, LA BARGE SPRING, CHARLEBOIS SPRING, AND BLUFF SADDLE

- ▲ **18.0 mile loop trip; 2580' elevation gain**
- ▲ **Moderate backpack (2-3 hiking days)**
- ▲ **Trailhead 4, Peralta**
- ▲ **Maps**
  Superstition Wilderness or *Weaver's Needle and Goldfield quadrangles*
- ▲ **Season: November to April**
  Water usually available at Whiskey Spring (mile 5.8), La Barge Spring (mile 8.6), and Charlebois Spring (mile 9.8); check with Forest Service during dry periods.

Features

This lengthy loop route is a fine choice for backpackers looking for a fairly challenging weekend outing. Climbs into the Superstition backcountry via Miners Summit. After passing several cottonwood- and sycamore-shaded seeps down in La Barge Canyon (where rainy-season trekkers might also find a clear, running stream), the trail climbs past classic vistas of Weaver's Needle to scenic Bluff Saddle, a fitting climax to this varied excursion.

Trailhead Route

Follow the trailhead route for Trip 9.

Description

From Peralta Trailhead (0.0; 2420), follow the Dutchman's/Miners Trail to Miners Summit (4.4; 3260) (see Trip 11), then proceed along the Whiskey Spring and Red Tanks trails to La Barge Spring (8.6; 2610) (see Trip 12). At a signed junction just beyond the spring we turn right, onto the Dutchman's/Miners Trail, then continue gently down La Barge Canyon, crossing the wash at frequent intervals and passing through sparse stands of oak, mesquite, sycamore and cottonwood, and an occasional Arizona walnut. Soon after passing the short, right-branching lateral to Music Canyon Spring (water during rainy periods only), the trail climbs moderately up the right-hand canyonside to meet the signed Peters Trail atop a minor ridge (9.7; 2580). We stay left at this junction and descend a short distance to the unsigned spur trail to Charlebois (locally pronounced "Charley-boy") Spring (0.2 mile up Charlebois Canyon to the right). Water is *almost* always available here, but during dry periods it should be checked out first with the Forest Service. There are several nice campsites in this area, shaded by some large sycamores and cottonwoods. (The Forest Service asks that you do not camp right at this spring.)

Continuing from here along the Dutchman's Trail, we soon recross La Barge Creek and resume descending gently down-canyon. Shortly after we pass a drift fence, a nice view opens up across the canyon to the steep basaltic cliffs of Black Mountain and, in the distance, the yellow rhyolite bluffs of Geronimo Head. At the head of Marsh Valley the signed Cavalry Trail comes in on the right (11.3; 2370); our route goes left here, and begins climbing gently away from La Barge Creek. Soon we reach a signed junction with the Bull Pass Trail, where we stay left again. There is a fabulous, head-on view of Weaver's Needle from here.

As we climb into Needle Canyon the route is temporarily confused by use-trails; the correct path trends steadily south along the left side of Needle Creek wash. When the track becomes once again unambiguous, we cut over to the right side of the creekbed and soon meet the Terrapin Trail at a junction marked only by a signpost (12.7; 2640). To complete our loop back to Peralta Trailhead, we turn left onto the latter and follow the directions for the second half of Trip 10 back to the parking area (18.0; 2420). (It is also possible to turn *right* here, reverse the steps of the *first* half of Trip 10, and return via Blacktop Pass and the Peralta Trail—20.1 miles total.)

TRIP 14
PERALTA TRAILHEAD TO CANYON LAKE VIA FREMONT SADDLE, BOULDER CANYON, AND INDIAN PAINT MINE

⌃ **15.6 miles one-way (31-mile car shuttle required); 2010' elevation gain**
⌃ **Strenuous dayhike or moderate backpack (2-3 hiking days)**
⌃ **Trailhead 4, Peralta (start)**
⌃ **Trailhead 1, Canyon Lake (finish)**
⌃ **Maps**
  Superstition Wilderness or *Weaver's Needle, Goldfield,* and *Mormon Flat Dam* quadrangles
⌃ **Season: November to April**
  Water is generally available along Boulder Creek (miles 7.1 to 10.9) during rainy periods only

Features

This transmontane trek climbs into the Superstition backcountry via Fremont Saddle, then traces Boulder Creek for virtually its entire length—from its eastern headwaters near Pinyon Camp, in the shadow of Weaver's Needle, to within a mile of its end at La Barge Creek. Dayhikers will have little time to linger along this long, sometimes rough route, but backpackers with a layover day (or two) will be able to make a number of fascinating side trips along the way.

Trailhead route

Start: follow the trailhead route for Trip 9. Finish: follow the trailhead route for Trip 1.

Description

From Peralta Trailhead (0.0; 2420) follow the Peralta Canyon Trail across Fremont Saddle to the signed trail junction in East Boulder Canyon (6.3; 2480) (see Trips 9 and 10). Here we turn left, onto the Dutchman's Trail, and proceed down-canyon, past occasional fair tentsites shaded by small hackberries and sugar sumacs. When East Boulder Creek has running water (a likelihood after a good, soaking winter rain or two), the music of riffles and cascades accompanies the hiker through this delightful section, the comparative lushness of which is attributable partly to the presence of the creek, and partly to the morning and evening shade provided by the high cliffs looming to either side. As you pass beneath the buff-colored precipices of Palomino Mountain (on your left), look for the small natural arch which has formed near its summit.

Where East Boulder Canyon begins to open up a bit, the Bull Pass Trail branches right at a signed fork. If you wish to make the strenuous but worthwhile sidetrip up to Black Top Mesa (1.2 miles one-way; see Trip 3), turn right here. Otherwise, continue straight ahead along the gently descending Dutchman's Trail, arriving in 0.1 mile at a signed junction with the Boulder Canyon Trail (7.1; 2480). Here we turn right and proceed down the rocky, brushy wash of East Boulder Creek, ignoring the occasional use-paths branching off to either side. After about 0.5 mile, West Boulder Creek comes in from the left and joins our wash. Beyond here the Boulder Canyon Trail, which was never really all that distinct to begin with, disappears into the boulders and sand of what is now Boulder Canyon. The next 3 miles of our route consist essentially of boulder-hopping cross-country down the canyon, though if you wish you may try to follow the disconnected snatches of use-trail that appear now and then on either side of the watercourse. These typically fade out after leading only a few hundred yards, but they make the going easier in many places. It is necessary to cross Boulder Creek several times in the miles ahead, and when the water is exceptionally high the route may be impassable.

A little less than a mile after leaving the Dutchman's Trail, Needle Canyon Wash can be seen emerging from a steep-walled slot on the right. The spooky, twisting gorge of lower Needle Canyon is well worth an exploratory visit (unless a heavy storm seems imminent). About 2.5 miles downstream from this point, Second Water Canyon will be seen coming down from the left (west); the Second Water Trail joins our route at a signed junction on a rocky bench near the confluence of Second Water and Boulder creeks (10.6; 1940). Second Water Spring (which generally has water from the first winter rains until April or May) is about 0.5 mile up Second Water Canyon (see Trip 5).

The next section of our route is crucial: rockhop ¼ mile downstream from the preceding junction, to a point where a minor drainage drops directly down from the gap (Paint Mine Saddle) between Battleship Mountain and the next peak to the north. Scramble up this drainage a few yards, until you spot the continuation of the Boulder Canyon Trail leading off to the left. A short climb up this now brings us to Indian Paint Mine and Paint Mine Saddle (11.1; 1970). To complete your trek from here, reverse the steps of Trip 1 the remaining 4.5 miles to Canyon Lake (15.6; 1680).

TRIP 15
JF Trailhead to Dripping Spring

- ▲ **5.6 miles round trip; 500' elevation gain**
- ▲ **Leisurely dayhike or backpack (2 hiking days)**
- ▲ **Trailhead 5, JF and Woodbury**
- ▲ **Maps**
  Superstition Wilderness or *Iron Mountain and Weaver's Needle quadrangles*
- ▲ **Season: November to April**
  Water available at Dripping Spring (mile 2.8) following rainy periods only

Features

Fraser Canyon, with its groves of hackberry, mesquite and cottonwood, provides the shortest and most pleasant route to Dripping Spring, a leafy oasis that attracts a wide variety of bird and animal life. This is a fine "warm-up" trip; not too taxing, yet providing enough exercise to prepare the hiker for more strenuous outings in the future, and offering a degree of solitude and wilderness "feel" that is more than commensurate with the modest effort involved.

Trailhead Route

Follow the trailhead route for Trip 17 to the trailhead parking for Woodbury Trailhead. The locked gate just beyond the turnoff spur to the parking area leads to JF Ranch Headquarters. Some hikers cross the gate and hike half a mile down Forest Road 172B to the JF Trailhead but U.S.F.S. personnel warn that ranchers do not like hikers to use this route. An alternative approach to the JF Trailhead is to follow the JF Trail from the parking area to a signed junction (0.6, 3560) and take the left turn. This is a bit confusing as the sign is located about 40 feet past the turnoff so go back 40 feet and turn right. This trail is not as well used as other trails in the area but is easy to follow if you attention. First it leads across fairly level terrain a bit south of due west. Then it drops into a tributary which soon leads to Fraser Wash. At one point this trail seems to cross Fraser Wash but all traces of trail soon fade. Instead of crossing the wash the trail goes down the wash about 100 feet then comes out on the left side and soon joins FR 172B, which approaches the ranch gate after a few hundred more feet. Just before the ranch gate bear right a few dozen feet to the trailhead sign and gate.

Description

The Coffee Flat Trail starts here (0.0; 3120), and we follow it first along a fenceline, then roughly parallel to Fraser Wash. Shortly after winding through a grove of mesquites this trail drops into shallow Fraser Wash (0.4; 3080) and promptly disappears among the boulders and sand of the creekbed. Here we turn right and boulder-hop our way downstream, past an exceptionally large cottonwood tree which serves as a helpful landmark for locating the trail again on the return trip.

Occasional stretches of trail can be found on either side of the wash as we proceed down-canyon, but unless the creek is running exceptionally high (it usually does not run at all), there is little reason for the foot-traveler to seek them out—it is just as easy to walk cross-country directly down the streambed. Fraser Canyon gradually grows deeper and better defined, and soon we must thread a narrow, cliffy bottleneck, or "box." (Those who are religiously tracing out the trail at this point may pick it up again on the right—north—side of the stream after passing through here.)

As we continue downstream two major tributary drainages open up on the left—first Whetrock Canyon, then Musk Hog Canyon. About 0.6 mile below the confluence of the Musk Hog drainage, Fraser Canyon ends at Randolph Canyon, the large defile heading up to the right. The Coffee Flat Trail is on the north side of Fraser Wash at this point; just before it crosses Randolph Creek a signpost marks a junction with the right-branching Red Tanks Trail (2.8; 2620). There are nice campsites in the vicinity, scattered among groves of sycamore, mesquite and netleaf hackberry. Dripping Spring is at the base of the south canyon wall a hundred yards or so downstream.

Return the way you came.

TRIP 16
JF Trailhead to Peralta Trailhead via Dripping Spring, the Red Tanks Trail, Upper La Barge Box, and Whiskey Spring

- 15.7 miles one-way (33-mile car shuttle required); 2160' elevation gain
- Moderate backpack (2-3 hiking days)
- Trailhead 5, JF and Woodbury, (start)
- Trailhead 4, Peralta (finish)
- Maps
  Superstition Wilderness or *Iron Mountain and Weaver's Needle quadrangles*
- Season: November to April
  Water is usually available at Whiskey Spring (mile 9.9), and, during rainy periods only, at Dripping Spring (mile 2.8), and along La Barge Creek (miles 8.0 to 9.1)

Features

Faint, twisting, at times perplexing and exasperating—the Red Tanks Trail is one to test the route-finding prowess of even the most experienced wilderness traveler. Those with the patience and skill to trace this rarely-trod route will find their efforts amply rewarded, however, for the solitude and the desolate beauty of the backcountry it traverses are commensurate with its difficulty. An added bonus is the delightful spring-season swimming that, during wet years, is to be had in the potholes of Upper La Barge Box.

Remember—this is no route for beginners.

Trailhead Route

Start: follow the trailhead route for Trip 15. Finish: follow the trailhead route for Trip 9.

Description

From JF Headquarters (0.0; 3120), follow the route of Trip 15 to the trail junction near Dripping Spring (2.8; 2620). Here we turn right, and follow the Red Tanks Trail as it climbs gently along the right-hand side of Randolph Canyon Wash, which sometimes contains running water during the rainy season (but not always—check with the Forest Service first). Where Red Tanks Canyon branches off to the left, the trail veers right and proceeds up Randolph Canyon a very short distance, to an exceedingly obscure junction marked with a cairn (3.4; 2720). Turning left here, we drop down a few yards, cross Randolph Canyon Wash, then climb up and over a low, cholla-covered ridge into Red Tanks Canyon.

The trail stays mostly to the left of Red Tanks wash as it proceeds up-canyon, sometimes winding through shady glens of oak and sugar sumac (nice camping), other times climbing high up on the grassy canyonsides, where early-morning and late-evening hikers might spot a herd of collared peccaries, or javelinas, feeding upon the prickly pear of which they are so fond. At a major split in Red Tanks Canyon we cross the creekbed to the right, walk up the right-hand fork a few dozen yards, then cross back to the left and clamber over a low ridge to intersect the left fork. The quickly steepening trail then follows this northwestward-trending drainage to its head at Red Tanks Divide (5.8; 3660), a wide saddle affording fine views of the long cliffs of Coffee Flat Mountains and across the pinyon- and juniper-forested headwaters of La Barge Creek.

From the divide we wind westward through a maze of small rock outcroppings, then swing right and drop into a canyon. After passing a drift fence the trail becomes quite obscure, (even more obscure than it has been heretofore), and ducks appear on occasion to help us keep our bearings. At doubtful forks, remember that the route tends to keep to the left of the drainage as it descends. Just before reaching a small basin visible below, we contour to the left across a broad ridge, following ducks, then drop down to and recross the drainage near its confluence with a tributary of La Barge Creek. From here the path strikes off westward, past the site of an old corral, then swings left and descends gently to the edge of a spacious, juniper-dotted basin. The trail grows considerably more distinct as it heads across the northern fringe of this basin.

Next to a northward-trending tributary of La Barge Creek, we meet the signed, right-branching Hoolie Bacon Trail (7.6; 3220), at which junction we stay left and proceed across relatively level terrain toward Upper La Barge Box, the cliff-edged narrows visible down-canyon. A number of faint sidetrails branch off to the left through here, leading to nice campsites along nearby La Barge Creek. Beyond this area the trail climbs up onto the north canyonside, preparing to avoid the more difficult passages of Upper La Barge Box. This routing unfortunately misses the many fine swimming holes which pool up in the Box when the water is high, and skilled cross-country travelers may prefer to temporarily abandon the trail and scramble directly down the bouldery throat of the narrows.

After emerging from the west end of Upper La Barge Box, we drop down to creek level, then continue about 0.5 mile down-canyon to a signed junction with the Whiskey Spring Trail (9.1; 2800). To complete your journey from here, turn left and walk part of the route of Trip 12 (in reverse) to Miners Summit (11.3; 3260). The reverse the steps of the first part of Trip 11 the remaining distance to Peralta Trailhead (15.7; 2420).

TRIP 17
WOODBURY TRAILHEAD TO ROGERS CANYON CLIFF DWELLINGS

▲ **11.4 miles round trip; 2580′ elevation gain**
▲ **Strenuous dayhike or backpack (2 hiking days)**
▲ **Trailhead 5, JF and Woodbury**
▲ **Maps**
  Superstition Wilderness or *Iron Mountain quadrangle*
▲ **Season: November to April**
  Water is generally available at Rogers Creek (mile 5.3) from the beginning of the winter rainy season until April or May

Features

This trip features a special destination: a set of ancient cliff dwellings tucked away beneath the precipitous walls of Rogers Canyon. But these ruins, fascinating as they are, are not the sole attraction of this route, for Rogers Canyon is a delight as well— threaded by a clear, sparkling stream (in season), shaded by leafy groves of oak and sycamore, as wild and serene today as it was in the time of the cliff dwellers themselves.

Trailhead Route/Camping

From Florence Junction drive east on U.S. 60 for 2 miles to Queen Valley Road (paved). Follow this north 1.7 miles, then veer right onto Forest Road 357. Follow the latter 2.5 miles and turn left onto Forest Road 172. Follow it north nearly 11 miles to a locked gate. The trailhead is a short distance down the spur road to the right. The trail to Tortilla Pass and Rogers Canyon begins on the north side of the trailhead. The last 13.7 miles of this approach are over dirt roads, and may not be negotiable by some passenger vehicles (or by any vehicles immediately following a heavy rain). Visitors will probably see passenger cars parked at the trailhead but a high clearance vehicle will mean fewer headaches. There are many good sites for car camping both at the trailhead parking lot and along the drive to the trailhead.

Description

From the signed Woodbury Trailhead (0.0; 3520), follow the JF Trail as it heads uphill along a rough old road toward the saddle that is the head of Randolph Canyon (0.6; 3480). First we walk between a cattle tank and a windmill, then we drop slightly, veer left, and enter Randolph Canyon not far before reaching a tilted Superstition Wilderness boundary sign. After crossing and recrossing the wash, the trail climbs up the left bank to a low ridge, which offers an unobstructed view of the rugged southern flanks of 5077-foot La Barge Mountain, off to the northwest. At the second crossing (1.4; 3250), we ignore a faint and fading spur, cross the creekbed (running water after heavy rains) and begin the long climb to Tortilla Pass.

The ensuing climb is very rough and steep in places. Partway up, the trail grows more distinct and passes Palmer Oaks, shrub live oaks, and some tenacious one-seed junipers—signs of our increasing elevation. Near the top of the climb we cross a wash that may contain a trickle of water during the wet season.

At Tortilla Pass (3.3; 4480) there is a trail junction. Here we turn right onto the Rogers Canyon Trail and climb a short distance farther to a second, unnamed pass (3.6; 4600). On a clear day the broad backbone of the Sierra Ancha Range, far to the north, can be seen from this point.

From this saddle the trail drops steeply down to the head of a tributary of Rogers Canyon Creek. The first part of this descent is exceptionally steep and rough. After threading a narrow, rocky gateway in this canyon the route swings right and levels off considerably. As it does so, the tenor of the landscape grows more congenial—the canyon walls are higher and they provide a measure of shelter from the winds which often whip across the highlands; there is occasionally running water down the creekbed; and single-leaf pinyons, Emory and Arizona white oaks, and tall Arizona sycamores appear in larger and larger groves. By the time we cross Rogers Canyon Creek in a small, grassy basin and meet the Frog Tank Trail at a signed junction (5.3; 3680), we are likely to blink our eyes and wonder if we are still in the same arid mountain range we started in. There are a number of excellent campsites here, and fair swimming when the water is high.

To reach the cliff dwellings, continue east along the Rogers Canyon Trail, boulderhopping across the stream several times. After 0.4 mile the trail should be on the right (south) side of the creek; just before it climbs up into a oak thicket beyond here, look for a sign on the left (5.7; 3800). The ruins are directly across the canyon from here, on the north side at the base of an overhanging cliff about 100 feet above Rogers Canyon Creek. Not a great deal of the old settlement remains, just a few walled-off rooms set here and there in recesses in the cliff. Yet their antiquity is immediately apparent, even to the most casual observer, and they are impressive enough if viewed in the proper perspective. They are, after all, thought to date back to about 1300 AD, some 200 years before the first glimmer of the Renaissance in Europe. The reason for their abandonment—and for the abandonment of hundreds of similar sites scattered across the Southwest—remains a mystery. We may never know precisely why the inhabitants of this particular set of dwellings left their lovely home, but the visitor who lingers awhile in Rogers Canyon, with its singing, crystalline creek and its serene groves of oak and sycamore, will readily understand why they chose to settle here in the first place.

The ruins are legally guarded by the Federal Antiquities Act, but the only real protection they have lies in the respect and common sense of visitors. Please do not damage or alter them in any way.

Return the way you came, or via the trail up Rogers Canyon to Rogers Trough (9.9 miles; 10-mile car shuttle required; see Trip 19).

Ancient cliff dwelling in Rogers Canyon

TRIP 18
ROGERS TROUGH TO REAVIS GRAVE

- Ɐ **4.8 miles round trip; 660' elevation gain**
- Ɐ **Leisurely dayhike**
- Ɐ **Trailhead 6, Rogers Trough**
- Ɐ **Maps**
  Superstition Wilderness or *Iron Mountain quadrangle*
- Ɐ **Season: all year; best in spring and fall**
  Water available in Rogers Canyon (miles 0.0 to 1.8) during rainy periods only

Features

The destination of this fine, leisurely excursion is the gravesite of Elisha Reavis, a remarkable recluse who, during the late 1800s, almost single-handedly homesteaded 60 acres of land on nearby Reavis Creek. Along the way we pass through the quiet, shady defile of upper Rogers Canyon, whose serene groves of sycamore and walnut help put the hiker in the proper frame of mind to visit the final resting place of the man who probably knew these mountains better than any other.

Trailhead Route/Camping

Note: 4-wheel-drive vehicles recommended. Follow the directions for Woodbury Trailhead (Trip 17) to the point where Forest Road 172A branches off of Forest Road 172 (8.1 miles from Forest Road 357). Turn right here, onto 172A. After 3.1 miles you will come to a junction with Forest Road 650. Turn left and drive just over a quarter of a mile to the trailhead. Forest Road 650 and the Reavis Ranch Trail are part of the route of the Arizona Trail. Eventually, the entire Arizona Trail, from the Mexican border to the Utah state line, will be closed to motorized travel. This may change the location of the trailhead parking area. A 4WD vehicle is recommended to negotiate most of this approach. However, any vehicle that makes it to the Forest Road 172A turnoff can probably handle the next half mile and there are pullouts for parking. A high clearance vehicle could probably go an additional mile or so but the road steepens and traction is needed for safety. While a new, sporty model of Ford Taurus was seen coming down from the trailhead, the driver did not look happy negotiating deep ruts. There are places to set up camp off Forest Road 172A and at the trailhead.

Description

From the trailhead parking area (0.0; 4840) the trail proceeds gently across two small creekbeds of Rogers Creek. After about a hundred yards from the start the West Pinto Trail branches right from a signed junction; we keep left here and follow the Reavis Trail downcanyon through a delightful riparian forest of hackberry, sycamore and walnut. About 1.5 miles later, after winding back and forth across the rocky creekbed a number of times, the trail swings northward toward a side canyon which can be seen opening up on the right. At a signed junction here (1.8; 4400) the Rogers Canyon Trail continues on; we stay right and follow the Reavis Ranch Trail as it passes a fence and climbs moderately up the tributary canyon. The surrounds here are less congenial than in Rogers Canyon—the few large trees are confined to widely spaced pockets down in the wash, and the shadeless stretches between them are bouldery and throttle with brush. (This entire area burned in the Iron Fire of 1966.)

About 0.6 mile beyond the preceding junction, immediately after crossing the tributary creekbed from its right to its left side, we arrive at an unsigned junction (2.4; 4620) marked with a cairn. The right-hand fork here is the continuation of the Reavis Ranch Trail, which leaves the streambed at this point and climbs up the canyonside to the north; to reach Reavis Grave we follow the left fork as it cuts steeply up a rocky hillside. After proceeding only a few dozen yards this rough pathway peters out between clumps of shrubbery; the grave is in an inconspicuous clearing just to the left of this area.

The cause of Reavis' death was never determined. When his remains were found here in 1896 the head was located some distance away from the rest of the body, and thus was born many a grisly legend concerning the "Curse of the Superstition Mountains." But probably coyotes or other scavengers were responsible for his "beheading."

Return the way you came.

TRIP 19
ROGERS TROUGH TO ROGERS CANYON CLIFF DWELLINGS

- ▲ **8.4 miles round trip; 1040′ elevation gain**
- ▲ **Moderate dayhike or leisurely backpack (2 hiking days)**
- ▲ **Trailhead 6, Rogers Trough**
- ▲ **Maps**
  Superstition Wilderness or *Iron Mountain quadrangle*
- ▲ **Season: all year; best in spring and fall**

Water is generally available along entire route from the beginning of the winter rainy season until April or May; check with Forest Service first

~~~~~~

Features

This route provides the easiest access to the ancient cliff dwellings in Rogers Canyon. Along the way it stays close to Rogers Canyon Creek, one of the leafiest and most congenial watercourses in all the Superstitions. With its lack of steep, tiring climbs, this trip is a good choice for the beginning hiker or backpacker, yet its beautiful setting and intriguing destination make it worthwhile for more experienced trekkers as well.

Trailhead Route

Follow the trailhead route for Trip 18.

Description

From the parking area at Rogers Trough Trailhead (0.0; 4840) our route proceeds along a well defined path. After about a hundred yards the West Pinto Trail branches right at a signed junction; we stay left here and follow the Reavis Trail down-canyon. Where a major side canyon opens up to the northeast we swing right, away from the stream, and meet the Rogers Canyon Trail at a signed junction (1.8; 4400). If you wish, you may go straight ahead here and make the side trip to Reavis Grave (1.2 miles round trip; see Trip 18). Otherwise we turn left, cross a rocky area back to Rogers Canyon, and continue downstream. Soon after we pass an old corral and stock fence, the canyon walls begin to steepen considerably, providing enough shelter to foster a fairly dense forest cover of stately sycamores, sturdy alligator junipers, Emory and white oaks and a few Arizona walnuts and velvet ashes. During later winter and early spring there is usually enough running water to permit some brisk swimming in the pools which, for the next mile or so, decorate the stream like beads on a necklace.

After skirting the base of a steep cliff the trail swings to the left, then drops down to a sign on the left (south) side of Rogers Canyon Creek (4.2; 3800). The cliff dwellings are just across the creek from here, 100 feet or so up the hillside at the base of a high, overhanging cliff. (For a description of these ruins, see Trip 17.) There are a few fair campsites in this area, but backpackers will find far better ones at the Rogers Canyon/Frog Tank Trail junction, 0.4 mile down the canyon from here.

Return the way you came, or via the trail to Tortilla Pass and JF Ranch (9.9 miles total; 7-mile car shuttle required; see Trip 17).

TRIP 20
TORTILLA TRAILHEAD TO PERALTA TRAILHEAD

- ▲ 15.7 miles one-way (43-mile car shuttle required); 2510' elevation gain
- ▲ Strenuous dayhike or moderate backpack (2-3 hiking days)
- ▲ Trailhead 3, Tortilla (start)
- ▲ Trailhead 4, Peralta (finish)
- ▲ Maps
  Superstition Wilderness or *Weaver's Needle quadrangle*
- ▲ Season: November to April
  Water is usually available at Charlebois Spring (near mile 7.4)
  (check with Forest Service during prolonged dry spells); during
  rainy periods, water may also be available at Kane Spring (mile 2.2),
  and in Peters Canyon (miles 3.7 to 5.0)

Features

After traversing a variety of peaceful, comparatively gentle terrain, this transmontane route crosses scenic Peters Mesa and twists down into the rugged heart of the Superstition Wilderness. Terrapin Pass offers the hiker one of the finest views to be had of the famous landmark of Weaver's Needle.

Trailhead Route

Start: follow the trailhead route for Trip 8. Finish: follow the trailhead route for Trip 9.

Description

From Tortilla Trailhead (0.0; 3080), follow the route of Trip 8 to the saddle atop Peters Mesa (5.3; 3580). From here the trail drops gently westward for 0.2 mile, then swings sharply left and continues downhill to the southeast. The path is occasionally faint through here, but cairns mark the way. You may spot some clusters of glinting quartz crystals in this area.

In 0.5 mile more we cross a small wash (5.8; 3340), then climb slightly to crest a minor ridge. The trail next descends moderately southward, staying just above the bottom of a bluff-lined ravine. Soon we veer to the right, crossing a flat area with a good view down the gulf of La Barge Canyon. The final descent into the canyon is quite steep in places.

At the bottom of this descent we meet the Dutchman Trail at a signed junction (7.4; 2580). Here we turn right and drop a short distance further to a sign pointing out the spur trail to Charlebois (locally pronounced "Charley-boy") Spring (0.2 mile up Charlebois Canyon to the right). Water is *almost* always available here, but during dry weather spells this should be checked out beforehand with the Forest Service. There are several nice campsites in the area, shaded by large sycamores and cottonwoods. The Forest Service asks that you camp a good distance away from the spring itself, as a variety of shy wildlife depend on it for water.

Continuing from here along the Dutchman's Trail, we soon cross La Barge Creek and descend gently down-canyon. Shortly after we pass a drift fence, a nice view opens up across the canyon to the steep basaltic cliffs of Black Mountain and, in the distance, the yellow rhyolite bluffs of Geronimo Head. In the area known as Marsh Valley, the signed Cavalry Trail comes in on the right (9.0; 2370). Our route goes left here and begins climbing gently away from La Barge Creek. Soon we reach a signed junction with the Bull Pass Trail, where we go left again. There is a fabulous, head-on view of Weaver's Needle from here.

As we climb into Needle Canyon, the route is temporarily confused by use-trails; the correct path trends steadily south along the east side of Needle Creek Wash. When the track becomes once again unambiguous, we cut over to the right side of the creekbed and soon meet the Terrapin Trail, at the junction marked only by a signpost (10.4; 2640). To complete our transmontane trek to Peralta Trailhead, we turn left onto the latter and follow the directions for the second half of Trip 10 to the trailhead (15.7; 2420). (It is also possible to turn *right* here, reverse the steps of the *first* half of Trip 10, and finish your trek via Blacktop Pass and the Peralta Trail—17.8 miles total.)

TRIP 21
TORTILLA TRAILHEAD TO ROGERS CANYON CLIFF DWELLINGS

- ▲ **19.2 miles round trip; 3540' elevation gain**
- ▲ **Moderate backpack (2 hiking days)**
- ▲ **Trailhead 3, Tortilla**
- ▲ **Maps**
  Superstition Wilderness or *Weaver's Needle and Iron Mountain* quadrangles
- ▲ **Season: November to April**
  Water is generally available at Rogers Canyon (mile 9.2) from the beginning of the winter rainy season until April or May; Clover Spring (mile 3.6) has water during rainy periods only

Features

This comparatively unfrequented route provides the hiker an alternative way (to Trip 17) to reach beautiful Rogers Canyon and its intriguing ruins. The trail offers open and varied views the entire way, and is a fine introduction to the northern Superstitions.

Trailhead Route

Follow the trailhead route for Trip 8.

Description

From the trailhead at the end of Forest Road 213 (0.0; 3080), follow the signed JF Trail as it climbs gently southeast. The route follows an old roadway through this stretch. In about 0.5 mile a very faint road branches right; we continue straight ahead. At a second junction just beyond an open gate, we veer a bit right and proceed uphill. Continue climbing to a signed junction with the Hoolie Bacon Trail (1.3; 3410). Our route goes left here, staying on the JF Trail and climbing steadily. The old roadbed narrows to a trail as we proceed, and a good view opens up across the great canyon of the Salt River to the rocky summits of the Four Peaks in the Mazatzal Range. The ground cover through here is a characteristic lower Sonoran mixture of prickly pear, paloverde, agave and mesquite.

Riparian forest in Rogers Canyon

For the next two miles the pathway stays on or near the crest of a long, gently ascending ridge. The many clusters of sparkling quartz crystals that will likely catch your eye in this area provide frequent excuses to stop and rest. At length the steadily ascending trail dips slightly to cross a tiny ravine well below the ridgeline. The thick growth of scrub oak here is a welcome indicator of our increasing altitude. At a second, larger watercourse (3.6; 3980) there is a fair campsite beneath a solitary mesquite tree. Clover Spring, which may be dry (check with the Forest Service if you will be depending on it for water) is 0.2 mile up the wash.

The trail now resumes its gradual ascent, again staying close to the ridgeline for the most part. After another two miles it tops out temporarily at a saddle (5.9; 4560) beneath chaparral-clad Peak 4893. From here we make a brief descent through scrub-oak forest to a second saddle (6.3; 4380). The trail passes through this gap, then descends a little further before climbing moderately to the head of Tortilla Creek at Tortilla Pass (7.2; 4480). At a signed junction where we turn left, onto the Rogers Canyon Trail, and follow the route of Trip 17 the remaining 2.4 miles to a sign across the canyon from Rogers Canyon Cliff Dwellings (9.6; 3800) (see Trip 17 for a description of the dwelling area).

Return the way you came.

TRIP 22
REAVIS TRAILHEAD TO REAVIS HEADQUARTERS

- ▲ **19.6 miles round trip; 1640' elevation gain**
- ▲ **Moderate backpack (2 hiking days)**
- ▲ **Trailhead 7, Reavis**
- ▲ **Maps**
  Superstition Wilderness or *Pinyon Mountain and Iron Mountain quadrangles*
- ▲ **Season: all year; hot in summer**
  Water available at Reavis Creek (mile 9.8) from the beginning of the winter rainy season until April or May; check with Forest Service first

Features

From 1872 until his death in 1896, Elisha M. Reavis homesteaded 60 acres of land in the pine-and-juniper-forested highlands of the eastern Superstitions. He was the perfect picture of a hermit, living and working alone, letting his hair and beard grow to prodigious lengths, appearing in town only at rare intervals to sell his home-grown vegetables. This trip follows an abandoned road up to his old ranch site, where backpackers can get a taste of the serene, undis-turbed life which Reavis enjoyed for nearly a quarter of a century. (The homestead was purchased by the Forest Service in 1967, and has been open to the public since then.)

Trailhead Route/Camping

From Apache Junction follow State Highway 88 approximately 30 miles to a Highway Department maintenance yard opposite Horse Mesa. Continue east along State 88 from here for 0.9 mile, then turn right onto Reavis Ranch Road (Forest Road 212) and follow it uphill 3.1 miles to the barricades which mark the beginning of the Reavis Ranch Trail. The last 3.1 miles of this approach might be troublesome for some passenger cars. Forest Road 212 can also be reached by dri-ving 14.4 miles southwest from Theodore Roosevelt Dam on Highway 88—the Apache Trail. When the trail is freshly graded, pas-senger cars can be driven to the trailhead. For the current road status contact the rangers at the Roosevelt Lake Visitor Center, (520) 467-3200, which is open daily 7:45 A.M.-4:30 P.M. except holidays. Be care-ful: at best this hard packed road is coated with loose sand and small gravel making for poor traction on curves and steep grades. Car camping is possible at the small trailhead parking area and at pull-outs along Forest Road 212.

Description

From the parking area at Reavis Trailhead (0.0; 3660), walk gently uphill, past the barricades that block the Reavis Ranch Road to vehicu-lar traffic. For the first few miles the trail-road ascends at an easy grade, a bit washed out in places, staying on or near the crest of a winding ridge, crossing from one side to the other frequently. Views are excellent from the start, both northward, across Apache Lake to the beautiful Four Peaks of the Mazatzals, and westward, across the maze of peaks and ridges surrounding Fish Creek and the Salt River Canyon. Vegetation is mostly sparse along this section, consisting chiefly of yucca, snakeweed, treacherous mats of agave and sotol, and a few hardy shrubs such as mountain mahogany and shrub live oak. After we pass through a major saddle (4.0; 4620) and begin traversing beneath the high northeast face of Castle Dome Mountain, the plant cover grows noticeably denser, and hoptree and single-leaf pinyon appear.

After passing through another saddle, the trail (actually still very much a road in appearance) drops a slight distance to Windy Pass (6.1; 4900), which offers an excellent view westward, across the central Superstitions of the seemingly ever-present landmark of Weaver's

Needle. From this gap we drop downhill along a minor drainage (a section of the road has washed away here, but the route is clear) to Plow Saddle, a broad, grassy notch containing a corral. Here the route resumes climbing, topping out at a small ridgecrest affording another good view of Weaver's Needle. After dropping a bit to a signed junction with the Frog Tank Trail (8.0; 4820), the trail-road swings gradually onto the east slope of a long ridge and traverses southward, paralleling Reavis Creek, down in the canyon some distance below. At a sycamore-shaded gate we meet the Reavis Gap Trail, branching left at a signed junction. Here we continue straight ahead on the old road, past some rusting, abandoned farm machinery and an apple orchard, relics of a bygone era which presage our arrival at Reavis Headquarters (9.8; 4860).

Reavis' original cabin no longer exists. The present ranch house was built by the Clements Cattle Company in the 1930s and later used by the Forest Service as an "administrative site". Architecturally this structure was quite a hodge-podge, with walls that are variously of adobe and stone, covered by a metal roof. An assortment of other building techniques and materials, some of them incongruously modern-looking, were applied over the years. The house was gutted by fire years ago. All that remains is a concrete floor. Those who prefer more natural surroundings will find a number of good tentsites nearby. This valley is one of the most pleasant areas in the Superstitions, sporting a spotty cover of ponderosa pine, single-leaf pinyon, some tall sycamores near the creek, and Palmer and white oak. Reavis Creek, which flows only after the winter rainy season has gotten well under way, is apparently the only source of water.

A number of tall tales revolve around Reavis, known to contemporaries as the "Hermit of the Superstitions." One writer reports that his cabbages grew to a phenomenal size, often weighing as much as ten pounds. Another rumor has it that he ran about naked at night, shouting and shooting bullets at the stars, and was thus never bothered by the local Apaches, who supposedly feared the evil spirits by which he was possessed. He died in 1896 on the other side of Reavis Saddle, and by the time his remains were located the head had been chewed off of the body by scavengers; this perfectly natural occurrence, widely reported as a "beheading," immediately got hitched on the legend of the lost Dutchman Mine as "The Dutchman's Revenge," the "Curse of the Superstition Mountains," and so on. In reality, one supposes, Reavis was nothing more than a harmless old recluse—a bit antisocial, no doubt, but neither a raving madman nor a victim of some fanciful curse.

Return the way you came.

AREA 2—The Southeastern Ranges

Arizona's southeastern ranges, for the purposes of this guide, consist of the Santa Catalina, Rincon, Santa Rita and Chiricahua Mountains. Each of these is an "island" range, rising out of a surrounding sea of desert and grassland to heights in excess of 8-9000 feet. With their broad latitudinal sweep, some parts of these mountains provide enjoyable hiking during every month of the year. Lower elevations are warm (hot in summer), dry, studded with cacti and, in spring and fall, awash with colorful wildflowers. In the middle regions you will find pretty forests of silverleaf oak, pinyon pine and alligator juniper, while the heights are crowned with ponderosa pine, Mexican white pine, Douglas-fir, quaking aspen and, in the Chiricahua Mountains, Engelmann spruce.

Trips in the Santa Catalina and Chiricahua mountains lie within the Pusch Ridge Wilderness, the Chiricahua Wilderness, and Chiricahua National Monument respectively, while those in the Santa Rita Mountains explore the Mount Wrightson Wilderness. The Rincon Mountains backcountry lies within Saguaro National Park, and has been set aside as wilderness by the National Park Service. Hikers will be glad to learn that cattle grazing is no longer permitted in any of these areas.

When hiking the higher trails in July or August, remember that afternoon thundershowers are an almost daily occurrence. Carry raingear even if the morning weather is clear, and plan your itinerary so as to avoid exposed peaks and ridges (prime targets for lightning) during the afternoon. You may wish to visit the high country during dry periods in the winter; if you do, be prepared for subfreezing nighttime temperatures and unexpected snowstorms. Trips with very wide elevation ranges have no "ideal" hiking season; you will have to decide if you wish to be hot down low or cold up high. Temperature extremes can be avoided somewhat by hiking in spring and fall.

Wildlife is still plentiful in these ranges. The huge herds of prong-horn antelope that once roamed the surrounding grasslands may be gone, but the mountains themselves still boast healthy populations of mule deer and Coues white-tailed deer, coatimundis, cougars and bobcats. A few black bears either inhabit or visit each area, and some 35 or so desert bighorn sheep—exceedingly shy creatures—cling to existence in a rugged corner of the Santa Catalina Mountains. A variety of colorful, subtropical birds migrate northward each spring from Mexico and Central America, to nest in the hardwood-forested canyons of the Chiricahua and Santa Rita ranges. There have even been rumors that jaguars—long extinct in the United States—occasionally stray into the Chiricahuas from the fastnesses of the Mexican Sierra Madre.

The present rugged relief of this section of the state is the result of massive thrusting and faulting that has been going on since at least the beginning of the Cenozoic era some 70 million years ago. Structurally, that relief is even greater than it appears to be, since eons of erosion have filled the valleys between the mountains with thousands of feet of alluvial deposits; today, some of the ranges are so deeply awash in this alluvium that they barely manage to poke up out of their own debris.

The areas covered in this chapter are essentially devoid of valuable mineral deposits. There is no particular geological reason for this however—it merely reflects the sad fact that only those few areas that *were* mineral-free have survived as official wilderness. An exception to this is the Santa Rita Mountains, where there are quite a few active mines. (The Mount Wrightson Wilderness, however, contains only a few, presently inactive workings.)

The southeastern ranges have long played an important role in the history of the region. In pre-Columbian times they provided the local Indians with plentiful game, reliable water, and relief from the sweltering heat of lowland summers. Later, following the invasion of the whites, they served as virtually impregnable wartime citadels. In Arizona's first "Indian uprising," a band of Pimas led by Luis Oacpicagua killed several Spanish settlers, then fled to the Santa Catalina Mountains. As a result of this revolt an army was stationed in the area, and a general escalation of hostilities promptly ensued. The Pimas were soon brought under military control, but not before the Apaches had joined the fray, and *they* were not to be so quickly conquered. For the next 80 years, in one of the longest wars in history, these hardened, highly skilled, and vastly outnumbered guerrilla fighters harassed first the Spaniards, then the Mexicans, and finally the Americans, holding continuous sway over vast tracts of disputed land, until the decimation of their ranks broke their resistance. Perhaps the most feared of the Apache bands were the Chiricahuas, who operated out of the mountains of the same name and, under the leadership of the likes of Cochise, Juh, and Golthlay (Geronimo), were the last to surrender to the whites.

Visit the ranges today and you will find not a trace of these bloody, protracted battles. What you *will* find is a penetrating sense of stillness and serenity, the excitement of storms, vistas that know no bounds, skies of the deepest blue. And you will come away feeling that these mountains are just as much worth fighting for today as they were during the heyday of the Apache.

Managing Agencies

Pusch Ridge Wilderness:

Santa Catalina Ranger District
5700 N. Sabino Canyon Road
Tucson, AZ 85715
(520) 749-8700
For Sabino Canyon shuttle information: (520) 749-2861

Rincon Mountains:

East Saguaro National Park
3693 S. Old Spanish Trail
Tucson, AZ 85730
(520) 733-5153

West Saguaro National Park
2700 N. Kinney Drive
Tucson, AZ 85743
(520) 883-6366

Santa Rita Mountains:

Nogales Ranger District
303 Old Tucson Rd.
Rio Rico, AZ 85621
(520) 281-2296

Chiracahua Wilderness:

Douglas Ranger District
RR #1, Box 228R
Douglas, AZ 85607
(520) 364-3468

Chiricahua Nat'l Monument
Dos Cabezas Route, Box 6500
Willcox, AZ 85643
(520) 824-3560

Further Reading

Watch for Me On the Mountain (biography of Geronimo) by Forrest Carter (Delacorte, New York, NY, 1978)

Guide to the Santa Catalina Mountains of Arizona, by Edgar G. Heylmun (Treasure Chest Publications, Tucson, Arizona, 1979

Tucson Hiking Guide, by Betty Leavengood (Pruett Publishing Company, Boulder, Colorado, 1997)

Hiker's Guide to the Santa Rita Mountains, by Betty Leavengood and Mike Liebert (Pruett Publishing Company, Boulder, Colorado, 1994)

Apaches, Eagles of the Southwest, by Donald E. Worcester (University of Oklahoma Press, Norman, Oklahoma, 1979)

Southern Arizona Wildflower Guide (Tucson Daily Citizen, Tucson, Arizona, 1974)

See also the Pusch Ridge and Chiricahua Wilderness management plans, available for inspection at local Forest Service offices.

Pusch Ridge Wilderness of the Santa Catalinas

The Santa Catalina Range towers over Tucson nearly 7,000 feet. When Tucson is baking in summer, the high parts of the range are cool, offering recreation opportunities as well as an escape from the heat. In winter it is not unusual for some Tucsonites to go swimming in unheated outdoor swimming pools while others grab the skis and head for the Mount Lemmon Ski Valley. At this time the lower levels of the range offer an ideal climate for hiking and camping.

TRIP 23
ROMERO CANYON TRAILHEAD TO ROMERO CANYON

- ▲ **5.6-12.4 miles round trip; 1120-3340′ elevation gain**
- ▲ **Moderate to strenuous dayhike or backpack (2 hiking days)**
- ▲ **Trailhead 8, Romero Canyon**
- ▲ **Maps**
  Pusch Ridge Wilderness or *Oro Valley and Mount Lemmon quad-rangles*
- ▲ **Season: November to April**
  Water always available at Romero Creek (mile 2.8); also from mile 5.0 to 6.2 during rainy periods only

Features

A fine introduction to the "front range" of the western Santa Catalinas, this route passes alternately along wildflower-dotted hill-sides and through leafy, intimate forest cloisters on the way to the head of Romero Canyon. En route we gain excellent views across the rough-cut skyline of Pusch Ridge, beneath which sprawls some of the wildest and most inaccessible country left in southern Arizona.

Trailhead Route/Camping

From Tucson, drive north along U.S. 77 (Oracle Road). About 6 miles beyond Ina Road, turn right into Catalina State Park. At the entry station you will be charged a day use fee of $4, or a camping fee of $9 or $15 (with electricity). Drive an additional mile and a half to the large trailhead parking area.

Description

From the parking area at Romero Canyon Trailhead (0.0; 2720) fol-low a well defined and signed path east as it crosses sandy Canada del Oro and swings up to a trail junction just beyond. Bear left from the Birding Trail along an old road smoothed into a wide footpath. Continue straight past the Canyon Loop Trail half a mile farther. Soon a sign proclaims the trail ahead to be within a bighorn sheep management area with no dogs allowed ever and hikers are not to leave the trail more than 400 feet during lambing season, January 1-April 30. A half mile later the road ends at a point overlooking Montrose Canyon Wash on the right (1.1; 2960). A glance into the wash may give some idea how much water to expect. Here we turn onto a foot trail which can be seen heading off to the left, and climb up to the Coronado National Forest boundary. Above here the trail climbs rather steeply, switchbacking occasionally and soon rising high above rugged Montrose Canyon. There are many side-use trails, usually blocked by a line of stones low enough that a rubbernecking hiker can easily step over them unnoticed. The vegetative cover here is dense and varied, consisting chiefly of statuesque saguaros, sprawling ocotillos, yellow (or foothill) paloverde and prickly pear. During the spring months there are bright patches of wildflowers all

Cascade and pool, Pima Canyon

through this section, including yellow-blossomed brittlebush and paperflower, as well as some narrowleaf aster. Views are excellent to the south, sweeping across the cliffy foothills of Pusch Ridge to steep-walled, square-topped Table Mountain. With luck you might spot one of the 40 or so bighorn sheep which inhabit the inaccessible fast-nesses of Pusch Ridge, particularly during the winter, when fierce snowstorms occasionally drive them off the heights.

After winding up and down through a jumbled, rocky area, the trail threads a narrow notch atop a ridge (2.4; 3640). From here we climb a short distance eastward along the ridge, gaining good views up the long defile of Romero Canyon, and then drop down to a sad-dle crest between Romero Creek and a drainage on the right (2.8; 3600). Shortly beyond the saddle, the trail reaches the pools and crosses the stream—though it appears to continue upstream. A series of potholes just downstream from here always have water, and pro-vide enjoyable swimming during warm weather. When these are too crowded there are less popular pools upstream. A few poor-to-fair campsites are located nearby.

For the next 0.5 mile we proceed up-canyon, crossing the creek on occasion but mostly staying on the dry flats to either side. The first crossing is on solid bedrock and the trail seems to end in an area of beautiful pools. Sycamore, walnut and velvet ash grow near the stream, while Mexican blue oaks and mesquites are predominant in the drier areas away from the water. The canyon quickly grows nar-rower and rougher, and the trail soon begins a steep, switchbacking ascent up the left-hand canyon wall. As we gain elevation there are good views of the craggy headlands surrounding 7952-foot Cathedral Rock.

After gaining some 800 feet the trail levels off and begins travers-ing high above the canyon floor. Approximately 0.5 mile later, after crossing a (seasonally) brushy flat (the site of an old corral), we drop down a few steep switchbacks to an old campsite featuring a couple of large stone fire rings (5.0; 4680). Other nice campsites can be found just up- or down-stream. Romero Creek, which runs only during the rainy season (and often intermittently even then), is just beyond the campsite. Romero Spring is a short distance down-canyon, at the con-fluence of a tributary wash which comes down from the south. It is apparently not a reliable source of water during the dry months.

To continue to the head of Romero Canyon, follow the trail as it proceeds moderately up-canyon, crossing the bouldery streambed frequently. About 0.5 mile later we switchback a short distance up the north canyonside, through a light forest cover of pinyon pine and alligator juniper, then drop back down to creekside. There are excellent campsites in this area, beneath a shady overstory of silverleaf and Arizona white oaks, velvet ash, walnut, and an occasional cypress or ponderosa. During the spring, delicate yellow columbines bloom in moist pockets by the water.

A few hundred yards above here the trail swings to the right and enters a side canyon (6.2; 5320), preparatory to beginning the ascent to Romero Pass. Here, at the end of today's excursion, there is one final campsite (water during rainy periods only).

Return the way you came.

TRIP 24
MAGEE ROADEND TO PIMA CANYON

▲ **6.4 miles round trip; 1020′ elevation gain**
▲ **Leisurely dayhike or backpack (2 hiking days)**
▲ **Trailhead 9, Magee Roadend**
▲ **Maps**
   Pusch Ridge Wilderness or *Tucson North quadrangle*
▲ **Season: November to April**
   Water available intermittently in Pima Canyon (miles 1. 1 to 3.2) during rainy periods only

Features

Pima Canyon, draining the "back side" of rugged Pusch Ridge, provides the easiest access to the front range of the Santa Catalinas. A good midwinter warmup, this leisurely trip samples the interesting desert country along the lower part of the canyon, reserving the high, forested region beyond for later, more strenuous excursions.

Trailhead Route/Camping

From the intersection of Ina and Oracle roads in Tucson drive north one mile on Oracle Road and turn right on Magee Road and follow it (and the signs) 1.6 miles to a timer-controlled, gated parking lot. The gate is open from 5 A.M.-9 P.M. The nearest car camping is at Catalina State Park, five miles north off Oracle Road.

Description

From the parking area at the end of Magee Road (0.0; 2940) walk along a path between two parallel barbed wire fences. Eventually, there will be houses built right up to the right hand fence. After a quarter mile the path passes through a hikers gate and proceeds across the rocky slopes at the south base of Pusch Peak then contours to the left into Pima Canyon. The ground cover here is a typical Lower Sonoran mixture of gangly ocotillos, tall saguaros, foothill paloverdes and prickly pears. Bright yellow brittlebush blossoms carpet the area in the spring.

Presently the trail switches back to the right and drops down to Pima Canyon Wash (1.1; 3180) (generally dry except during rainy periods). Above here we work our way gradually up-canyon, winding in and out among large boulders and frequently crossing the creekbed. Here and there in the smooth bedrock you may see metates, small pits in which the Indians once ground acorns into meal. A wide variety of birdlife congregates in this canyon at various times of the year, including robins, cardinals, kestrels and black phoebes. A number of mammals are to be found here as well: desert mule deer, Harris ground squirrels, javelinas and blacktail rabbits. The large, debris-shrouded nests of the Mexican woodrat are sometimes found in brushy thickets by the creek, though the architects themselves are not so frequently seen.

Near where a major, northward-trending tributary joins the wash there is a nice campsite beneath some robust cottonwoods. Above here the trail gradually grows steeper and not as well used but not much harder to follow. Soon, we come to another, steeper tributary drainage (3.2; 3960) which comes down from cliffy Point 6628 (off to the right, or southeast). Here there are a few stunted Mexican blue oaks, fair camping, and a nice view of Tucson through the deep "V" of Pima Canyon.

Return the way you came, or continue up the trail (which soon becomes even steeper and less well traveled) to the high country at Mount Kimball (see Trip 25).

Metate ground in bedrock, Pima Canyon

TRIP 25
MAGEE ROADEND TO MOUNT KIMBALL

▲ **14.2 miles round trip; 4320' elevation gain**
▲ **Strenuous dayhike or backpack (2-3 hiking days)**
▲ **Trailhead 9, Magee Roadend**
▲ **Maps**
   Pusch Ridge Wilderness or *Tucson North and Oro Valley quadrangles*
▲ **Season: all year, except after snowstorms**
   *Water is almost always available at Pima Canyon Spring (mile 5. 3);
   check with Forest Service during dry weather periods*

Features

Standing like a sentinel above the western end of the Santa
Catalina front range, 7255-foot Mount Kimball commands a fine view
of some of the roughest, most beautiful country in Arizona. Because
the latter half of the Pima Canyon Trail up to the peak is exceptionally steep and difficult to follow, this trip is recommended only for very
experienced hikers.

Trailhead Route

Follow the trailhead route for Trip 24.

Description

From Magee Roadend (0.0; 2940), follow the route of Trip 24 up
Pima Canyon to the tributary (3.2; 3960) which comes down from
Point 6628. As we continue up-canyon from this point, the trail grows
progressively steeper, more overgrown with brush, and harder to
follow. After crossing the creekbed in Pima Canyon near a small
catchment dam built by the Arizona Game and Fish Commission, the
narrow track rollercoasters steeply up and down (mostly up) the
canyonsides on either side of the stream, passing occasional clumps of
Mexican pinyon pine and one-seed juniper, signs of our rapidly
increasing elevation. Presently we enter a narrow, cliff-bound defile,
within which is Pima Canyon Spring (5.3; 5600), a reliable source of
water except possibly during prolonged spells of dry weather. A poor
campsite is nearby.

About 0.4 mile up-canyon from the spring is an unsigned junction
marked with a cairn. The left-forking path climbs straight ahead a
short distance to the head of Pima Canyon at Pima Saddle; a point
just to the north of here commands a fabulous vista across the almost
unbelievably tough-cut north slopes of Pusch Ridge. This is desert
bighorn country, one of the few remaining sanctuaries for a race of

wild, sure-footed mountaineers that once ranged widely over the Santa Catalinas and many of the other high mountains of the Southwest. The fact that these exceptionally shy animals have managed to hang on here, within a few miles of a major metropolitan center, testifies to the ruggedness and inaccessibility of this area.

Back at the cairn, the main trail sneaks out of Pima Canyon to the right, then switchbacks up to the lip of a small, pinyon-forested basin. The path is very difficult to follow in places as it strikes off southward up this basin; take your time through here, and look for ducks and cairns at confusing spots. After crossing a small drainage to its right (southwest) side we climb up a bit to a minor ridge, then climb steeply southeastward. Soon this ridge melts into a larger ridge at a broad saddle; here we swing to the left and climb the remaining distance to the comparatively level crown of Mount Kimball (7.1; 7255). Most of this mountaintop is forested with ponderosa pine; the clearest views are obtained by following a faint use-trail to a rocky promontory at the north edge of the flat summit area. From here there is an excellent vista across the chopped-up country drained by Montrose and Romero creeks. Cathedral Rock and Window Rock are both visible as well, rising beyond the head of Ventana Canyon. Those who are willing to carry food, water and bedding up this far will be rewarded with an opportunity to view the sunrise as it unleashes its splendors on the vast landscape sprawling below. At night the lights of Tucson put on a fine show, winking and shimmering between the black silhouettes of the pines. Caution: do not remain in the summit area if a thunderstorm seems imminent.

Return the way you came.

TRIP 26
CACTUS PICNIC GROUND TO BRIDALVEIL FALLS

- ▲ **11.0 miles round trip; 3000′ elevation gain**
- ▲ **Strenuous dayhike or backpack (2 hiking days)**
- ▲ **Trailhead 10, Cactus Picnic Ground**
- ▲ **Maps**
  Pusch Ridge Wilderness or *Sabino Canyon quadrangle*
- ▲ **Season: November to April**
  Water available in Esperero Canyon (miles 4. 1 to 5.5) during rainy periods only

Features

This trip, best done during the late-winter-early-spring wet season, ascends the front range of the Santa Catalinas to tiny, graceful Bridalveil Falls. This wispy cascade, a fine destination in its own right, makes a fine base for backpackers wishing to continue to The Window or Cathedral Rock.

Trailhead Route/Camping

From the intersection of Sabino Canyon and Sunrise roads in Tucson follow signs a short distance to the Sabino Canyon Visitor Center. Here, one may catch the Sabino Canyon shuttle for $5 to the first stop, after 9 A.M. (a late start during a high temperature period); hike Sabino Canyon Road (closed to private vehicles) northeast 0.6 mile to the original trailhead (just after Cactus Picnic Ground); or take the nature trail to the east of the visitor center, then follow the new trail to the original trailhead. This route is three quarters of a mile but avoids walking on pavement. There is no car camping near the trailhead. Forest Service campgrounds start at milepost 5.5 on the Mount Lemmon Highway. Each campground is open its own portion of the year. Ask for the campground information sheet at the visitor center.

Description

From the trailhead at Cactus Picnic Ground (0.0; 2840) follow the Espero Trail as it heads gently uphill to the north. A faint unsigned spur trail soon branches left; we go right, climb up to a low saddle, and then cross a level section planted with prickly pear, ocotillo, paloverde, brittlebush and some impressive saguaros and mesquite trees. After swinging back down to the right we reach a signed junction, 0.7 mile from the trailhead, where we continue straight. (The right-hand fork leads in 0.6 mile down to Sabino Canyon Road at the first shuttle stop, and may be used as an alternate approach to the Espero Trail.) Shortly beyond here the trail climbs steeply up a ridgeline, where we start to get a good view of Tucson, then cuts left across a flat and drops into shallow Bird Canyon. At a fence here we temporarily leave Coronado National Forest (please do not camp in this privately-owned area), then resume climbing steeply up another ridge. After gaining some 600 vertical feet the path works its way left into an unnamed gulch and continues, for at least a short distance, a bit less relentlessly, uphill. Where this canyon forks, the trail follows the left branch, eventually reaching a saddle near its head (2.9; 4420). The last few hundred feet of this ascent are again quite steep. Here there is a nice view down into Espero Canyon, and up to the cliff-bound heights of Window Rock and Cathedral Rock. During periods of strong runoff a cascade is visible from this point.

From this gap we ascend moderately up-canyon, staying high above Esperero Creek and passing a few mesquite trees, one-seed junipers, and clumps of shrub live oak. Soon the trail tops out at another small saddle, then drops down to the floor of Esperero Canyon (4.1; 4640), where there are sycamores and some comparatively large oaks growing among the jumble of canyon-bottom boulders. A few fair campsites can be found nearby, but do not expect to find any water except during and immediately following rainy periods.

After crossing the creekbed, the trail meanders up-canyon, rising and falling over short distances and crossing the watercourse at frequent intervals. About a mile later we pass a side drainage in which some maps show Mormon Spring. (This spring apparently no longer flows, but some potholes in the streambed above it often hold water when the rest of Esperero Creek is dry.) Esperero Canyon branches here; our route goes left, into the west fork, and climbs 0.5 mile farther to Bridalveil Falls (5.5; 5360), off to the left of the trail. This fall is hardly spectacular as waterfalls go, being only about 30 feet high and rarely flowing with enough volume to produce even a mild roar (in fact, it is likely to dry up completely by early spring), yet is has a soothing, unpretentious beauty of its own, especially early in the day when the falls are briefly in direct sunlight. Some impressive specimens of Arizona cypress grow just across the creek, some of them leaning out slightly across the pool at the base of the falls. There is an excellent campsite here, shaded by an arching canopy of Emory oaks, within earshot of the quiet cascade. A variety of wildlife frequents this area; Harris ground squirrels scamper up and down the tree trunks, Coues deer and desert mule deer occasionally

Esperero Trail to Bridalveil Falls

come to drink out of the stream, and ringtail cats, striped skunks and other nocturnal prowlers may pay a visit to your camp if you elect to spend the night—drawn by curiosity and, as often as not, by the alluring aroma of the food stored in your pack.

Return the way you came, or continue on to The Window or Cathedral Rock (see Trips 28 and 30).

TRIP 27
CACTUS PICNIC GROUND TO THE WINDOW

▲ **16.8 miles round trip; 5140′ elevation gain**
▲ **Strenuous dayhike or backpack (3 hiking days)**
▲ **Trailhead 10, Cactus Picnic Ground**
▲ **Maps**
   Pusch Ridge Wilderness or *Sabino Canyon and Mount Lemmon quadrangles*
▲ **Season: all year, except after snowstorms**
   Water available in Espereo Canyon (miles 4.1 to 5.5) during rainy periods only

Features

After climbing up to Bridalveil Falls, this very strenuous route continues uphill to The Window, a small natural arch in a blade of rock perched nearly a vertical mile above Tucson. Even without this unusual feature for its destination, this trek would still be highly worthwhile, by simple virtue of the many fine vistas it affords along the way.

Trailhead Route

Follow the trailhead route for Trip 26.

Description

From Cactus Picnic Ground (0.0; 2880), follow the route of Trip 25 to Bridalveil Falls (5.5; 5360). Here the trail veers right, proceeds a short distance up a tributary of Espereo Canyon, then commences climbing very steeply up a ridge to the left. This ascent continues unbroken for some 600 vertical feet, after which the trail temporarily levels off at a dry campsite on a flat atop the ridge. At a trail fork here we swing to the left and climb more moderately along the rather faint path, through a thickening forest cover of ponderosa pine, spiny Schott's yuccas and overarching white oaks to a signed junction with the Cathedral Rock Trail (6.4; 6120). The route now goes left, and continues ascending moderately to a saddle (7.2; 6680) at the head of Esperero Canyon. From this point one looks directly down into the rugged headwaters of Montrose Canyon, which fall away abruptly northward; to the southeast, the view stretches across the Catalina foothills to the graceful pyramid of Rincon Peak, rising above Tanque Verde Ridge in the Rincon Mountains.

From this gap the trail switchbacks steeply up the rocky northeast ridge of Window Rock. After gaining 600 feet of elevation we top out at a point just south of this peak's summit rocks (peakbaggers may wish to scramble up to the top from here). The trail next circles westward to a minor gap, then plunges downward, through much brush and past some spectacular cliffs and pinnacles, to The Window (8.4; 7000), a 15-foot-high, wind- and water-eroded perforation in a large fin of rock. There is a register here, of the type usually reserved for mountaintops, in which you may read the comments of others who have labored up to this lofty point, and in which you may record your own strenuous accomplishment. Be careful if you go scrambling around in the arch; it is a sheer, 100 foot drop out of the far side. When the sunlight strikes it at the proper angle, this natural "hole in the wall" is clearly visible from parts of Tucson; once you have been there, it is a pleasant sensation to view it from city level and mentally relive this excursion.

Return the way you came.

TRIP 28
Cactus Picnic Ground to Magee Roadend via Bridalveil Falls, The Window, and Mount Kimball

- ▲ **19.0 miles one way (13-mile car shuttle required); 5240′ elevation gain**
- ▲ **Strenuous backpack (3 hiking days)**
- ▲ **Trailhead 10, Cactus Picnic Ground (start)**
- ▲ **Trailhead 9, Magee Roadend (finish)**
- ▲ **Maps**
  Pusch Ridge Wilderness or *Sabino Canyon, Mount Lemmon, Oro Valley, and Tucson North quadrangles*
- ▲ **Season: all year, except after snowstorms**
  Water is almost always available at Pima Canyon Spring (mile 13.7) (check with Forest Service during dry weather spells); Esperero Canyon (miles 4.1 to 5.5) and Pima Canyon (miles 15.8 to 17.9) have water during rainy periods only

Features

After climbing up past Bridalveil Falls, this strenuous backpacking route stays high on the crest of the Santa Catalina front range, traversing across The Window and Mount Kimball before dropping back to the desert via Pima Canyon. With fine wet-season campsites located at Bridalveil Falls and near Pima Canyon Spring, this makes a good, albeit strenuous, 3-day outing.

Trailhead Route

Start: follow the trailhead route for Trip 26. Finish: follow the trailhead route for Trip 24.

Description

From Cactus Picnic Ground (0.0; 2880), follow the route of Trip 27 to The Window (8.4;7000). After dropping steeply past The Window's base, the trail descends more gradually along a broad, open ridgetop. After a little over 0.5 mile we cut sharply to the left and switchback down into the head of Ventana Canyon. At a signed junction with the Ventana Canyon Trail we turn right, then climb gently past a pair of switchbacks to the saddle dividing Montrose and Ventana canyons. Several more switchbacks now bring us up onto a wide, gently sloping shelf just east of Mount Kimball, along which we climb very gradually, through an open forest cover of wind-tossed Mexican pinyon pines, sturdy alligator junipers and a variety of oaks. After 0.6 mile this gentle ascent suddenly ends, and the trail swings to the right and twists steeply uphill some 200 feet to a saddle with a good dry campsite and a nice view of Tucson (11.4; 6860).

At a signed junction in this gap, we turn right and follow a faint path that scrabbles steeply 0.5 mile up to the flat summit of Mount Kimball (11.9; 7255). To complete your journey from here, reverse the steps of Trip 25 the remaining 7.1 miles to Magee Roadend (19.0; 2940).

TRIP 29
CACTUS PICNIC GROUND TO ROMERO CANYON TRAILHEAD VIA BRIDALVEIL FALLS AND ROMERO PASS

⌃ **17.7 miles one-way (20-mile car shuttle required); 5260' elevation gain**
⌃ **Strenuous backpack (3 hiking days)**
⌃ **Trailhead 10, Cactus Picnic Ground (start)**
⌃ **Trailhead 8, Romero Canyon (finish)**

▲ **Maps**
Pusch Ridge Wilderness or *Sabino Canyon, Mount Lemmon, and Oro Valley quadrangles*
▲ **Season: all year, except after snowstorms**
Water available in Esperero Canyon (miles 4.1 to 5.5) and Romero Canyon (miles 11.5 to 12.6) during rainy periods only

Features

After climbing up to Bridalveil Falls in the Santa Catalina front range, this route crosses two high saddles and drops into Romero Canyon. Both Cathedral Rock and The Window are accessible via short sidetrips from the main route, and magnificent views alternate with shady forest closures almost the entire way. With delightful campsites located at convenient intervals in Esperero and Romero canyons, this makes a fine 3-day trek for the backpacker in good physical condition.

Trailhead Route

Start: follow the trailhead route for Trip 26. Finish: follow the trailhead route for Trip 23.

Description

From Cactus Picnic Ground (0.0; 2880), follow the route of Trip 25 to Bridalveil Falls (5.5; 5360). Here the trail veers right, proceeds a short distance up a tributary of Esperero Canyon, then commences climbing very steeply up a ridge to the left. This ascent continues unbroken for some 600 vertical feet, after which the trail temporarily levels off at a dry campsite on a flat atop the ridge. At a trail fork here we swing to the left and climb more moderately along the rather faint path, through a thickening forest cover of ponderosa pine, Schott's yucca and white oak, to a signed junction with the Cathedral Rock Trail (6.4; 6120). Turn left here if you wish to make the highly worthwhile, 4.0 mile round-trip detour to The Window (see Trip 27). To continue on the main route, we turn right and climb moderately along a rocky, brushy path, past good views of the distant Rincon Mountains, to a saddle (7.4; 6920) southeast of Cathedral Rock. Very experienced cross-country scramblers may wish to try for Cathedral's craggy, 7952-foot summit (the highest in the front range) from here. (This route is neither straightforward nor easy. Some technical rock-climbing experience is necessary to reach the highest point, and many climbers will want a rope.)

There is an obscure, unsigned junction in this saddle. Our route turns left and heads west a short distance, then drops north into a small basin forested with ponderosa pine, Douglas-fir and white fir.

After passing a nice campsite (a creeklet nearby generally has water following heavy rains), we reach the lip of this basin, where we are treated to a nice view across the gap of Romero Pass to the Wilderness of Rocks and the heavily forested Mount Lemmon area. Red-tailed hawks can often be seen soaring and hunting above the brushy slopes below.

The trail now switchbacks steeply down a series of nearly shadeless, chaparral-covered slopes some 1000 vertical feet to a signed junction at the head of West Fork Sabino Canyon (9.1; 5500). The path which branches right from here is a variant of the West Fork Sabino Trail; our route goes left, across the bed of West Fork Sabino Creek (generally dry at this point), then proceeds uphill a short distance to the main West Fork Sabino Trail (signed). Here we take the left fork, and follow it a few hundred yards onto a ridge, whose crest is then followed the remaining 0.5 mile to often-windy Romero Pass (10.5; 6040), a major saddle separating the Santa Catalina front range from the main mountain mass. At a junction here we turn left, onto the signed Romero Canyon Trail, drop steeply down switchbacks into a

Trail through ocotillo, Pusch Ridge Wilderness

tributary of Romero Canyon (usually dry), and then proceed more moderately down-canyon beneath a pleasantly shady forest overstory of tall ponderosa pines, lots of silverleaf and Arizona white oaks, and some velvet ash. About 1 mile beyond Romero Pass the trail reaches the main branch of Romero Canyon (1 1.5; 5320), where there is a good campsite and, during rainy periods, running water.

To complete your journey from here, reverse the steps of Trip 23 the remaining 6.2 miles to Romero Canyon Trailhead (17.7; 2720).

TRIP 30
CACTUS PICNIC GROUND TO SABINO CANYON ROADEND VIA BRIDALVEIL FALLS, AND WEST FORK SABINO CANYON

▲ **16.7 mile near-loop trip (use Sabino Canyon shuttle to make a complete loop); 4280′ elevation gain**
▲ **Strenuous dayhike or backpack (3 hiking days)**
▲ **Trailhead 10, Cactus Picnic Ground (start)**
▲ **Trailhead 11, Sabino Canyon Roadend (finish)**
▲ **Maps**
  Pusch Ridge Wilderness or *Sabino Canyon and Mount Lemmon quadrangles.*
▲ **Season: all year, except after snowstorms**
  Water is available year-round at Hutch's Pool (near mile 12.7); Esperero Canyon (miles 4.1 to 5.5) has water during rainy periods only

Features
Beginning amid the cacti and shrubs of the Sonoran desert, this strenuous trek climbs past pretty, oak- and cypress-shaded Bridalveil Falls to the pine-forested crest of the Santa Catalina front range. The West Fork of Sabino Canyon provides a convenient return route, one made all the more attractive by the easy access it provides to Hutch's Pool, a delightful, year-round swimming hole.

Trailhead Route
Start: follow the trailhead route for Trip 26. Finish: follow the trailhead route for Trip 31.

Description
From Cactus Picnic Ground (0.0; 2880), follow the Esperero and Cathedral Rock trails to the signed fork near the head of West Fork Sabino Canyon (9.1; 5500) (see Trip 29). Here we turn right, onto a

variant of the West Fork Sabino Trail, and descend gradually 0.2 mile to the main West Fork Sabino Trail. The route now follows the latter down-canyon, crossing the rocky bed of West Fork Sabino Creek at frequent intervals (water during rainy periods only). This section of the trail is somewhat overgrown with mimosa and hikers in shorts will quickly learn to give these sharp-spined plants a wide berth. Occasional good campsites, partially shaded by overarching Emory oaks and sycamores, can be found near the stream. A lengthy lunch stop (or an overnight stay) in this pleasant area will allow you to become acquainted with the boldest, noisiest member of the local wildlife fraternity—the Mexican jay, a bird readily identifiable by its raucous call and impudent manners.

About 2 miles beyond the last junction, the trail crosses the creek from its left to its right side, climbs a bit, then traverses along the canyonside as the streambed gradually falls away below. The forest cover thins out as we leave the watercourse, with hardy one-seed junipers, shrub, live oaks and some beautiful Mexican blue oaks now forming its major components. Sharp-spined amole, sotol, and yucca begin to appear in the rocky, sunny spaces between trees. After winding in and out of a pair of minor side canyons we reach a saddle atop a low ridge, then drop down into and cross a small drainage. From here a few switchbacks bring us to an unsigned junction (12.7; 3920) near Sabino Creek. Hutch's Pool, with its good campsites, perennial water, and excellent warm-weather swimming, is a few hundred yards up the spur trail to the left (see Trip 31).

To complete your journey from here, reverse the steps of Trip 31 the remaining 4.0 miles to Sabino Canyon Roadend (16.7; 3330).

TRIP 31
SABINO CANYON ROADEND TO HUTCH'S POOL

- ▲ **8.4 miles round trip; 950′ elevation gain**
- ▲ **Moderate dayhike or backpack (2 hiking days)**
- ▲ **Trailhead 11, Sabino Canyon Roadend**
- ▲ **Maps**
  Pusch Wilderness or *Sabino Canyon and Mount Lemmon quadrangles*
- ▲ **Season: all year; hot in summer**
  Water available all year at Hutch 's Pool (mile 4.2)

Features

Hutch's Pool, in the opinion of many, is by far the finest swimming hole in the Santa Catalinas. But it is not the only attraction of this route; along the way to the pool there are fine views down into rugged Sabino Canyon, and equally good vistas across the high, rough-cut ridges which drop abruptly from the high country to Sabino Basin.

This trip's season is given as all year, even though the route can be fiercely hot during the summer. Those wishing to enjoy the cool waters of Hutch's Pool during the hottest weather usually plan on being gone the entire day, leaving early in the morning and returning as the temperature drops in late afternoon. But be sure to get back to the trailhead in time to catch the last shuttle out of Sabino Canyon.

Trailhead Route

Follow the trailhead route for Trip 26. Sabino Canyon Roadend trailhead is four miles past the Sabino Canyon Visitor Center; take the Sabino Canyon shuttle to the trailhead.

Description

From the trailhead at the end of Sabino Canyon Road (0.0; 3330) the signed Sabino Canyon Trail switchbacks moderately uphill through a sparse ground cover consisting mainly of saguaro, paloverde, amole, ocotillo and prickly pear. After climbing steadily for 0.5 mile we arrive at a signed junction with the Phoneline Trail, where we take the left fork and begin traversing the east wall of Sabino Canyon some 300-400 feet above the creek. About ¾ mile beyond here the trail climbs up to a notch (1.2; 3800) behind a large granite outcropping which stands like a sentinel above a narrow horseshoe bend in the canyon.

A few hundred feet beyond this saddle a steep, rough trail of use drops down a ravine to some deep pools and good campsites along the creek. Our route continues traversing up-canyon, making a number of ups and downs as it winds in and out of a side drainage and passes behind some minor outcroppings. Presently we drop down a few switchbacks and step across Palisade Creek (water during rainy periods only) to a signed trail junction in Sabino Basin (2.5; 3680). Here the route turns left, then crosses the rocky wash of Box Camp Creek and a low ridge just beyond, and begins climbing gently up the sycamore-dotted floor of the basin. There are occasional good campsites in this area, off to the left by the stream. Watch out for the poison ivy which abounds here.

After proceeding a little over a mile upstream we cross Sabino Creek from its north to its south side. Shortly beyond here the trail prepares to switchback up the left-hand canyonside, but just before it begins this climb an unsigned spur trail branches right. We now turn onto the latter and follow it a few hundred yards to Hutch's Pool (4.2; 3860), a delightful, year-round swimming hole. There are several excellent campsites nearby, though this popular area has been picked clean of firewood. During the cooler months of the year, when there are not enough human swimmers here to keep the local brown and rainbow trout in a perpetual panic, the stream offers fair angling. Several more deep pools can be found upstream from Hutch's.

Return the way you came.

TRIP 32
SABINO CANYON ROADEND TO LOWER BEAR CANYON PICNIC GROUND

- 11.3 miles one-way (use of Sabino Canyon and Bear Canyon shuttles required or add 5.7 more miles; see Trip 31); 1740' elevation gain
- Moderate dayhike or backpack (2 hiking days)
- Trailhead 11, Sabino Canyon Roadend (start)
- Trailhead 12, Lower Bear Canyon Picnic Ground (finish)
- Maps
  Pusch Ridge Wilderness or *Sabino Canyon quadrangle*
- Season: November to April
  Water available all year at Seven Falls (near mile 9.0); Palisade Creek (mile 2.5) and Sycamore Creek (near mile 4.6) have water during rainy periods only

Features

Hikers looking to stretch their legs during the winter months will appreciate this route, which features a very short car shuttle and samples a variety of pleasant country. The highlight of the trek is Seven Falls, a series of high cataracts which puts on an awesome spectacle following heavy rains.

Trailhead Route

Start: follow the trailhead route for Trip 31. Finish: follow the trailhead route for Trip 33.

Description

From Sabino Canyon Roadend (0.0; 3330), follow the route of Trip 31 to the signed trail junction at Palisade Creek in Sabino Basin (2.5;

3680). Turn right here, then proceed gently up-canyon beneath a pleasant riparian overstory of tall oaks and sycamores. Several excellent campsites can be found through here (and for the next mile or so up the trail), but water is available only during rainy periods. Soon we pass the signed, left-branching Box Camp Trail, where we turn right again and climb a single switchback onto a sunny slope planted with hardy one-seed junipers, low-growing mats of agave and sotol, and some small Mexican blue oaks and shrub live oaks. After gaining only a little elevation, we traverse eastward and presently find ourselves walking alongside the bed of Pine Creek, which has risen to our level. At the signed junction with the Palisade Trail (parts of which are visible descending from the high country to the north) the route turns right and climbs a moderate switchback up the canyonside, gaining some nice views back across Sabino Basin to the Romero Pass area.

From the top of this switchback the trail climbs southeast to Sycamore Saddle (4.6; 4600), where there is a fork. Backpackers looking for tentsites may wish to follow the left-branching pathway a short distance downhill to Sycamore Creek, which offers running water (during rainy periods only) and delightful camping beneath tall oaks, rustling sycamores, and some nice stands of Arizona cypress. Water is always available at Sycamore Spring Reservoir, about 1 mile down this trail from where it first meets the creek.

Sabino Creek below Hutch's Pool

To continue on the main route, turn right at the junction in Sycamore Saddle and climb gently southward to nearby Thimble Saddle (5.2; 4840). From this, the high point of our trek, the trail proceeds very gradually downhill for 0.5 mile, then begins a long, switchbacking descent into Bear Canyon. A mile later (and some 700 feet lower) we cross Bear Creek (water during rainy periods only), then climb up the opposite canyonside a bit, and work our way down-canyon, staying about 50 feet above the streambed. Occasional fair campsites can be found among the jumble of flood debris in the watercourse below.

Soon a drop-off looms ahead in the canyon; now we climb slightly, and traverse around a rocky projection high above Seven Falls. The falls are not yet visible, but if Bear Creek is running high their roar will be easily audible from this area. After we descend moderately across the head of a large amphitheater, the falls come into view across the canyon, and we drop down a series of switchbacks to a signed junction near their base (9.0; 3320). The lowest fall is 0.2 mile down the right-branching trail. A string of deep potholes worn into the creekbed here offer water year-round and provide enjoyable swimming during warm weather. The continuation of our route goes left at the fork and descends gently the remaining 2.3 miles to Lower Bear Canyon Picnic Ground (11.3; 2800) (reverse the steps of Trip 33).

TRIP 33
Lower Bear Canyon Picnic Ground to Seven Falls

- ▲ **5.0 miles round trip; 480' elevation gain**
- ▲ **Leisurely dayhike**
- ▲ **Trailhead 12, Lower Bear Canyon Picnic Ground**
- ▲ **Maps**
  Pusch Ridge Wilderness or *Sabino Canyon quadrangle*
- ▲ **Season: all year; hot in summer**
  Water available all year at Seven Falls (mile 2.5)

Features

Right after a heavy rain, when the resurrected creeks of the Santa Catalinas are high and rolling—that is the ideal time to go see Seven Falls. At other times these steep cataracts are not so spectacular (or are even completely dry), but they may still be worth a visit to enjoy the fine swimming in the deep, perennially filled pools at their bases.

Trailhead Route

Follow the trailhead route for Trip 26 to the Sabino Canyon visitor Center; either take the Bear Canyon shuttle to the trailhead or walk the nature trail on the east side of the visitor center 0.1 mile to the start of the 1.6 mile path to the trailhead.

Description

From the end of the road at Lower Bear Picnic Ground (0.0; 2800), follow the wide, well-maintained trail as it drops gently toward Bear Creek, through a typical Lower Sonoran plant cover of honey mesquite, the omnipresent saguaro and prickly pear, low-growing pincushion cactus, yellow paloverde, ocotillo, teddybear and jumping cholla, and brittlebush. A few medium-sized sycamores and cotton-woods grow along the creek, which is soon crossed via the first of a series of low, rock-and-cement dams. The trail proceeds gently upstream for the next mile and a half, past several more crossings (the stream is generally dry or intermittent except during rainy periods), and then switchbacks moderately a short distance up the right-hand (south) canyon wall.

Seven Falls, Bear Canyon

We now continue our way up-canyon, keeping 100 feet or so above the creek, until we arrive at a signed junction from where Seven Falls is visible in the deeply recessed, steep-walled amphitheater across the canyon. Here our route turns left and drops down slightly to Bear Creek, just below the lowest of the falls (2.5; 3280). It is possible to scramble up past several of the falls from here, although care should be taken when climbing the slippery, water-worn rocks. The potholes beneath the falls contain water all year long, and offer excellent swimming during warm weather.

Return the way you came.

TRIP 34
SHOWERS POINT CAMPGROUND TO MUD SPRING

▲ **5.4 miles round trip; 1420′ elevation gain**
▲ **Moderate dayhike or backpack (2 hiking days)**
▲ **Trailhead 13, Showers Point Campground**
▲ **Maps**
   Pusch Ridge Wilderness or *Mount Bigelow quadrangle*
▲ **Season: April to November**
   Water available all season at Mud Spring (mile 2. 7)

Features
This route passes through tall forests of pine and fir on its way to an all-year spring perched high above the Catalina foothills and the city of Tucson. It is an excellent choice for dayhikers seeking an introduction to the middle reaches of the range, and for backpackers who appreciate a camp with a view.

Trailhead Route/Camping
Follow the Mount Lemmon Highway from Tucson to milepost 19.5, turn left onto Organization Ridge Road, and drive 0.5 mile to the trailhead parking just past Showers Point Group Campground. If there are no parking spaces you will have to park opposite the Palisades Information Station and walk the half mile to the trailhead. Do not park in the campground. Campgrounds are found off the Mount Lemmon Highway at mileposts 5.5, 12.0, 17.0, and beyond the Organization Ridge Road turnoff.

Description
From the signed trailhead just after Showers Point Campground (0.0; 7760) follow the well-maintained Palisade Trail as it drops along

the slopes immediately above the head of Palisade Canyon. The trail works its way in and out of a few minor drainages as it passes well below the group campgrounds up on Organization Ridge. In about half a mile the trail crosses a very rocky area and cairns mark a faint spur trail that descends right to the base of the cascade you will hear in wet seasons. Soon, the main trail crosses a junction; down to the right are the Hidden Pools. The trail that rises to the left is off limits as it leads to the girl scout camp. After passing through some majestic stands of ponderosa pine, Mexican white pine, Douglas-fir and Gambel oak, and perhaps seeing some of the Coues white-tailed deer that frequent these slopes during the summer, we swing out onto the crest of Organization Ridge, gaining some nice views to either side through the pines. After dropping a short distance along the gently descending ridgeline, the route veers off to the left, then drops more steeply down a brushy slope to a minor, oak-covered ridge. From here we switchback into a small ravine just west of Pine Canyon.

Shortly after crossing this ravine from east to west the trail passes an excellent campsite (2.5; 6600) just above the streamcourse to the left. This camp, in a pleasant mid-mountain forest of ponderosa pine, Schott's yucca, and silverleaf and Arizona white oak, is situated just above a rocky dropoff in the drainage, and it affords a grand view of spirelike Thimble Peak, lower Sabino Canyon, and much of metropolitan Tucson. This vista is even better at night, when a vast, sparkling sea of lights floats above the jagged, jet-black silhouette of the foothills—as though the stars had fallen from the sky and collected in a pool at your feet.

Thimble Peak from near Mud Peak

During the rainy season there is often water here, and sometimes a series of dashing falls below the dropoff. If not, water is always available at the cement tank of Mud Spring (2.7; 6480), about 0.1 mile down the moderately descending, switchbacking trail. There are a couple of campsites near this spring, though they are not as nice as the one above.

Return the way you came.

TRIP 35
SHOWERS POINT CAMPGROUND TO
SABINO CANYON ROADEND

- 10.0 miles one-way (35-mile car shuttle required); 4520' elevation loss, negligible gain
- Moderate dayhike or backpack (2-3 hiking days)
- Trailhead 13, Showers Point Campground (start)
- Trailhead 11, Sabino Canyon Roadend (finish)
- Maps

    Pusch Ridge Wilderness or *Mount Bigelow, Mount Lemmon, and Sabino Canyon quadrangles*
- Season: April to November

    Water available all season at Mud Spring (mile 2.7); Palisade Creek (mile 7.5) has water during rainy periods only

Features

Beginning amid the pines and firs of the Catalina high country and ending among the shrubs and cacti of the foothills, this route transects four life zones—Canadian, Transition, and Upper and Lower Sonoran. Most of this long descent is made via open ridgelines, making for excellent vistas all the way down.

Trailhead Route

Start: follow the trailhead route for Trip 34. Finish: follow the trailhead route for Trip 31.

Description

From the trailhead just beyond Showers Point Campground (0.0; 7760), follow the Palisade Trail to Mud Spring (2.7; 6440), continue moderately downhill past a few switchbacks, and then traverse to the right, onto the broad divide between Pine and Palisade creeks. There are excellent views from this ridge of Thimble Peak in the Catalina foothills, and across Sabino Canyon to the front range, dominated by craggy, 7952-foot Cathedral Rock. The plant cover here is thinner than above, with scrubby clumps of Mexican pinyon pine, one-seed juniper, shrub live oak, alligator juniper and manzanita growing in place of the ponderosa forests from which we have descended.

At a small rock shelf overlooking Palisade Canyon we resume switchbacking steeply downhill, passing many fine vistas. A surprising variety of wildflowers bloom in the spring on these dry, rocky slopes, including bright red Indian paintbrush, purple-tufted thistle, parry penstemon and aster. As you continue to lose elevation, look also for brittlebush, desert marigold, and low-growing mats of verbena. At length the trail makes a long traverse to the southeast, then drops down into lower Pine Canyon. Here we cross Pine Creek (water during rainy periods only) to a signed junction (6.4; 4080), where we turn right. There are several good campsites nearby land for a mile or so downstream), shaded by a healthy riparian growth of large Mexican blue oaks and sycamores. As we proceed gently down-canyon from the last fork, Pine Creek falls away gradually below, and the trail drops down a switchback or two to keep pace. After 1 mile the Box Camp Trail branches right, but we continue straight ahead a few hundred feet farther to the signed junction with the Sabino Canyon Trail (7.5; 3680). To complete your trek from here, turn right and reverse the steps of the first half of Trip 31 the remaining 2.5 miles to Sabino Canyon Roadend (10.0; 3330).

TRIP 36
MOUNT LEMMON HIGHWAY TO SABINO CANYON ROADEND VIA THE BOX CAMP TRAIL

▲ **9.3 miles one-way (37-mile car shuttle required); 4700' elevation loss, negligible gain**
▲ **Moderate dayhike or leisurely backpack (2 hiking days)**
▲ **Trailhead 14, Mount Lemmon Highway (start)**
▲ **Trailhead 11, Sabino Canyon Roadend (finish)**
▲ **Maps**
  Pusch Ridge Wilderness or *Mount Bigelow, Mount Lemmon, and Sabino Canyon quadrangles*
▲ **Season: April to November**
  Water available all season at Box Spring (near mile 1.8); Palisade Creek (mile 6. 7) has water during rainy periods only

Features

Before the construction of the Mount Lemmon Highway, the Box Camp Trail provided the quickest access to the Soldier Camp area in the high country. Today this historic track is a bit overgrown, though still easy to follow, and hikers will find it an interesting and highly scenic route through the heart of the wild Santa Catalinas.

Trailhead Route/Camping

Start: drive up the Mount Lemmon Highway from Tucson to milepost 21.7. The trailhead parking lot is on the left side of the road. Just before the trailhead you will pass Spencer Canyon Campground. If this is closed, campgrounds lower on the mountain will be open. Finish: follow the trailhead route for Trip 31.

Description

From the Box Camp Trailhead on Mount Lemmon Highway (0.0; 8010), climb steeply a short distance, pass beneath a power line, and then proceed gently up and down through a forest of magnificent ponderosa and Mexican white pines, intermixed with some white fir and Douglas-fir. After passing beneath the summit of Spencer Peak we follow a broad ridgeline southward, gaining occasional glimpses of the forested Santa Catalina high country through the trees to either side. During the autumn months, small stands of frost-yellowed aspens add flecks of color to the dark green slopes beneath Marshall Peak, across the deep gap of Sabino Canyon to the west. About a mile beyond the highway we drop steeply a short distance into a minor drainage, which we follow more gently downhill through a grassy, parklike area. Camping would be delightful here, but water is generally available only on the heels of the spring snowmelt and following very heavy rains.

After crossing this drainage a few times the trail winds steeply downhill to a signed junction (1.8; 7440) with the right-branching spur to Box Spring. The spring, 0.3 miles down the sidetrail, apparently flows year-round. This area is the site of old Box Camp, a late 19th century military way-station of which very few traces remain.

Beyond here the trail passes through a minor saddle, then commences switchbacking moderately-to-steeply down a ridgeline. As we lose elevation the forest cover steadily thins out, and good views open up across the Catalina foothills to the Rincon and Santa Rita mountains. After descending some 1800 vertical feet, we drop into a rocky, oak-and-pinyon-forested drainage, which contains unreliable Apache Spring (4.5; 5560) (water only during very wet periods). The trail climbs out of this small watercourse via a saddle to the west, then descends the slopes above Box Camp Canyon, alternating long,

Sabino Canyon Roadend

downhill traverses with spates of very steep (and somewhat brushy) switchbacks. The ground cover continues to grow sparser as we drop, and by the time the trail levels off temporarily to cross a minor drainage basin, saguaro, prickly pear, mesquite and ocotillo have begun to appear.

Soon the trail resumes its very steep, switchbacking descent, bottoming out at Palisade Creek (6.6; 3760). There is delightful camping hereabouts, in a nice riparian forest of rustling sycamores and shady Mexican blue oaks. The creek flows only during rainy periods. After crossing the streambed, we proceed a short distance to a fork, turn left, and continue about 200 yards to a signed junction with the Sabino Canyon Trail. To complete your journey from here, turn left again and reverse the steps of the first half of Trip 31 the remaining 2.5 miles to Sabino Canyon Roadend (9.3; 3330).

TRIP 37
MARSHALL GULCH PICNIC AREA TO SABINO CANYON

- ▲ **6.4 miles round trip; 1420′ elevation gain**
- ▲ **Moderate dayhike or backpack (2 hiking days)**
- ▲ **Trailhead 15, Marshall Gulch Picnic Area**
- ▲ **Maps**
  Pusch Ridge Wilderness or *Mount Lemmon quadrangle*
- ▲ **Season: April to November**
  Water available all season along entire route

Features

Sabino Creek is one of only two perennial streams in the Pusch Ridge Wilderness, and this trip is included mainly for the benefit of anglers who wish to match wits with the trout that were stocked in it. Nonanglers need not stay at home, however; they will find enjoyable camping at many spots, or can simply come and enjoy the quiet company of the stream for a few hours.

This route is cross-country all the way, and recommended for very experienced hikers only. Many sections of the creekbed are quite rough, and the going is often slow, so allow yourself plenty of time for this one.

Trailhead Route/Camping

Drive the Mount Lemmon Highway from Tucson past milepost 24.8, the Ski Valley/Summerhaven junction. Drive through Summerhaven plus an additional mile to the end of Marshall Gulch Picnic Area. When the gates are locked (in winter), you will have to find legal parking outside and walk in—almost half a mile. On the drive up you pass several campgrounds.

Description

From Marshall Gulch Picnic Area (0.0; 7420) follow Sabino Creek directly down Sabino Canyon. The canyonsides above the stream are heavily forested with towering Douglas-firs, Gambel oaks and a few ponderosa pines, but the creekbanks themselves are too rocky and floodswept to support much more than water-loving willows and alders and an occasional stubborn bigtooth maple or two. It is possible to make reasonably rapid progress at first, but the canyon bottom soon becomes a maze of giant boulders which must be patiently scrambled over, around, and occasionally under. After the first mile or so the gorge widens out considerably and the going gets a bit easier. Scattered between here and the end of our route are occasional good campsites. (Because of the summer homes upstream, water from the creek should be purified before drinking.)

The Arizona Game and Fish Department used to stock this part of Sabino Creek by helicopter with brown and rainbow trout, and anglers will want to test their skills at the many pools here. Because so few anglers get to this remote spot some fish are quite large. One grew so big that it got written up in the local newspaper. It became quite a crusade to catch it. Finally, a lucky angler got the prize and spent two days carrying it out. By time the trophy arrived home it had started to rot. Getting into and out of some stretches of the creek can be difficult because of boulders and brush.

At a point about 3 miles from the start—a distance that may seem twice as long because of the many brushy "boxes" and small falls which must be negotiated en route—a major tributary drainage drops down from the right (north) into Sabino Canyon (3.2; 6000). This point marks the end of our excursion. It is possible for skilled bushwackers to continue downstream from here to Hutch's Pool and the West Fork Sabino Trail, but the going is exceptionally difficult, even dangerous in places. Most hikers will probably have gotten enough of a taste of this rugged canyon by the time they get this far, anyway.

Return the way you came.

TRIP 38
ASPEN LOOP (MARSHALL GULCH PICNIC AREA TO MARSHALL SADDLE AND RETURN)

- ▲ **3.7 mile loop trip; 780' elevation gain**
- ▲ **Leisurely dayhike**
- ▲ **Trailhead 15, Marshall Gulch Picnic Area**
- ▲ **Maps**
  Pusch Ridge Wilderness or *Mount Lemmon quadrangle.*
- ▲ **Season: April to November**
  Water available all season in Marshall Gulch (miles 3.2 to 3. 7)

Features
This trip, a fine, leisurely introduction to the varying moods of the Santa Catalina high country, has two chief attractions: a lovely grove of tall, straight-trunked aspens, and the lush, maple-lined defile of Marshall Gulch. Portions of the route are particularly beautiful during the fall, when sharp frosts nip at the yellowing, reddening leaves.

Trailhead Route
Follow the trailhead route for Trip 37.

Description
From lower left end of the final parking area of the Marshall Gulch Picnic Area (0.0; 7420) follow the signed Aspen Trail as it climbs steeply across a hillside to the southeast. The severe gradient quickly eases, and we climb more moderately through a dense forest cover of Gambel oak, white fir and Douglas-fir, and some sun-loving Mexican white pine. Keep your eyes open for the Coues white-tailed deer that are occasionally seen through here. In a little less than half a mile the

path drops slightly, then enters an open, parklike grove of mature aspens—an excellent spot to lay out a picnic spread, or simply to lie beneath the trees and enjoy the peace and quiet. Young aspens thrive in recently burned areas—this very opening may well have been cleared by a small blaze started by summer lightning—where they serve to enrich the blackened soil for the conifers that will eventually, in the course of natural succession, replace them. Beautiful in any season, aspen groves can be particularly striking during the fall, when the leaves turn, and in early spring, when the bone-white, leafless trunks stand in ghostly contrast to their dark-green coniferous surroundings.

A short distance beyond this grove the trail switchbacks very steeply up an oak- and ponderosa-forested ridgeline. After gaining several hundred feet of elevation the route levels off and traverses westward past a few minor ups and downs. At a signed junction with a spur trail to Lunch Ledge we stay right, and soon begin an occasionally steep descent that presently brings us to Marshall Saddle (2.5; 7960), a broad gap in a sunny, airy forest of ponderosa. At a signed, 5-way junction here our route turns right and drops into the head of Marshall Gulch. Soon we sidle up alongside a streamcourse, which usually contains at least intermittent pools of water. The canyonsides here are forested with pines and firs, and nice copses of Arizona alder and bigtooth maple line the banks of the tiny creek. A variety of wildflowers bloom in this lush area throughout the summer, including fleabane, aspen sunflower, and exuberant blue spikes of lupine.

Take your time in ambling through this serene, leafy canyon, for all too soon the trail leads us back to Marshall Gulch Picnic Area (3.7; 7420), just across the parking lot from where our trip began.

TRIP 39
MARSHALL GULCH PICNIC AREA TO LEMMON CREEK AND THE WILDERNESS OF ROCKS

- ▲ **7.8 miles round trip; 1740′ elevation gain**
- ▲ **Moderate dayhike or leisurely backpack (2 hiking days)**
- ▲ **Trailhead 15, Marshall Gulch Picnic Area**
- ▲ **Maps**
  Pusch Ridge Wilderness or *Mount Lemmon quadrangle*
- ▲ **Season: April to November**
  Water available all season at Lemmon Creek (mile 3.6)

Features

This route climbs up lushly-forested Marshall Gulch to Marshall Saddle, then drops into the headwaters of Lemmon Creek, where backpackers will find perennial water and excellent camping. Just beyond is the Wilderness of Rocks, a fantasyland of weirdly eroded granite outcroppings that will whet the curiosity of the explorer.

Trailhead Route

Follow the trailhead route for Trip 37.

Description

From Marshall Gulch Picnic Area (0.0; 7420), follow the signed Marshall Saddle/Wilderness of Rocks Trail up the shady defile of Marshall Gulch. The trail climbs gently-to-moderately through here, staying to the right of a small creek, which almost always flows at least intermittently. The slopes above the stream support some nice stands of ponderosa pine, Mexican white pine and white fir, while bigtooth maples and tangles of willow and alder flourish along the watercourse. Aspen sunflower, lupine and fleabane are among the wildflowers which dot the canyonsides during the summer.

The angle of ascent steepens as we approach the head of the gulch, and presently we top out at Marshall Saddle (1.2; 7960), where, in an open forest of ponderosa, there is a signed 5-way junction. Our route goes straight ahead at this crossroads, and then drops moderately to the west. After 0.25 mile we pass a large rock outcropping—a precursor of many such formations to be met below. Beyond here we cross Lemmon Creek (which may be dry at this point) near its head, then continue descending more gently. As we gradually lose elevation, the forest cover of pines and firs is invaded

Wilderness of Rocks

by increasing numbers of silverleaf oak and Arizona white oak. A little over a mile after leaving Marshall Saddle the trail recrosses the
creek and passes a good campsite by a copse of diminutive aspens.
About 0.5 mile and several creek crossings later we reach a signed
junction by the stream (2.9; 7280). Our route stays left here and continues down the creek a bit, then angles to the left and meanders
across the exposed tops of some low rock outcrops. The trail is often
faint in rocky areas through here, but ducks and blazes generally
show up to guide you at critical junctures.

Beyond this section we drop down and make one final crossing of
Lemmon Creek. There is an excellent campsite here, and water is
always available in pools along the streambed. After crossing the latter, the trail makes a short, steep climb up a ridge, then descends
southwestward into the Wilderness of Rocks (3.9; 7100), an extensive
maze of water-sculpted granitic domes, pinnacles and "balanced
rocks" of every manner and shape. Several layover days could be
spent exploring this delightful area. Cozy, secluded campsites can be
found everywhere, but water generally has to be packed in from
nearby Lemmon Creek.

Return the way you came.

TRIP 40
MARSHALL GULCH PICNIC AREA TO SABINO CANYON
ROADEND VIA THE WILDERNESS OF ROCKS, ROMERO PASS,
AND HUTCH'S POOL

- ▲ **15.8 miles one-way (40-mile car shuttle required); 5520' eleva-
  tion loss, 1440' gain**
- ▲ **Strenuous dayhike or moderate backpack (3 hiking days)**
- ▲ **Trailhead 15, Marshall Gulch Picnic Area (start)**
- ▲ **Trailhead 11, Sabino Canyon Roadend (finish)**
- ▲ **Maps**
  Pusch Ridge Wilderness or *Mount Lemmon and Sabino Canyon*
  quadrangles.
- ▲ **Season: April to November**
  Water available all year round at Lemmon Creek (mile 3.6) and
  Hutch 's Pool (near mile 11.8)

Features
Roaming the mountains from top to bottom, this fine ramble gives
the hiker a taste of everything the Santa Catalinas have to offer:

hushed, cathedral-like forests of pine and fir; picturesquely eroded pinnacles and crags; wide-open vistas across rugged ridges and canyons; oak- and sycamore-shaded creeks; and rocky hillsides studded with saguaro cacti. The presence of perennial water and good campsites at Lemmon and Sabino creeks makes this an excellent choice for a 3-day backpack, even during spells of dry weather.

Parts of this route are rather hard to follow, and it is recommended only for reasonably experienced wilderness travelers.

Trailhead Route

Start: follow the trailhead route for Trip 37. Finish: follow the trailhead route for Trip 31.

Description

From Marshall Gulch Picnic Area (0.0; 7420), follow the route of Trip 39 to the Wilderness of Rocks (3.9; 7100). As we skirt the edge of this wonderfully sculpted area, most of the rock formations are off to the right, or north. Soon a pair of short, steep climbs bring us to an ill-defined saddle, where we exit the Wilderness of Rocks and proceed to meander up and down across the next basin. The trail is occasionally faint through here—look for ducks to guide you. After another short ascent we arrive at a signed junction with the Mount Lemmon Trail (5.4; 7280), atop a high ridge affording a nice view down the western Catalina slope. Our route goes left here and, after climbing for ¼ mile, passes just to the left of a huge, flat rock. Those who scramble out to the edge of this rock will be rewarded with a fabulous overview of the rugged bighorn-sheep country sprawling at the base of craggy Pusch Ridge.

Beyond here the rough trail drops, very steeply at times, toward Romero Pass, through a mixed forest cover of Arizona white oaks, silverleaf oaks, some thick-girthed alligator junipers, Mexican pinyon pines, ponderosa pines and, near the top of the descent, a few Douglas-firs. Views are excellent much of the way down: to the west lies the deep defile of Romero Canyon, and to the south and east, rising in the distance beyond the Catalina foothills, stand the Santa Rita and Rincon ranges.

At length we drop into Romero Pass (6.6; 6040). From a junction here our route goes left, descends moderately down a ridgeline for 0.5 mile, then cuts back right and reaches another junction near the head of West Fork Sabino Canyon. Here we turn left, proceed downhill 0.6 mile, and cross the usually dry bed of West Fork Sabino Creek to yet another junction (8.4; 5280). To complete your journey from here, turn left and follow the second half of Trip 30 past Hutch's Pool to Sabino Canyon Roadend (15.8; 3330).

Saguaro National Park East and the Rincon Mountains

Although they not tower as high as the Santa Catalinas, the Rincons have their own appeal. There are no roads into these mountains, hence, one does not often run into large crowds and there is more of a feeling of wilderness once the first few miles are left behind. The recreation map published by the Southern Arizona Hiking Club is probably the most useful, accurate, and up-to-date map of this area. See the Appendix for locations where maps are sold.

TRIP 41
DOUGLAS SPRING TRAILHEAD TO DOUGLAS SPRING

▲ **11.8 miles round trip; 2050' elevation gain**
▲ **Moderate dayhike or backpack (2 hiking days)**
▲ **Trailhead 16, Douglas Spring**
▲ **Maps**
  Rincon Mountains Trail and Recreation Map or *Tanque Verde Peak and Mica Mountain quadrangles*
▲ **Season: November to April**
  Water available at Douglas Spring (mile 5.9) during rainy periods only

Features
Beginning in a region which is a veritable showcase of Lower Sonoran vegetation, and part of Saguaro National Park, this route soon climbs into the foothills of the Rincon Mountains and wanders through open forests of oak and juniper to Douglas Spring, where the Park Service maintains a trail camp. Along the way there are a number of pleasant vistas, both of the forested tops of the Rincons, swelling high above the hiker, and of metropolitan Tucson, sprawling across the flatlands so far below.

Trailhead Route/Camping
Drive east on Tucson's Speedway Boulevard to the end of the road—about 14 miles past Country Club Drive. Just before the road ends at a private gate to a guest ranch there is a parking area to the right. Although not posted against camping this is probably not a safe place to car camp as it is just off a main road. You may hike into the park and camp only if you have gotten the required permit obtainable from rangers at the park entrance. Even the shaded

ramada adjacent to the trailhead is within the park. The nearest good places to car camp are off the Mount Lemmon Highway.

Description

From the trailhead at the end of East Speedway Road (0.0; 2750), walk a little south of east through a beautiful vegetative cover of exuberant, red-blossoming ocotillos, yellow paloverdes, creosote bushes, pale green prickly pears, staghorn, jumping and teddy-bear chollas, and some magnificent saguaros. During the spring months one can spend hours here identifying wildflowers; some of the more common ones you will likely see are brittlebush blossoms, delicate yellow paperflowers, narrowleaf asters and desert marigolds, not to mention the blossoms on all the trees, shrubs and cacti mentioned above.

As the current recreation map shows, there is a regular maze of trails around the Douglas Spring Trail. All of these in the early section are either signed (at 0.2, 0.4, 0.8, and 2.3 miles) or have a line of rocks to designate a spurious status. After ¾ mile the trail begins climbing moderately up a low ridge. Soon we work our way up a drainage to a minor saddle (2.2; 3720), where we pass through a fence that is part of the old Aguila Corral. From here the trail drops slightly, then winds back and forth across a wash that supports a few mesquite trees and some seepwillows. After exiting this wash we continue climbing moderately until we reach the crest of another low ridge, just beyond which is an unsigned trail junction (3.0; 4360). The faint spur trail that branches south leads in about 300 yards to Tina Larga Tank, an artificially augmented catchment basin that used to hold water for a surprising length of time after heavy rains. In the early 1980's it was washed out and can no longer be depended on as a water source. It is still shown on many maps.

Staying left at this junction, we climb a short distance, then meander up and down across a rolling area, through a light forest cover of doughty alligator junipers, one-seed junipers and Mexican blue oaks. The rocky protuberance of Helens Dome is visible straight ahead, as is the high, pine-forested country around Mica Mountain. Off to the right stands Tanque Verde Peak, while far below to the left one can see Portoritas Tank, an artificial pond of similar construction to Tina Larga Tank.

After topping a low, rather ill-defined ridgeline, the trail drops very gently down to Douglas Spring (5.9; 4800), where there are campsites equipped with grills and a toilet. A few velvet ash trees grow along the creekbed, along with the preponderant oaks and junipers, and the bright blossoms of thistle, parry penstemon, and desert marigold provide touches of color here and there during spring. The creek is the only source of water here, and it runs only during the rainy season. A camping permit is necessary for overnight stays.

Return the way you came.

TRIP 42
DOUGLAS SPRING TRAILHEAD TO MANNING CAMP

▲ **24.4 miles round trip; 5250' elevation gain**
▲ **Moderate to strenuous backpack (2-4 hiking days)**
▲ **Trailhead 16, Douglas Spring**
▲ **Maps**
  Rincon Mountains Trail and Recreation Map or *Tanque Verde Peak and Mica Mountain quadrangles*
▲ **Season: March to November**
  Water available all season at Manning Camp (mile 12.2); Douglas Spring (mile 5.9) has water only during rainy periods

Features

This fine backpacking route, a good choice for a 3-5 day outing, climbs into the Rincon Mountains high country via Douglas Spring Campground and Cow Head Saddle. Along the way it passes through vegetation communities representing four distinct life zones—Lower Sonoran, Upper Sonoran, Transition and (if you elect to visit the north slope of Mica Mountain) Canadian. Manning Camp is a delightful campsite that offers hikers a choice of layover day activities—those with energy to burn can visit Mica Mountain, the highest point in the Rincons, while less energetic hikers can stretch out in the shade of a tall ponderosa pine, resting their bones, watching the sun track slowly across the deep blue sky, and listening to the wind as it sighs in the boughs.

Trailhead Route

Follow the trailhead route for Trip 41.

Description

From Douglas Spring Trailhead (0.0; 2750), follow Trip 41 to Douglas Spring Campground (5.9; 4800). From here we continue along the Douglas Spring Trail, which swings southward and climbs—gently at first, then more steeply—through a scrubby vegetative cover of small Mexican pinyons, hardy alligator junipers, manzanita, cliff rose, Emory and shrub live oak, and Arizona rosewood. Shortly after working our way into a small canyon we pass through a fence, then climb steeply on a few switchbacks to Cow Head Saddle (8.3; 6100). The forest overstory is denser and shadier at this altitude, with silverleaf oak and ponderosa pine beginning to supplant the pinyons and junipers.

At a signed junction in the saddle we turn left and climb moderately-to-steeply in the direction of Helens Dome, the rocky crag which now and then can be seen ahead through the trees. After about 2.5 miles of continuous climbing the trail suddenly drops slightly, then crosses a minor drainage. There may be a trickle of water here in early spring; if so, you may see some Coues white-tailed deer stepping cautiously out of the surrounding forest for a drink. We next follow this watercourse gently uphill for a short distance, then climb more steeply to a signed junction with the North Slope Trail (11.6; 8040). Our route goes right at this fork, climbs a bit, and then drops steadily past the clearly signed, left-branching Fire Loop Trail to Manning Camp (12.2; 8000), where you will find perennial water, camp grills, a toilet, and a cabin and corral used by the Park Service, all shaded by a dense forest of mature ponderosa pines. A camping permit is needed for overnight stays.

Manning Camp makes an excellent base for exploring the surrounding high country. A number of fine side trips are possible. Perhaps the best of these is the 5.3-mile loop hike up to Mica Mountain and Italian Spring (mileages given below indicate distances from Manning Camp, not from Douglas Spring Trailhead): At the signed junction just north of the Park Service cabin at Manning Camp, turn right and walk northeast up the floor of a minor drainage. At a succession of two signed forks we stay left; at a third,

Desert landscape, Rincon Mountains

unsigned split, we veer right. As the trail climbs gradually up and around the east shoulder of Mica Mountain we catch occasional glimpses through the trees of Spud Rock. Just below Mica's summit is a signed junction, where the trail to Italian Spring branches right; here we turn left and proceed 0. 1 mile to the top of Mica Mountain, the highest point in the Rincons and, formerly, the site of Mica Fire Tower. (The tower was removed some years ago.)

When ready to continue our sidetrip, we retrace our steps 0. 1 mile to the preceding junction, turn left, and descend gently along a grassy ridgetop. At a fork about ¼ mile later the route goes left, then switchbacks down to Italian Spring (2.3; 8000), a dependable year-round water source. At a junction here we turn left, onto the North Slope Trail, and climb a few switchbacks to a saddle between small rock outcroppings. In early spring a few patches of snow may linger in this area. For the next 2 miles the trail traverses the northwest shoulder of Mica Mountain, gently rising and falling over short distances and passing through some magnificent stands of ponderosa pine, Mexican white pine, Douglas-fir and white fir. The latter two species, generally associated with the Canadian life zone, are not at all common elsewhere in the Rincons, but they flourish on this high, north-facing slope.

At the end of this traverse we climb a few switchbacks, detouring above a smooth, sloping slab of rock (the top of which affords an excellent view of the distant Santa Catalina range). After switchbacking back down the far side of the slab, the North Slope Trail reaches a gap behind the monolith of Helens Dome, just beyond which is the junction with the trail coming up from Cow Head Saddle (4.7; 8040). Here we turn left and complete our sidetrip by retracing the steps of our earlier route back to Manning Camp (5.3; 8000).

Return the way you came.

TRIP 43
TANQUE VERDE TRAILHEAD TO JUNIPER BASIN AND TANQUE VERDE PEAK

~~~~~~

- ▲ **17.6 miles round trip; 3940′ elevation gain**
- ▲ **Strenuous dayhike or backpack (2-3 hiking days)**
- ▲ **Trailhead 17, Tanque Verde**
- ▲ **Maps**

   Rincon Mountains Trail and Recreation Map or *Tanque Verde Peak quadrangle*

▲ **Season: all year, except after snowstorms**
Water available at Juniper Basin Campground (mile 6.9) during
rainy periods only; check with Park Service first

Features

This strenuous route follows the broad, gradually rising back of Tanque Verde Ridge to 7049-foot Tanque Verde Peak, which affords a commanding view of both Tucson and the Rincon Mountains backcountry. Along the way the trail winds among tall saguaros, climbs wildflower-dotted slopes, and passes through delightful forests of oak, pinyon and juniper.

Strong hikers can make it to Tanque Verde Peak and back in a single day, but this trip is best done as a 2- or 3-day backpack.

Trailhead Route

From Tucson follow Old Spanish Trail east to Saguaro National Park. The visitor center has recreation and topographic maps for sale and you can get current information about the status of water sources and camping permits. Just past the entrance station take the first right. (If you go straight you will be committed to an eight mile, one way scenic loop.) After 1.6 miles you will come to the trailhead, just before a picnic area. There is no camping in the park except in the backcountry—with a permit.

Description

From the trailhead near Javelina Picnic Ground (0.0; 3100), walk gently downhill through a varied ground cover of magnificent saguaros, ocotillos, foothill paloverdes, hedgehog cacti, teddy-bear and staghorn chollas, prickly pear, brittlebushes, desert zinnias, purple-tufted thistles, narrowleaf asters, delicate yellow paperflowers, and desert marigolds. This rich panoply of Lower Sonoran zone vegetation puts forth a magnificent display of blossoms during the spring months, especially in wet years. After descending a short distance we cross a pair of small, shallow drainages, then climb, steeply in places, past a fence to a ridgetop saddle (1.0; 3480) atop the southwest extremity of Tanque Verde Ridge. Here there is a nice view eastward, across Rincon Valley to 8482-foot Rincon Peak, and westward to Tucson and the Santa Catalina Mountains. On a clear day it is possible to make out the distant spire of Picacho Butte, poking above the horizon beyond the city.

At an unsigned junction in this saddle we turn left along the crest of the saddle and begin the long climb up Tanque Verde Ridge. The trail stays either on top of or just to the left of the top of the broad ridge, paralleling a fence much of the way. The grade along this ascent varies from level to steep, with very few switchbacks to even things out. As we gain elevation the saguaros and paloverdes of the Lower Sonoran life zone give way to sotol, amole and nolina, indicating that we have climbed into a grassland community of the Upper Sonoran zone. Shiny flecks of mica, a silicate mineral common in the Rincons, appear underfoot here and there.

After passing through a gate (3.3; 4800) we continue climbing, a bit less steeply now, then top out at a hump on the ridge and descend a short distance to a gap. Beyond here we climb again, soon entering a patchy forest cover of Emory oaks, hardy Mexican pinyons, spiny Schott's yuccas and stout-trunked alligator junipers that grows increasingly dense as we gain elevation. After rollercoastering over a few ups and downs the trail crosses a small, sandy wash (usually dry), then proceeds across a comparatively level section a mile or so to Juniper Basin Campground (6.9; 6000), where there are grills, toilets, and the ruin of an old cement cabin, all set in the dappled shade of an oak-juniper woodland. The only source of water here is a tiny creeklet that generally flows only during rainy periods (and sometimes not even then; check it out with the Park Service if you will be depending on it for water). A camping permit is needed for overnight stays.

To continue to Tanque Verde Peak from here, follow the trail as it climbs gently onto the ridge east of Juniper Basin. Once on this ridge we climb more steeply, gaining some nice views of Rincon Peak, looming closer now than before, and of the heavily forested crown of Mica Mountain, rising above the Manning Camp area. A smattering of ponderosa pines can be seen down in a basin to the right.

Presently we round a bend on the ridge, and the rocky cap of Tanque Verde Peak appears directly ahead. A few short, steep climbs now bring us to a signed junction (8.8; 7040), where we turn right and climb a short distance farther to a register at the base of the peak's summit monolith. A tricky 10-foot rock scramble is necessary to reach the highest point from here. Those who figure out how to get on top are rewarded with a spectacular 360-degree vista that fully compensates for the laborious hike up. Included in this panorama are the Santa Rita and Huachuca Mountains, the Little Rincons (peeking above Happy Valley Saddle, the wide gap between Mica Mountain and Rincon Peak), the Galiuro and the Santa Catalina Mountains, and the city of Tucson. Foregrounding these views are the broad, sweeping slopes of Tanque Verde Ridge, which fall away in gentle waves in every direction. This isolated aerie is an excellent place from which to observe red-tailed hawks and golden eagles, a few of which can almost always be seen soaring and hunting against the vast backdrop of desert and mountains sprawling below. Caution: do not remain in the summit area if a thunderstorm appears to be brewing.

Return the way you came.

TRIP 44
TANQUE VERDE TRAILHEAD TO MANNING CAMP

- ▲ **30.8 miles round trip; 6960' elevation gain**
- ▲ **Strenuous backpack (4 hiking days)**
- ▲ **Trailhead 17, Tanque Verde**
- ▲ **Maps**
  Rincon Mountains Trail and Recreation Map or *Tanque Verde Peak and Mica Mountain quadrangles*
- ▲ **Season: March to November**
  Water available year-round at Manning Camp (mile 15.4); Juniper Basin Campground (mile 6.9) has water following rainy periods only

Features

After making the long, stiff climb up to Tanque Verde Peak, this route drops into Cow Head Saddle and then climbs into the high country at Manning Camp, where, in a delightfully shady forest of ponderosa, hikers will find relief from the searing heat of lowland summers. Plan on spending at least one layover day exploring the cool, pine- and fir-forested highlands surrounding nearby 8666-foot Mica Mountain, the highest point in the Rincons.

Trailhead Route

Follow the trailhead route for Trip 43.

Description

From the trailhead near Javelina Picnic Ground (0.0; 3100), follow the Tanque Verde Ridge Trail past Juniper Basin Campground to the trail junction just below Tanque Verde Peak (8.8; 7040) (see Trip 43). After making the short sidetrip up to Tanque Verde Peak's isolated, commanding summit, continue along the main trail, which descends moderately-to-steeply eastward through a semishady forest cover of ponderosa pine and silverleaf oak. After about a mile, the angle of this descent eases, and the trail makes a few ups and downs before dropping into Cow Head Saddle (11.5; 6100). At a signed junction here we go straight ahead and climb moderately-to-steeply in the direction of Helens Dome, the craggy monolith that can be glimpsed on occasion through the thickening forest cover. After about 2.5 miles of continuous climbing the trail drops slightly, then crosses a minor drainage which may contain a trickle of water during early spring. We next follow this watercourse gently uphill for a short distance, then climb more steeply to a signed junction with the North Slope Trail (14.8; 8040), coming over from Italian Spring. Our route goes right at this fork, climbs a bit, and then drops steadily (past the clearly signed, left-branching Fire Loop Trail) to Manning Camp (15.4; 8000), where there are year-round water, grills, and a toilet. Manning Cabin is used to house Park Service backcountry personnel. Camping is delightful here, beneath a shady forest of Arizona white oak, silverleaf oak, and dense stands of mature ponderosa pine. A number of worthwhile side trips can be made from this centrally located spot; one of the finest of these, the 5.3 mile loop trip up to Mica Mountain and Italian Spring, is described in Trip 42. A camping permit is needed for overnight stays.

Return the way you came, or via the Douglas Spring Trail to Douglas Spring Trailhead (9-mile car shuttle required; see Trip 42).

Manning Cabin

TRIP 45
MILLER CREEK TO HAPPY VALLEY CAMPGROUND AND RINCON PEAK

▲ **16.2 miles round trip; 4280' elevation gain**
▲ **Strenuous dayhike or backpack (2-3 hiking days)**
▲ **Trailhead 18, Miller Creek**
▲ **Maps**
   Rincon Mountains Trail and Recreation Map or *Happy Valley, Mica Mountain, and Rincon Peak quadrangles*
▲ **Season: April to November**
   Water available at Happy Valley Campground (mile 4.9) and at mile 6.7 during early spring and following periods of heavy rain

Features

This trip follows the shortest and least strenuous route to Rincon Peak, whose lofty, isolated crown affords one of the finest vistas in the entire state. It is still far from easy, however, entailing an elevation gain of over 4000 feet, and should be attempted only by those in good physical condition. Hikers who are both able and willing to invest the effort required to teach the top can be sure of reaping a commensurate dividend—the pride and satisfaction which are not earned with the attainment of easier summits.

Trailhead Route/Camping

From Tucson, drive southeast on Interstate Highway 10 about 45 miles and take the Mescal/J-Six ranch exit. Go over the interstate highway and drive past Mescal. In three miles the road becomes Forest Road 35, which although signed as unmaintained, shows strong signs of being graded. At its best, this road is suitable for passenger cars. High clearance is necessary when the streams are flowing, or when the streams have moved rocks into the roadbed. Get the current road conditions by phoning the rangers at Saguaro National Park. In 15.7 miles from the highway there is a signed turn to the left and the trailhead is only 200 yards farther. There are many suitable places to camp both during the drive in and near the trailhead. Do not camp within park boundaries without a permit.

Description

From the trailhead (0.0; 4200) follow the Miller Creek Trail up the imperceptibly sloping floor of Miller Canyon. After the first half mile or so, this canyon temporarily deepens and narrows; above this section, where the defile begins to open out again and after we pass the second Arizona Trail sign, we reach a place where the creek flows over a short rocky area and then seems to continue on the right side. Here, we cross to the left and climb out of the main canyon. After passing up a drainage, then following a low ridge between two drainages, we reach a fence with a hikers gate and the park boundary. The route bears left, crosses a drainage and then begins climbing steeply uphill, through a scrubby forest cover of emery oak, Mexican blue oak and Mexican pinyon. As we gain elevation a nice view opens up across Happy Valley to the Little Rincon Mountains.

At length, after negotiating several short, steep climbs interspersed among lengthy sieges of switchbacks, we arrive at a saddle of sorts (3.6; 5800). Here the trail swings left onto the wall of a small ravine, which is then followed to its head at Happy Valley Saddle (4.4; 6200). After turning left at a signed junction in this broad, ponderosa-forested gap, we follow a gently descending, usually dry streambed to a junction with the signed Rincon Peak Trail (4.9; 6080). A hundred yards or so down the right-branching trail, in a serene forest of ponderosa pine, silverleaf and Arizona white oak, and Schott's yucca, is Happy Valley Campground. Here there are grills, a toilet and, in early spring, running water. Backpackers will need a permit from the Park Service to spend the night here.

To reach Rincon Peak from the campground, retrace your steps to the last junction. Turning right here (left, if coming directly from the Miller Creek Trail), we next follow the Rincon Peak Trail southward as it winds over a few ups and downs, then strikes off through a nice forest of oak and alligator juniper. Once beyond this rather flat area the trail begins climbing again, alternating long, uphill traverses with spates of steep switchbacks. At a small, rocky drainage (6.7; 7000) there may be a trickle of water.

As we continue to gain elevation we enter the partial shade of a moderate forest cover of Douglas-fir, white fir and, in the sunnier spots, Mexican white pine.

About 2.5 miles beyond Happy Valley Saddle the gradient suddenly grows exceptionally steep (so steep that the Park Service has closed this section of the trail to equestrian use). After grunting and straining up numerous dizzily canted switchbacks, we skirt a small copse of aspens (some of the very few aspens to be found in the Rincons), and then arrive at a trail register just below Rincon Peak. From here a rudimentary path wanders the remaining 200 yards up to the high point (8.1; 8482), where you will find a tall cairn, a summit register, and a world of mountains and valleys sprawling across the vast landscape at your feet. On a clear day, when a storm has cleansed the air of its dusty burden and a legion of broken clouds trail their deep blue shadows behind them across the refreshed earth, the view from this commanding summit can be unforgettable. With the aid of a detailed map it is possible to identify at least a dozen distinct mountain ranges, including the Babequivaris, the Galiuros, the Santa Catalinas, and the Santa Ritas, to name just a few.

This peak is an obvious target for lightning bolts; should a thunderstorm appear to be brewing, vacate the summit immediately.

When thoroughly sated with vistas, return the way you came.

TRIP 46
MILLER CREEK TO DOUGLAS SPRING TRAILHEAD VIA HAPPY VALLEY SADDLE, MANNING CAMP, AND DOUGLAS SPRING CAMPGROUND

▲ **23.0 miles one-way (50-mile car shuttle required); 4780' elevation gain**

▲ **Strenuous backpack (3 hiking days)**

▲ **Trailhead 18, Miller Creek (start)**

▲ **Trailhead 16, Douglas Spring (finish)**

▲ **Maps**
   Rincon Mountains Trail and Recreation Map or *Happy Valley, Mica Mountain, Tanque Verde Peak, and Rincon Peak (for an optional spur hike) quadrangles*

▲ **Season: March to November**
   Water available all season at Manning Camp (mile 10.6); Happy Valley Campground (near mile 4.4) and Douglas Spring Campground(mile 16.9) have water during rainy periods only

Features
This lengthy transmontane route can be rushed through in as few as two days, but ideally it should be stretched out over at least five, with layover days spent at Happy Valley Saddle and Manning Camp campgrounds. This pace allows one to make the highly scenic detours to Mica Mountain and Rincon Peak. Happy Valley and Tanque Verde peaks are also easily accessible from points along the route. This trek is thus a peakbagger's delight, passing within side-tripping distance of all of the Rincons' highest and most prominent summits.

Trailhead Route
Start: follow the trailhead route for Trip 45. Finish: follow the trailhead route for Trip 41.

Description

From Miller Creek Trailhead (0.0; 4200), follow the route of Trip 45 up to the signed trail junction in Happy Valley Saddle (4.4; 6200). Most backpackers will want to spend the first night of their trek at Happy Valley Campground, 0.6 mile down the trail to the left. A lay-over day here will allow you to make the strenuous but highly rec-ommended side trip to 8482-foot Rincon Peak (6.4 miles round trip from the campground; see Trip 45). A camping permit is required for overnight stays.

When ready to continue our journey, we proceed northwest from Happy Valley Saddle and soon commence switchbacking steeply uphill, through a mixed forest cover of stunted ponderosa pine, Mexican pinyon, Emory oak, Arizona white oak, silverleaf oak, spiny Schott's yucca and alligator juniper. At length, after gaining 1000 feet of elevation, the trail swings left onto the west shoulder of Happy Valley Peak, levels off, and traverses across to a signed junction (6.3; 7200) just below Happy Valley Lookout. An 0.2-mile-long, switch-backing spur leads from here to the 7348-foot summit, which affords fine views of Rincon Peak, Tanque Verde Peak, Mica Mountain, the Galiuro Mountains and the Little Rincons.

From this junction the trail drops slightly onto Heartbreak Ridge, whose mostly shadeless crest is then followed northwestward, up and over three minor rises, to a fork (7.9; 7120), where the signed Deerhead Spring Trail veers right. We stay left here, on the Heartbreak Ridge Trail, and climb steeply up a brushy slope to a signed, 4-way junction (8.4; 7560). Our route now turns left, travers-es a few hundred yards to a minor, ponderosa-forested ridgecrest, then drops slightly and crosses a tiny creeklet (9.1; 7440) (water dur-ing early spring and after heavy rains only). Just downstream from here is Devils Bathtub, where the creek (when it is running) spills down a 50-foot waterfall into a small pool at the bottom of a smooth, water-worn granite bowl. During warm weather, hikers may wish to scramble down into this bowl for an impromptu dip.

About 0.5 miles beyond the Bathtub we meet the signed Manning Camp Trail coming up from Grass Shack Spring; here we turn right and ascend a few switchbacks into a rockbound stream channel. After paralleling a streamlet (water in early spring and following heavy rains) for a short distance, the trail crosses to the left and climbs steeply into a thickening forest of ponderosa pine. The angle of this ascent soon eases, and shortly we arrive at Manning Camp (10.6; 8000), where there are grills, a toilet and year-round water. Manning Cabin is used by Park Service backcountry personnel. As at all campgrounds in the Rincons, a Park Service camping permit is required for spending the night here. Many fine side trips can be made from here; one of the best of these, the 5.3 mile loop trip up to lofty Mica Mountain and Italian Spring, is described in Trip 42.

To complete your trek across the Rincons, reverse the steps of Trip 42 to Douglas Spring Campground (16.9; 4800) and Douglas Spring Trailhead (22.8; 2750). Alternatively, follow the Tanque Verde Ridge Trail from Cow Head Saddle out to Javelina Picnic Ground (26.0 miles total; reverse the steps of Trip 44).

Santa Rita Mountains

Less than an hour's drive from Tucson, The Santa Ritas and Madera Canyon offer a variety of recreational opportunities including world class birdwatching opportunities, hiking, and camping. Mount Wrightson tops out at 9543 feet, offering stupendous views in all directions.

TRIP 47
BOG SPRINGS CAMPGROUND TO BOG SPRINGS, KENT SPRING, AND SYLVESTER SPRING

▲ **4.8 mile semiloop trip; 1600' elevation gain**
▲ **Moderate dayhike or leisurely backpack (2 hiking days)**
▲ **Trailhead 19, Bog Spring Campground**
▲ **Maps**
Santa Rita Mountains Trail and Recreation Map or *Mount Wrightson quadrangle*
▲ **Season: all year, except following snowstorms**
Water is usually available at Bog, Kent, and Sylvester springs (miles 1.4, 2.7 and 3.1); check with Forest Service during spells of very dry weather

Features
Easily completed in half a day, yet encompassing a variety of fine vistas, this pleasant ramble is a good introduction to the Santa Rita Mountains. Included on the itinerary are four near-perennial watering holes, making this an especially good route for observing wildlife.

Trailhead Route/Camping

Drive about 25 miles south of Tucson on Interstate Highway 19 and take the Continental exit. Drive under the interstate highway and take the right turn 1.1 miles later. Just after milepost 12, take the left turn and drive 0.5 mile uphill to the Bog Springs Campground. The trail starts after the third campsite on the right. Day use parking and/or camping costs $5 which can be paid at the self-registration station past a couple of more campsites on the left. Pick up the free (non-topographic) map that shows the major trails and trailheads of the Santa Ritas. If you do not wish to pay a $5 fee for camping or parking, use the free day use parking adjacent to the campground turnoff. Then, either walk up the road or take the shorter (but steeper and rockier) trail to the camping area. This is the only car camping area in Madera Canyon.

Description

From the trailhead at Bog Springs Campground (0.0; 5080) follow a rocky jeep track (now closed to motor vehicles) as it crosses a small drainage, then ascends moderately through a forest cover of emery oak, Arizona white oak, alligator juniper and silverleaf oak. The road steepens a bit as it climbs up to a saddle (0.7; 5340). Bear left at the signed junction onto a narrow trail which can be seen sneaking off to the left; from here we work our way up onto a hillside that affords a pleasant view across Madera Canyon to the tawny grasslands beyond. About 0.6 mile along this trail we cross a small drainage, then climb a short distance to Bog Springs (1.4; 5880). Here there are a few fair campsites, beneath a shady overstory of Arizona walnuts, rustling sycamores, silverleaf oaks, some tall Apache pines, and a few Douglas-firs. This is a good spot to observe wildlife; Mexican jays are common (as are a variety of other birds—see Trip 48 for a partial listing of species that might be seen in this area), and wild turkeys and Coues white-tailed deer are frequent visitors during the cooler months of the year. The spring almost always has water, but check it out with the Forest Service if you will be depending on it during dry weather. There is a faucet just beyond the spring so you need not take water from the tank-where wildlife drinks. Many people trust water from this faucet but an ounce of caution is worth a pound of cure.

From here the trail proceeds up a ravine a short distance, then climbs out steeply to the right. After gaining a ridge, we switchback more moderately uphill, and an impressive view opens up across the densely forested headwaters of Madera Canyon to the rugged, cliff-bound summit of 9453-foot Mount Wrightson. Presently the switchbacks cease, and we traverse across a sunny, south-facing slope

Mt. Wrightson from Bog Springs Campground

planted with Chihuahua pine and Mexican pinyon pine to signed Kent Spring (2.7; 6640), about as reliable as Bog Springs. There are campsites here, but they are not as attractive as the ones at Bog Springs. At one time the Civilian Conservation Corps constructed a trail to a saddle high above. The Forest Service was planning to restore the washed out trail until the saddle was burned off in a fire. Now, plans to restore the trail are being resurrected.

Here our route rejoins the abandoned jeep road, which leads very steeply downhill, following the pleasantly forested ravine draining Kent Spring. In about 0.5 mile we pass Sylvester Spring, climb out of the ravine to the left, and drop into a tributary of Madera Creek. This tributary often has running water, but it offers only poor campsites. At an unsigned fork in the road we go right, and proceed a short distance back to the same saddle we crossed earlier in the day (4.1; 5340). To complete your trek, retrace your steps 0.7 miles to Bog Springs Campground (4.8; 5040).

TRIP 48
MADERA CANYON ROADEND TO LODE STAR MINE

- ▲ **3.2 miles round trip; 960' elevation gain**
- ▲ **Leisurely dayhike or backpack (2 hiking days)**
- ▲ **Trailhead 20, Madera Canyon Roadend**
- ▲ **Maps**
  Santa Rita Mountains Trail and Recreation Map or *Mount Wrightson and Mount Hopkins quadrangles*
- ▲ **Season: all year, except after snowstorms**
  Water available intermittently along Madera Creek, except possibly during very dry periods

Features

Nominally, this trip's destination is Lode Star Mine, an abandoned working near the head of leafy Madera Canyon. But far more attractive than the mine is the canyon itself—threaded by a near-perennial creek, shaded by a mixed forest of hardwoods and conifers, and famous across the nation for the variety of its birdlife. This short hike can be rushed through in just two hours, but its lush, sylvan setting warrants a more relaxed pace. Birdwatchers—and others—will find enough here to occupy them all day, and may even wish to spend the night.

Trailhead Route

Follow the trailhead route for Trip 47 but instead of turning left for the Bog Springs Campground, continue on the main road an additional 1.1 miles to the TRAILS sign. Turn left and drive a short distance. The trails depart from the upper parking lot but there is better shade for the car (morning hours only) in the lower parking area. If all parking is taken (which may happen during weekends and holidays), there is additional trail parking in the Roundup Picnic Area, just after the TRAILS sign.

Description

From the far end of the upper parking area, (0.0; 5440), walk gently uphill, south, along an old road, now closed to motorized traffic, through a varied vegetative cover of prickly pears, saw-edged agaves, Emory oaks, sycamores, Arizona madrones and some Apache pines. In 0.3 mile the signed Old Baldy Trail branches off to the left; our route continues straight ahead here, on the Very Steep Trail (which is not steep at all at this point). Nearby Madera Creek, shown as a perennial stream on the topo, generally dries up into a series of disconnected pools during spells of dry weather, but a single heavy thunderstorm can turn it into a torrent in less than an hour. The creek is perhaps at its best in early spring, when it gurgles softly with the last of the high country snowmelt, and when its banks are graced here and there with showy yellow columbine blossoms.

The forest overstory grows lusher as we proceed up-canyon, and during the spring and summer the air comes alive with the songs and calls of the many birds that nest hereabouts. Among the many species you might spot (bring along binoculars and a field guide) are the solitary vireo, acorn woodpecker, Mexican jay, black-headed grosbeak, red-shafted flicker, western tanager, sulfur-bellied flycatcher, Mexican junco and coppery-tailed trogon. The last three birds on this list are essentially Mexican species, and are rarely seen in the U.S. outside of the southeastern Arizona mountains. A sighting of the rare coppery-tailed trogon, an iridescently plumed relative of the fabulous quetzal of Mexico and Central America, is especially prized among birdwatchers.

Presently we reach a signed junction (0.9; 5880) where we leave the Very Steep Trail and continue straight ahead, up Madera Canyon.

The road pinches out, the trail is washed out, then reappears on the far side of the creek. Soon, this trail is washed out as well and we continue via the creekbed. In a short distance (that seems more while boulder hopping) there are three sycamores in a line-two close together, one farther. Here, the trail resumes on the right bank, cutting sharply to the right. It climbs steeply a short distance up a wooded ridge, then traverses to the left, back toward the creek. There are some pleasing vistas along this section, down the length of Madera Canyon to the grassy flatlands beyond. A few Gambel oaks grow on this north-facing hillside, along with Apache pines, Arizona pines and, down in the streambed, some velvet ash. Shortly after swinging into near-contact with the creek we arrive at Lode Star Mine (1.6; 6400). Molybdenum, along with traces of gold and silver, were taken from this mine during its active years, but it is no longer being worked. A rusting boiler and lots of other relics remain in the area. Fair campsites can be found nearby, and water is almost always available in the stream (check with the Forest Service during dry periods, or pack up your own supply).

Return the way you came.

Note: the U.S. Forest Service is planning to re-route the Very Steep Trail so that it ascends more gradually and becomes more popular. If this happens, these directions should still make it possible to find the Lode Star Mine.

TRIP 49
MADERA CANYON ROADEND TO VAULT MINE AND JOSEPHINE SADDLE

- ▲ **6.3 mile loop trip; 1840′ elevation gain**
- ▲ **Moderate dayhike or backpack (2 hiking days)**
- ▲ **Trailhead 20, Madera Canyon Roadend**
- ▲ **Maps**
  Santa Rita Mountains Trail and Recreation Map or *Mount Wrightson and Mount Hopkins quadrangles*
- ▲ **Season: April through November**
  Water almost always available at Sprung Spring (near mile 4.1); check with Forest Service during dry weather spells

Features

After sampling a portion of leafy Madera Canyon, this trip climbs steeply past Vault Mine to a pretty aspen grove high on the slopes of

Mount Hopkins. Returning via Josephine Saddle and the Old Baldy Trail makes for a varied, scenic loop route.

Trailhead Route

Follow the trailhead route for Trip 48.

Description

From the upper parking area (0.0; 5440), follow the route of Trip 48 to the signed trail fork in Madera Canyon (0.9; 5880). Take a sharp right here, just after the sign, and proceed a short distance up a ravine, then swing to the left and switchback exceptionally steeply uphill (one can now see why the Forest Service calls this the "Very Steep Trail"). As we gain elevation, occasional nice views open up across a densely forested basin draining into Madera Canyon.

Some ¾ mile after leaving the floor of the canyon, the trail passes the mouth of Vault Mine (1.6; 7000), which produced gold and silver before its short vein "pinched out." The shaft is not deep at all, and may be safely entered. From here the route continues steeply uphill, along a minor ridgeline, about ¼ mile to an unsigned junction marked with a cairn. We now turn left, onto the Agua Caliente Trail, and traverse across the shady northeast face of 8585-foot Mount Hopkins. This section offers several good views down the length of Madera Canyon to the distant Rincon and Santa Catalina ranges. Mount Wrightson's rocky, 9453-foot summit is also visible. Soon after leaving the Very Steep Trail we arrive at the edge of a beautiful grove of tall aspens—perhaps the finest such grove in the Santa Rita Mountains. This spot makes a fine lunch stop for dayhikers.

Beyond here the trail proceeds past a number of minor ups and downs, touching but not crossing three saddles on the ridge between Hopkins and Wrightson. Each of these gaps has a fair campsite (no

Summit of Mt. Hopkins

water), and affords a grand vista to the south, across Sonoita Valley and on into Mexico. Presently we drop a short distance into often-windy Josephine Saddle (4.1; 7080), where there are several good campsites, beneath a shady forest cover of silverleaf oak, Arizona pine and Apache pine. Water is usually available at Sprung Spring, ¼ mile down the signed Super Trail from the saddle. (During spells of dry weather, this spring should be checked out with the Forest Service.) A pair of plaques here memorialize three Boy Scouts who, on November 15, 1958, "passed this way on their way to the Better Place" (the trio perished in an uncommonly fierce, early-season snowstorm).

Several trails come together in this saddle. Our route turns left, onto the signed Old Baldy Trail, and switchbacks moderately down the wall of a ravine. Stay on the reworked trail where it tangles with an older, steeper pathway. Presently we traverse to the left, across several minor ridges and drainages, then drop past a treeless area affording an open view of Mount Wrightson. Shortly after passing a covered water tank we reach the signed junction with the Very Steep Trail back in Madera Canyon; to complete your trek from here, turn right and retrace the morning's route the remaining 0.3 mile to the trailhead (6.3; 5440).

Note: The U.S. Forest Service is currently planning to re-route the Very Steep Trail. The new route is planned to ascend more gradually, which should help to give the route more popularity. At this time, it is not known if the new route will still go past Vault Mine.

TRIP 50
Madera Canyon Roadend to Mount Wrightson

⌃ **12.8 miles loop trip; 4020' elevation gain**
⌃ **Strenuous dayhike or backpack (2-4 hiking days)**
⌃ **Trailhead 20, Madera Canyon Roadend**
⌃ **Maps**
   Santa Rita Mountains Trail and Recreation Map or *Mount Wrightson quadrangle*
⌃ **Season: May through October**
   Water almost always available at Sprung Spring (miles 3.5 and 10.6), Bellows Spring (mile 4.9), and Baldy Spring (mile 7.5); check with Forest Service during spells of dry weather

Features

9453-foot Mount Wrightson, the goal of this fine trip, is the highest and by far the most prominent summit in the Santa Rita Mountains. The route is fairly strenuous, but the trails used are well maintained and moderately graded all the way, and the great view from the top fully justifies the effort required to reach it.

Trailhead Route

Follow the trailhead routes for Trip 48.

Description

From the north end of the upper parking area, (0.0; 5440), follow the signed Super Trail as it climbs moderately a short distance, then swings right to a tributary of Madera Creek, where the gradient eases. This creeklet often has running water, and supports a nice riparian growth of sycamore, walnut, and velvet ash. In spring, showy yellow columbine blossoms grace the moist streambanks here and there. Soon we cross the creek to its left side, then climb through a forest cover of silverleaf oak, emery oak, Arizona white oak and alligator juniper onto the dry slope above. After a single switchback the trail cuts up-canyon, staying at about the level of the tops of the broadleaf trees lining the watercourse. About 1 mile from the trailhead we I temporarily return to creekside, then begin switchbacking moderately uphill. At length, after gaining an excellent view down the length of Madera Canyon, we reach an unnamed saddle (2.2; 6440). There is a good view of the long, rocky crest of Mount Wrightson from this gap.

Apache pines, Mexican white pines and Chihuahua pines gradually integrate themselves into the forest cover as we climb gently southward from the saddle. In 1.2 miles we arrive at Sprung Spring, which almost always has potable water (check with the Forest Service if you will be depending on this spring during very dry spells). About ¼ mile farther along is Josephine Saddle (3.6; 7080), where there is a memorial to three Boy Scouts who lost their lives in a fierce November snowstorm back in 1958. Several good campsites can be found in this forested, sometimes windy gap. The nearest water is at Sprung Spring.

At a signed junction in this saddle we turn left, onto the combined Super Trail/Old Baldy Trail. In 0.2 mile, where these two paths part ways, we turn left again, and follow the Old Baldy Trail as it switchbacks onto the west slope of Mount Wrightson. After we round a ridge containing a good but dry campsite, the steep cliffs of Wrightson's rugged northwest face loom directly ahead. A short traverse and a few more switchbacks now bring us to Bellows Spring, about as reliable as Sprung Spring. It may be necessary to do some rock scrambling to get water from Bellows Spring as the pipe no longer flows. From here we traverse northward a bit, past some avalanche-harried aspens and Gambel oaks, then ascend many tight switchbacks through a break in the spectacular cliffs. This climb tops out at Baldy Saddle (5.5; 8880). At a signed junction here we turn right and walk a short distance south to a second junction, where the Super Trail comes in from the left. Backpackers will find a number of windy, exposed campsites in this area; more sheltered ones are available at Baldy Spring, just down the Super Trail (see below).

To continue on to Mount Wrightson, go straight ahead here, and climb gently along a shady slope forested with Mexican white pine and a smattering of Douglas-fir. The trail soon steepens, then twists up several short, rocky switchbacks to the treeless summit (6.4; 9453). Views from this lofty, isolated mountaintop are as beautiful as they are extensive. The distinctive spire of Baboquivari Peak pokes above the desert flats to the west, while the Santa Catalina, Rincon and Galiuro mountains rear up in the north. The dark, forested cap of Chiricahua Peak is clearly discernible on the eastern horizon. To the south, long chains of ridges and peaks recede to the vanishing point, deep in Mexico. The view to the southwest is spoiled somewhat by a raw road scar that cuts across the face of nearby Mount Hopkins. The cement foundation here is almost all that remains of old Baldy Lookout, which was removed in 1958. There is also a concrete lined hole that may be the remains of a cistern. Remember that this peak is a prime target for lightning strikes; be sure to head back down the trail if you see a thunderstorm building up nearby.

After taking in the view (and signing the summit register), retrace your steps for 0.9 mile, turn right onto the signed Super Trail and proceed a short distance downhill to Baldy Spring (7.5; 8760). This spring does not produce much water during the summer months, at most a trickle from a pipe that no longer supplies its tank. Sometimes it dries up completely; check it out with the Forest Service if you plan to camp in this sheltered area. A lookout cabin stood here until 1974, when it was burned down by an arson fire.

From Baldy Spring we drop down a pair of switchbacks, then descend moderately through a forest of tall pines and firs to a signed junction with the Gardner Canyon Trail, where we stay right. Just beyond here we are treated to a good view of Mount Wrightson's "back" side—as rocky and cliffbound as its "front"—and of the swelling waves of bluish mountains receding southward, nicely framed by Riley Saddle, the forested gap to the right of 8474-foot Josephine Peak. Hopefully, these views are adequate compensation for the brushiness of this section. After traversing beneath the east face of Wrightson, the trail crosses Riley Saddle, then drops very gently across a sunny, south-facing slope densely planted with netleaf, silverleaf and white oak. About a mile beyond the saddle, we drop down a few switchbacks, rejoin the Old Baldy Trail, and continue a short distance farther to Josephine Saddle (10.6; 7080). To complete your journey from here, follow the signed Old Baldy Trail the remaining 2.2 miles back to Madera Canyon Roadend (12.8; 5440), just across the parking lot from where the hike began (see Trip 49).

TRIP 51
FLORIDA CANYON TRAILHEAD TO FLORIDA SPRING

- ▲ **7.4 miles round trip; 2760′ elevation gain**
- ▲ **Strenuous dayhike or backpack (2 hiking days)**
- ▲ **Trailhead 21, Florida Canyon**
- ▲ **Maps**
  Santa Rita Mountains Trail and Recreation Map or *Helvetia and Mount Wrightson quadrangles*
- ▲ **Season: all year, except following snowstorms**
  Water available at Robinson Spring (mile 1.7) and Florida Spring (mile 3.7) during rainy periods only

Features
Beginning at the edge of an Upper Sonoran grassland region, this route climbs quickly up the north slope of the Santa Rita Mountains to a dense, shady grove of Douglas fir near the head of Florida Canyon. Here, in a hushed, cathedral-like atmosphere, the hot, sun-drenched lowlands seem light-years away. Florida Spring makes an excellent base for backpackers on their way to Mount Wrightson.

Trailhead Route/Camping
Follow the trailhead route for Trip 47—except that after milepost 7.8, where the paved road takes a curve right, our route continues straight on Forest Road 62 for 0.3 mile. When Forest Road 62 curves away to the left we continue straight on Forest Road 62A. Both roads are suitable for most passenger cars. After 2.7 miles we reach a parking lot just outside the gate of the Florida Work Center. Camping is not permitted here. Either camp at Bog Springs Campground (see the trailhead route for Trip 47) or farther east off Forest Road 62.

Description

From the Florida Canyon Trailhead (0.0; 4240), follow an abandoned road as it crosses the usually dry bed of Florida Creek and proceeds gently uphill along the east bank. The watercourse supports a lush riparian growth of Mexican blue oak, sycamore and hackberry, while on the parched slopes just a few yards away, little can survive besides ocotillo, prickly pear, and a few other drought-tolerant shrubs and cacti. After climbing over a small rise we drop to a signed junction near the Florida Canyon Experimental Range Headquarters / Florida Work Center. Here we turn left, and work our way, on a trail now, into a tributary drainage. The forest cover is sparser in this smaller, apparently drier canyon, and consists mostly of mesquite, Emory oak and some diminutive Mexican blue oaks. Among the many wildflowers that bloom here in the spring are pinkish-red parry penstemon, verbena, filaree, white-blossomed sacred datura, brittlebush and prickly poppy. During the summer thunderstorm season, water sometimes pools up behind the many small catchment dams along the streambed. These once held a considerable amount of water but are now largely filled with silt. We also pass several tanks including a large circular one, now dry, and a smaller circular tank, about a mile from the trailhead, which uses an ingenious design in which a toilet tank float allows water to fill the tank to a certain level and no higher. Above this point we will often spot pipe leading down from Robinson Spring.

After crossing the wash a few times, the trail climbs steeply up a series of ridgelines to the left. As we gain elevation a nice vista opens up across the tawny, oak-dotted Santa Rita foothills to the north. About 1 mile after leaving the Florida Creek tributary, the trail threads a minor saddle, then drops a short distance back into the same drainage and climbs a bit to Robinson Spring (l.7; 5320), an unsigned, unreliable seep down in the canyon bottom (water during rainy periods only). Sycamore, velvet ash, Arizona walnut, hanging tendrils of canyon grape, silverleaf oak and alligator juniper all grow in this area. At one point the trail crosses tailings from a mine shaft that seems to be caved in but is still signed (in two languages) as dangerous. Camping is poor.

At the canyon forks just above the spring, the trail heads up the left branch a short distance, then crosses over to the right-hand prong and switchbacks steeply up to a small saddle. From here we swing left, continue climbing steeply along a ridgeline, then traverse southward across a shallow ravine and ascend to a larger saddle with a dry campsite and a good view across the rugged amphitheater drained by Florida Creek. As we continue south from this saddle, Apache pine, Mexican pinyon pine, Arizona pine and Chihuahua pine become predominant in the forest cover. But not for long—soon a few Douglas firs appear, and by the time we approach the head of Florida Canyon these trees form a dense, nearly pure stand. There is a fine campsite in this shady, soothingly quiet grove. Just beyond is a ravine, in which is found Florida Spring (3.7; 7000) about 50 feet above the trail (water during rainy periods only). Coues white-tailed deer and wild turkeys are frequent visitors to this area, and camping is delightful.

Return the way you came.

TRIP 52
FLORIDA CANYON TRAILHEAD TO MOUNT WRIGHTSON

- ▲ **15.2 miles round trip; 5540' elevation gain**
- ▲ **Strenuous dayhike or backpack (2-4 hiking days)**
- ▲ **Trailhead 21, Florida Canyon**
- ▲ **Maps**
  Santa Rita Mountains Trail and Recreation Map or *Helvetia and Mount Wrightson quadrangles*
- ▲ **Season: May through October**
  Water almost always available at Baldy Spring (near mile 6.7) (check with Forest Service during dry weather periods); Robinson Spring (mile 1.7) and Florida Spring (mile 3.7) have water during rainy periods only

Features

This trek reaches lofty Mount Wrightson via Florida Saddle and the Crest Trail—a route that is more strenuous, more scenic, and less-traveled than the more popular trails beginning in Madera Canyon. With delightful camping available at Florida Spring, this trip makes an excellent choice for the summit-bound backpacker.

Trailhead Route

Follow the trailhead route for Trip 51.

Description

From the Florida Canyon Trailhead (0.0; 4240), follow the route of Trip 51 to Florida Spring (3.7; 7000). After crossing the ravine below the spring, the trail switchbacks, very steeply at first, through more Douglas firs to Florida Saddle (4.7; 7880). At a signed intersection here we go right (west) and follow the Crest Trail a bit less steeply

0.3 mile to the signed, right-branching spur to Armour Spring (0.4 mile down the spur; water during rainy periods only). There is a good campsite here.

From this junction the trail climbs moderately along the east side of the long ridge that drops northward from Mount Wrightson. It is instructive to note how the forest cover varies along this crest— Arizona pine and Mexican white pine are predominant in windy, exposed areas and on south-facing slopes, while Douglas-fir prefers sheltered pockets on north-facing slopes, where one would expect deep drifts of snow to accumulate in winter. Views are excellent from several points, across the eastern Santa Rita foothills to the wrinkled landscape drained by Cienega Wash, with the Whetstone and Huachuca mountains rising in the distance. About 1.7 miles beyond Florida Saddle, the trail tops out near a rocky ridgelet, then descends to Baldy Saddle (6.7; 8880) where, at a quick succession of signed forks, the Old Baldy Trail branches right and then the Super Trail goes left. To reach the bald summit of Mount Wrightson we proceed straight ahead at each junction, and follow the rocky, switchbacking

horned owl

trail the remaining 0.9 mile to the top (7.6; 9453). For a description of the summit area, see Trip 50.

Return the way you came, or via either the Super Trail or Old Baldy Trail to Madera Canyon Roadend (9-mile car shuttle required; see Trip 50).

Chiricahua Wilderness and the Rattlesnake Fire

In 1994 the Rattlesnake Fire killed an estimated one million plus trees in the Chiricahua Wilderness. Several hundred thousand more trees were singed but not killed by the fire.

This has had several adverse effects on hiking in the Chiricahua Wilderness. First, the fire killed the root systems which held soil together allowing accelerated erosion. Besides the erosion of existing trails, there are damaged areas far from burned sections resulting from sediment deposited on trails, in drainages, and in water tanks— even a lake was sedimented full to the status of a meadow. Currently, only the Crest Trail receives much in the way of maintenance. Other trails have had sections partially or totally washed out, cut by ravines, and crossed by fallen trees. So far, only a tiny fraction of the dead trees have fallen. In the years ahead, a million dead trees will fall. Some will fall across trails.

Hikers have been going elsewhere. Weeds have grown up on once popular trails making them harder to follow. Springs that were formerly dependable, at least seasonally, have silted in.

However, the situation is not quite as bad as it sounds. Routes along the Crest Trail are only about half burned. Many of the other trails described in this section sustained much less damage. On most of these trails one can walk miles before reaching a seriously burned area. There are still some magnificent stands of old growth forest. However, due to extensive erosion, neither the South Fork nor the Snowshed Trails should be used to access the Crest Trails unless and until these trails are restored (though both trails have a lot to offer day hikers).

Once new growth has re-anchored soil and rocks on slopes, the forest service will start to restore trails. In many cases, this will mean rerouting trails onto more stable ground. Some trails may be abandoned.

A Chiricahua Wilderness map is scheduled for release in 1998. Since the map will be planned during a period of transition—when routes are in the planning stage, the map will be partially guesswork. However, it will be much more accurate than the old recreation and topographic quadrangle maps.

The trails in this section were surveyed for this edition in April, 1997—before the trail rangers had begun a maintenance schedule survey for summer, 1997. Call the rangers for current information about trail status.

Trail descriptions have been added for Chiricahua National Monument, at the north end of the range. These trails may not have the remote wilderness appeal of Chiricahua Wilderness—but the Rattlesnake Fire did not reach this area.

TRIP 53
RUSTLER PARK TO FLYS PEAK

▲ **6.4 miles round trip; 1420' elevation gain**
▲ **Moderate dayhike**
▲ **Trailhead 22, Rustler Park**
▲ **Maps**
   Chiricahua Wilderness (due out in 1998) or *Rustler Park and Chiricahua Peak quadrangles*
▲ **Season: May to October**
   No water available along route

Features

Rustler Park is the highest trailhead in the Chiricahua Mountains, and provides the most convenient access to the range's loftiest peaks. This trip, an excellent introduction to the Chiricahua high country, passes through dense stands of spruce and fir before climbing up to 9666-foot Flys Peak, where gaps in the forest cover provide glimpses across the vast expanse of mountains and desert sprawling below. An added bonus is the opportunity of detouring to highly scenic Centella Point.

Trailhead Route/Camping

From Willcox, drive southeast on Highway 186 for 33 miles. Turn left (east) on Highway 181 and drive 3 miles to Pinery Canyon Road. Turn right onto this road, which becomes Forest Road 42 (usually in good shape for passenger cars). After 12 miles, at Onion Saddle, turn right on FR 42B and proceed 3.1 miles to the trailhead—just after the first loop of the campground. There is parking near the outhouse adjacent to the trailhead. Signs warn that bears now seem to recognize cars as food containers, and have damaged cars while trying to reach the food.

Description

From the campground (0.0; 8410) the trail begins climbing gently. Very shortly we come to a fence with a hikers' gate and a junction to the Bootlegger Creek Trail. Here, we bear left, circling around a peak to our right. As the path ascends gently onto a shady, north-facing slope, the gradual change that has been taking place in the forest cover reaches its climax, and the hiker will notice that the sun-loving Chihuahua and Apache pines, which were so dominant on the drive up to Rustler Park, have been almost wholly supplanted by Douglas-fir, Engelmann spruce and quaking aspen—snow-tolerant trees of the Canadian life zone. We soon start to see trees that have been singed by fire but the vast majority are still living and most were not touched by fire.

Soon we meet the Rock Creek Trail coming up from the west to a saddle, (1.5; 8880), as well as an old forest road coming in from the left. We stay left—following the old road as it continues up slope out of the saddle. This road comes in from the cabin area near the campground and is still used by some people to avoid 1.5 miles of hiking. This approach should only be used with a high clearance vehicle. The U.S. Forest Service plans to close this route at some time in the future. About three quarters of a mile past this saddle you will pass a very singed wilderness boundary sign. Within a few hundred yards we come to another junction where five trails come together (2.4; 9080). If you are low on water at this point, you may wish to detour to usually reliable Tub Spring, 0.3 mile east down the left-branching trail. To reach Flys Peak, take the signed fork leading southeast and follow a series of broad switchbacks to a junction one eighth of a mile before the top (3.2; 9666). Take the left fork. From a distance Flys Peak appears to be largely burned off but this is deceptive. About half the distance along the trail is either only lightly singed or untouched. On the summit you will find a cement foundation and some rusting metal posts set in the ground, remnants of the cabin and lookout tower that once stood here. (The lookout became outmoded with the advent of airplanes and helicopters as firefighting aids, and the abandoned tower was dismantled to preserve the surrounding area's wilderness character.)

Flys' gently rounded summit is forested, and the only clear vista it offers is through a break in the trees to the south where the fire almost reached the summit. Those who hanker for a better view should make the side trip to strategically perched Centella Point. Retrace your steps 0.8 mile to the last junction before the ascent began and turn right (east) onto the path to Tub Spring. About 0.5 mile beyond the spring you will come to two junctions in quick succession; stay left at each, and continue for 1 mile to the airy overlook of 9320-foot Centella Point. Here you will find excellent views across the deep, beautifully sculptured canyon of Cave Creek, with its broad, forested basins and needle-sharp ridges and pinnacles.

Return the way you came.

TRIP 54
RUSTLER PARK TO FLYS PEAK, ANITA PARK, AND CHIRICAHUA PEAK

- ▲ **11.8 miles round trip; 2020' elevation gain**
- ▲ **Moderate dayhike or backpack (2 hiking days)**
- ▲ **Trailhead 22, Rustler Park**
- ▲ **Maps**
  Chiricahua Wilderness (due out in 1998) or *Rustler Park and Chiricahua Peak quadrangles*
- ▲ **Season: May to October**
  Water available all season (except possibly during very dry years) at Booger Spring (near mile 3.7) and Anita Spring (near mile 5.3)

Features

Picking up where the preceding trip left off, this fine route continues on to bright green Anita Park, a good base from which to explore the forested tops of the Chiricahuas, and culminates at 9796-foot Chiricahua Peak, the highest point in the range. Less than half the forest cover along this route was killed by the fire and the spots of shade and the coolness of the air at this altitude provide welcome relief from the heat and glare of lowland summers; the most difficult part of this excursion may well come at the very end, when you must convince yourself to return to the hot desert below.

Trailhead Route

Follow the trailhead route for Trip 53.

Description

Follow the directions for Trip 53 to the summit of Flys Peak (3.2; 9666). To continue to Chiricahua Peak, go back down the trail one eighth mile to the last junction and continue straight. After passing through an area mostly burned off we arrive at Round Park, a small meadow studded with aspen sunflowers and the nodding yellow heads of cutleaf coneflower. Coues white-tailed deer are often spotted here during the summer months. When the trail you have been following begins to fade out in the grass, move a few steps to the right onto the obvious Crest Trail. (If you wish, you may bypass Flys Peak by following the well signed, but largely burned, Crest Trail from the preceding junction directly to this point.)

Before proceeding south we may wish to seek water. At the far left end of Round Park is the signed spur trail to Booger Spring (a short distance east; water except in extremely dry years).

Continuing along the Crest Trail, it soon reaches the broad Cima Saddle where we find the signed junction with the Greenhouse Trail (4.4; 9240). Cima Park is just to the right. Our route continues south along the Crest Trail, past the right-branching Mormon Ridge Trail, and then arrives at the signed spur to Anita Park and Anita Spring (5.3; 9520). Anita Park, with its delightful camping, lies a short distance up this trail to the north-northeast; the almost always reliable spring is a few hundred yards beyond the park, down the hillside to the east. This is a good area in which to observe wildlife—deer frequent the meadow, and the surrounding forest is often alive with darting, singing Mexican chickadees, a species rarely seen elsewhere in the U.S. Black bears have also been known to visit occasionally, and campers should safeguard their food supply by suspending it out of harm's reach from a high tree limb. In hiking to Anita Park we traversed a lot of burned off trail, but the fire did not quite reach Anita Park.

Just south of the Anita Park spur trail is Junction Saddle. To reach Chiricahua Peak (which is not burned off, though the fire did approach too close for comfort) we turn first left, then right, at a succession of forks here, passing a dry campsite. About 0.4 mile more of moderate climbing brings us to the forested summit of Chiricahua Peak (5.9; 9796), where there is a good campsite for those who wish to spend the night at the loftiest point in the Chiricahuas (and who pack up enough water from Anita Spring). Trees limit the view in every direction, and a USGS benchmark next to the campsite is about the only evidence we have that we are indeed on top of this corner of the world.

To return to Rustler Park, retrace your steps to Round Park, staying left at the junction with the faint path used to descend Flys Peak, and follow the Crest Trail back to the trailhead (11.8; 8400). The bypass goes through some very burned off terrain but is shorter than climbing over Flys Peak again.

TRIP 55
TURKEY CREEK TO ANITA PARK AND CHIRICAHUA PEAK VIA THE SAULSBURY TRAIL

▲ **13.1 mile near-loop; 3640' elevation gain**
▲ **Strenuous dayhike or backpack (2 hiking days)**
▲ **Trailhead 23, Turkey Creek**
▲ **Maps**
   Chiricahua Wilderness (due out in 1998) or *Chiricahua Peak and Rustler Park quadrangles*
▲ **Season: May to October**
   Water available all season (except possibly during extremely dry years) at Anita Spring (near mile 6.3)

Features

An abundance of airy, exposed ridges over closed-in drainages makes this one of the most scenic routes in the Chiricahuas. Covering a much greater altitudinal sweep than the preceding two trips, this trek gives the hiker a more balanced feel for the range as a whole—from the oaks and cypresses of the midaltitude canyons to the aspen and spruce of the high country. If some of that "feel" tends to lodge in one's knees and ankles during the bone-jarring descent of steep Mormon Ridge, well, that too is an integral part of the Chiricahua experience.

Trailhead Route/Camping

Twelve miles east of the U.S. 191 and Highway 181 intersection, Highway 181 makes a 90 degree turn from straight east to north. From this point, Turkey Creek Road (Forest Road 41) heads east. Follow this graded dirt road almost nine miles to the left branching spur to the Saulsbury Canyon Trailhead. The sign is difficult to see from the main road as it is several dozen feet up the spur on the right side—with no sign at the junction. Start looking for the spur after passing a one lane bridge, a private gate on the left, and a cattleguard (all in quick succession). The 0.5 mile spur is rocky in places and not suitable for low-slung cars. If it does not get maintenance, it may not stay suitable for passenger cars. Camping is possible at the trailhead but there are more suitable places, both in established campgrounds, and dispersed camping off Forest Road 41 beyond the Saulsbury turnoff.

Description

From the Saulsbury Canyon trailhead at Turkey Creek (0.0; 6320) we walk gently uphill along an abandoned dirt road through a forest cover of silverleaf and emery oak, Apache and Chihuahua pine, Schott's yucca and a few Arizona cypresses. After the first half mile or so, the track assumes the more congenial dimensions of a trail and begins crossing and recrossing the usually dry bed of Saulsbury Creek. A mile from the start, we begin climbing moderately up the right-hand wall onto a low ridge between two drainages. Several hundred feet higher, after making a few token switchbacks (where we get a view of burned off Little Bald Mountain) the trail finally snakes up into wooded Saulsbury Saddle (1.9; 7480). At a sign here we turn right to another sign visible nearby, then move to the right again onto the southwest slope of the rocky ridge east of the saddle. The ensuing steep climb offers good views across the deep canyon of Turkey Creek. Soon we cross a minor saddle to the ridge's Gambel oak-shaded north side, trading the preceding vista for an equally rewarding overlook of Rock Canyon and distant Sulphur Spring Valley. Here, we begin to encounter trees singed by the Rattlesnake Fire.

As we approach the rocky crown of Little Bald Mountain the trail levels out a bit, allowing us to catch our breath for the first time since leaving the floor of Saulsbury Canyon some 1500 feet below. Here we come to a sunny notch from which we can see the rounded, invitingly forested, only partially burned tops of Flys and Chiricahua peaks, still 1300 feet above us. After traversing beneath Little Bald Mountain the trail suddenly leaves the oaks, pinyons and agaves of the foothills behind and enters the welcome shade of a dense copse of Douglas-fir, New Mexican locust and Engelmann spruce. As we begin climbing again, we pass our first quaking aspen—a sure sign that we have made it to the high country at last—and presently we arrive at a signed junction with the Crest Trail (4.4; 9280). (Hikers should make it a point to get here well before noon, as the trail to this point can get quite hot by midday.)

Here we turn right and then walk south along the Crest Trail to the still forested saddle that contains Round Park. Those who wish to make the sidetrip to Flys Peak should search for an unmarked junction at the north end of this wildflower-studded meadow, then follow the path that leads north 0.5 mile to the summit (see Trip 54). Much of this approach is through a burned area but the peak area is largely untouched. To reach Chiricahua Peak we stay on the Crest Trail, continuing south past several well-signed turnoffs until we arrive at a signed junction with the Anita Park/Anita Spring Spur Trail— where we reach green forest after passing through a burned area. Backpackers will find good camping at Anita Park, a few hundred yards north. Anita Spring, down on the hillside east of the park, has potable water except in the driest of times.

To continue to Chiricahua Peak, walk south a short distance to Junction Saddle (6.4; 9540). Stay left here, then go right at an unsigned turnoff just beyond and ascend moderately the remaining distance to the top (6.9; 9796). Here, at the highest point in the Chiricahuas, there is a good dry campsite. Views are unfortunately blocked by the heavy forest cover. Although approached by the fire, the peak area is largely untouched.

Burned section of the Crest Trail

To return to Turkey Creek, we retrace our steps to the last junction, where we turn right and begin a traverse of Chiricahua Peak's east slope. In 0.7 mile we reach another fork, turn right again, and continue along the peak's south face. After dropping moderately a short distance, the trail brings us to Chiricahua Saddle (9.0; 9200), where we turn right onto the signed Mormon Ridge Trail, a heavily forested route that plunges down some 3000 feet in less than 4 miles. From the saddle the trail descends, crossing a talus-choked ravine. About 0.7 mile later we meet the Mormon Canyon Trail on our left, and another branch of the Mormon Ridge Trail on our right; we go straight ahead, and soon begin dropping steeply. Most of this descent is made on the ridge's south side, keeping below the crest, and with only an occasional switchback to ease the gradient. In a few places the trail becomes merely a trace, often overgrown with weeds-especially where the slope traversed by the trail is very steep. Because the trail is the only level ground between the steep down slope to the left and the steep up slope to the right the feet seem able to follow the trail even where weeds are too thick for the eye to see the trail. Be careful with foot placement here. While descending, the hiker will doubtless be struck by the sharp contrast between Mormon Canyon's densely forested south wall and the hot, brushy north wall upon which, unfortunately, our trail happens to have been built.

A small expanse of burned pines (pre-Rattlesnake Fire) marks the halfway point of the descent. About a mile beyond this burn area the ridge begins to level out, large oaks and junipers appear on the park-like flats, and the walking gets easier and easier until we at last cross tiny Turkey Creek and climb up to the road just beyond(13.1; 6160). To place a car here for a shuttle, drive 0.4 mile beyond the spur turnoff for the Saulsbury Canyon Trailhead.

TRIP 56
TURKEY CREEK TO MONTE VISTA LOOKOUT VIA THE MORSE CANYON TRAIL

▲ **7.8-13.4 miles, round trip or shuttle trip; 2720-3760' elevation gain**
▲ **Strenuous dayhike or backpack (2 hiking days)**
▲ **Trailhead 23, Turkey Creek**
▲ **Maps**
   Chiricahua Wilderness (due out in 1998) or *Chiricahua Peak quadrangle*
▲ **Season: May to October**
   Water available all season (except possibly during very dry years) at Anita Spring (near mile 6.9) and Booger Spring (near mile 8.7). No reliable water along Morse Canyon and Mormon Ridge return routes.

Features
Monte Vista Peak is not the highest point in the Chiricahua Mountains, but it is strategically located, and the views from its summit are among the best in the range. This route makes a stiff climb up to the peak, then traverses across the spine of rocky, sunny Raspberry Ridge into the heart of the spruce- and fir-forested high country, where hikers who linger are presented with a wide variety of side-trip possibilities.

Trailhead Route/Camping
Follow the trailhead route for Trip 55 but drive 1.7 miles beyond the Saulsbury Canyon Trailhead spur—to the end of Turkey Creek Road. During this drive keep an eye out for good campsites.

Description
From the end of the Turkey Creek Road (0.0; 6640) the trail enters a moderately dense forest cover of Chihuahua pine, Apache pine and Douglas-fir as it curves into Morse Canyon. Almost immediately an unidentified spur trail branches off to the right; we stay left and continue up-canyon to a second spur off the old road. First we switchback up to the right of the old road, then to the left. This ascent continues

unbroken for 1900 vertical feet, until we suddenly top out at lofty Johnson Saddle (2.3; 8560). At a signed junction here we turn left and continue climbing, more gently now, along the ridgecrest leading to the lookout tower visible in the southeast. About ¼ mile farther is the wilderness-area boundary sign, and a mile after that is a junction just below Monte Vista Peak, where we stay right, as we do at a second fork just beyond. The trail now doubles back and continues uphill a few hundred yards to the summit (3.9; 9357).

On top you will find the lookout tower, a cabin and some small outbuildings, and fine vistas to the west and south across Sulphur Spring Valley and the rugged chain of peaks and ridges that recedes southward into Mexico. Views to the north and east are obscured by trees; one could obtain a 360-degree panorama from atop the lookout, but a sign at its base requests that you not climb the tower.

After soaking up the view, retrace your steps ¼ mile to the signed junction with the Crest Trail. Here, we begin to encounter trees burned by the Rattlesnake Fire of 1994. If you cannot manage the very short car shuttle between the beginning of this route and either the Saulsbury Canyon or the Mormon Ridge Trailhead, turn left here and retrace your steps back to the Morse Canyon Trailhead (7.8 miles total). Otherwise, follow the Crest Trail as it veers to the right, then doubles back and continues gently downhill to a junction with the Raspberry Ridge Trail coming up from the south (4.7; 9240). Turning left, our route now eases onto Raspberry Ridge, the high divide between Rucker Canyon Creek, in the deep canyon to the right, and Turkey Creek. This area is largely burned on the right all the way to the crest but is still green below the crest to the left. With a pair of binoculars it is usually possible to spot several golden eagles soaring in the vast airspace on either side of this ridge, especially now that excessive trapping of coyotes has reduced the eagles' chief competition for the small rodents on which they feed.

Soon we pass the thumblike projection of Paint Rock on its east side, then make a few rough ups and downs as the ridge temporarily grows jagged and narrow. A short, moderate ascent brings us to Chiricahua Saddle (6.0; 9200), where we have a choice of routes. Backpackers will wish to continue northeast along the Crest Trail and a spur trail 1 mile to Anita Park and Spring, where there is good camping, and then return to Turkey Creek via the Saulsbury Trail (walk the first 6.4 miles of Trip 55 in reverse; 13.3 miles total). Dayhikers will probably prefer to return via the shorter Mormon Ridge route, in which case they should turn left at Chiricahua Saddle and follow the directions for the last leg of Trip 55 back to the road (10.1 miles total). In either case the "shuttle" involved is short enough to be walked, if necessary; if you elect to do this, you may want to park your car at your destination, rather than at Morse Canyon, thus saving your tired legs the trouble of walking back up the dusty, dreary road in the heat of the afternoon.

TRIP 57
RUCKER CAMP TO RUCKER CANYON CREEK

▲ **5.2 miles round trip; 440′ elevation gain**
▲ **Leisurely dayhike or backpack (2 hiking days)**
▲ **Trailhead 24, Rucker Camp**
▲ **Maps**
   Chiricahua Wilderness (due out in 1998) or *Chiricahua Peak quadrangle*
▲ **Season: all year; best in spring and fall**
   Water available intermittently along entire route

Features
Only two perennial streams reach back significantly into the Chiricahua backcountry. One of them, Rucker Creek, graces the entire length of this fine, leisurely outing. The creek's reliable water supports a variety of wildlife and a dense, diversified forest of conifers and hardwoods. The mood here is tranquil, relaxed; the murmuring creek and rustling leaves foster an air of carefree repose not to be found in the harsher realms of desert and mountaintop. This trip is a good choice for the hiker seeking to "warm up" for the coming season—or for one who has wearied of the strenuous exploits of seasons past.

Trailhead Route/Camping
From the junction of U.S. 191 and Highway 181, drive 8 miles south on U.S. 191, turn left (east) on well-graded Rucker Canyon Road (Forest Road 74 and 74E), and drive 27 miles to Rucker Camp, where the road ends. Just after the campground entrance is a hikers' parking area where no camping or day use fee is required. Parking in a campsite requires paying the camping fee. From here, walk through the campground to the far left end. On the way in you will see a sign for Rucker Lake but will see only a meadow. This is the sediment-filled Rucker Lake.

Description
From the trailhead above Rucker Camp (0.0; 6160) walk up-canyon along the continuation of the Rucker Road. In a short distance

you will pass the signed Bear Canyon Trail branching left, then a campground water tank, beyond which the road begins to deteriorate. Soon the track begins crossing and recrossing bouldery Rucker Creek—whose flow may be intermittent at this point, particularly in the fall. A wide variety of trees flourish along the alternately sunny and shady stretches of the canyon bottom, with species representing three distinct life zones (Upper Sonoran, Transition and Canadian) growing side by side with the riparian species one would expect to find here—silverleaf oak and Schott's yucca with Douglas-fir, cypress with maple, Apache pine with velvet ash, all in a mix that may disappoint the hiker who prefers that nature adhere strictly to the rigid divisions of textbook biology. Among the animals which make their homes here are the night-prowling ringtail cat and coatimundi, the bold Mexican jay, and a few rare Chiricahua fox squirrels. The iridescently plumed, coppery-tailed trogon, a relative of the renowned Mexican quetzal, occasionally nests here in the spring, though it is more commonly seen in South Fork Cave Creek Canyon. At one time the pools of the creek were stocked with fish but sediment has largely filled the pools. Though traces of the fire are miles from the trailhead, the resultant erosion has had an effect here.

After 1½ miles all traces of the old road are behind us. The canyon grows narrower as we proceed upstream, and just before it makes a pronounced swing to the left, the trail doubles back and begins switchbacking up the south wall (2.6; 6600). This point marks the end of today's excursion; there are fair campsites here, but better ones may be found a short distance either up or downstream. Explorations up the remainder of Rucker Creek's rugged, cliffbound canyon can be rewarding, but just how far you will be able to go depends on your cross-country scrambling ability.

Return the way you came.

TRIP 58
RUCKER CAMP TO RUCKER CREEK, CHIRICAHUA PEAK, AND JUNCTION SADDLE

- ▲ **17.1-mile loop trip; 4200′ elevation gain**
- ▲ **Strenuous dayhike or backpack (2-3 hiking days)**
- ▲ **Trailhead 24, Rucker Camp**
- ▲ **Maps**
  Chiricahua Wilderness Map (due out in 1998) or *Chiricahua Peak quadrangle*
- ▲ **Season: May to October**

*Water available all season along Rucker Creek (to mile 2.6) (creek
may be intermittent); at Lone Juniper Spring (mile 7.7) until late
summer; and at Anita Spring (near mile 10.1) (except possibly during very dry years)*

Features

This long, strenuous loop trip samples all the varied aspects of the
Chiricahuas: deep, thickly wooded canyons; exposed, scenic ridges;
oddly sculptured cliffs and pinnacles; and the crisp air of the conifer-
topped peaks. Grand vistas alternate with intimate forest closures the
entire way.

Dayhikers will have to move right along—all day—on this lengthy
route, but backpackers may wish to take the time to explore the numerous side-trip possibilities available. Peakbaggers especially should
take advantage of the ready access this trip provides to Sentinel,
Snowshed, Chiricahua, Flys and Monte Vista peaks—the highest summits in the range.

Trailhead Route

Follow the trailhead route for Trip 57.

Description

Follow the directions for Trip 57 to the point where the Rucker
Canyon Trail begins switchbacking away from Rucker Creek (2.6;
6600), then continue along the trail as it climbs steeply up the right-
hand canyon wall. Near the middle of this 1000-foot ascent the path

Rucker Canyon

winds back and forth across a rocky ravine, and is occasionally brushy but not hard to follow. At the top of the climb we meet the Red Rock Canyon Trail (3.9; 7640) at a signed junction beneath an overhanging, curiously eroded rock outcropping. Make a sharp left here, passing below the large rock. The sign for this junction will probably still be lying downslope from the turn. The route now leads to a brushy, shadeless ridgetop past a slight rise, a venerably aged boundary sign, and then descends almost a hundred feet into Price Canyon, the invitingly shaded gorge on the right. Here we join the Price Canyon Trail (4.6; 7480), turn left at the drainage, try to follow the faint, washed out trail—which comes and goes—until it climbs steeply above the creek bed on the left side. You might spot some wild turkeys or Coues deer in this area, particularly early in the season, when there is generally a trickle of water down in the streambed. Here, you also start seeing singed trees. As you proceed uphill the burnoff becomes more serious and starts having an effect on the trail.

After a mile or so Price Canyon widens a bit, burned pines and firs begin to replace the oaks, and the hiker begins to see the full effect of a forest fire. In places, ravines have eroded across the trail, making cautious detours necessary. The trail always resumes after eroded sections-but one must sometimes search about rather than just wandering. Here and there small burned trees have fallen across the trail. Both erosion and fallen trees will worsen trail conditions in time. After surmounting a series of broad switchbacks at the head of the canyon we meet the signed trail to Sentinel Peak (6.5; 8960), where our route goes left, on the eastern branch of the Crest Trail. A little over a mile of easy walking through a sunny (and only partially burned) forest of Apache, Chihuahua and Mexican white pines brings us to a junction near Juniper Spring (water until late season), where we bear right and continue a few yards to a signed junction (8.5; 9480). (If Juniper Spring is dry there may be water 0.2 mile up the left fork, but Anita Park is a better bet.) Stay on the clearly signed Crest Trail here, and follow it for 0.7 mile (mostly heavily forested with old growth trees) northwest to the point where the Chiricahua Peak Trail branches off to the left (southwest). This trail then climbs moderately 0.4 mile to the forested summit of Chiricahua Peak (9.6; 9796). Here, at the highest point in the Chiricahua Mountains, there is a good campsite (but no water and no open views).

To return to Rucker Camp, retrace your steps to the Crest Trail, then turn left and walk a short distance north to Junction Saddle (10.1; 9540). Backpackers looking for campsites—and dayhikers who are low on water—will want to continue north along the Crest Trail a few hundred yards to the signed Anita Park/Anita Spring Spur Trail (see Trip 54). Otherwise we turn left and proceed gently downhill to Chiricahua Saddle (10.9; 9200), where we turn neither left nor right, but follow the Crest Trail as it descends straight ahead onto the spine of rocky, sunny Raspberry Ridge. The monolithic crown of Paint Rock is soon passed on its left flank, and 1.4 miles later we reach the signed turnoff to Monte Vista Lookout (12.2; 9240). If you have sufficient time and energy remaining, you can make the 1.6-mile round trip to the lookout, which offers unexcelled views across the southern Chiricahuas (see Trip 56). If not, turn left here and continue along the crest of Raspberry Ridge. Here, the burn was more complete and the trail becomes more rocky and harder to follow. Burned trees still show blaze marks and the trail stays just below the crest of the ridge, on its left, staying fairly level where hills along the ridge raise its height. Here and there are small patches of trees that survived the fire. The ridge will come to a false end where the trail seems to run into a tree with a small burned sign just past a cairn. The cairn marks the "elbow" of the first of several switchbacks that descend to a continuation of the ridge. These switchbacks are experiencing erosion and have fallen trees and must be negotiated with care. From just beyond the switchbacks the trail descends with the ridge, moderately until reaching a wooded (largely unburned) saddle at the head of precipitous Bear Canyon (14.3; 8280). Here the trail abruptly plunges downward, switchbacking irregularly and passing several steep, tricky sections where washouts have occurred. As we lose elevation, agaves and Schott's yuccas begin to appear in the sunny patches between the pines and firs—a sign that we have left the Canadian life zone far behind and reentered the Transition zone. After a mile the switchbacking ceases and the trail descends steeply at first, then less steeply and we emerge onto a gently sloping, widebottomed canyon which is heavily forested with silverleaf, Emory and Arizona white oak. From here the walking grows easier and easier as we march the final ¾ mile to the Rucker Road. Rucker Camp (17.1; 6160) is just down-canyon to the right.

TRIP 59
SOUTH FORK PICNIC AREA TO MAPLE CAMP

- ▲ **3.2 miles round trip; 280' elevation gain**
- ▲ **Leisurely dayhike or backpack (2 hiking days)**
- ▲ **Trailhead 25, South Fork Picnic Area**
- ▲ **Maps**
    Chiricahua Wilderness (due out in 1998) or *Portal Peak quadrangle*

▲ **Season: all year; best in spring and fall**
Water available intermittently along entire route
∿∿∿∿∿∿∿∿∿∿∿∿∿∿∿∿∿∿∿∿∿∿∿∿∿∿∿∿∿∿∿∿∿∿∿∿

Features

The South Fork of Cave Creek is one of only two perennial streams that penetrate significantly into the roadless Chiricahuas. It is thus something of an oasis, both for the solitude-seeking human visitor and for the wide variety of man-shy wildlife that has been driven here by the steady encroachment of roads, fences, and predator traps into the surrounding country. It is also a haven for migrating birds—over 200 distinct species have been spotted in the area, including the rare, spectacularly colored eared trogon and the coppery-tailed trogon. This trip is a must for birdwatchers, but the beautiful and serene South Fork Canyon contains enough nonavian attractions to recommend itself to all other hikers as well.

Trailhead Route/Camping

From the town of Portal, northeast of Douglas, drive west on Forest Road 42 nearly 3 miles and turn left (southwest) on South Fork Road (FR 42B). Continue just over a mile to the parking area. The trailhead starts from an old dirt road at the right side of the main parking area. Birdwatchers get here early and grab the parking spaces; however, theirs are the feet that maintain this trail—keeping it clear of weeds and making it easy to follow. There are three convenient campgrounds off FR 42; two between Portal and the FR 42B turnoff and one just after the turnoff, access to the latter requires driving across a rocky streambed.

Description

From the end of the road at South Fork Picnic Area (0.0; 5300) our route follows a wide, well-used but unobtrusive trail up the imperceptibly sloping floor of South Fork Canyon. The forest cover in this sheltered, well-watered area is a fabulous montage of disparate species—rustling sycamores, walnuts, towering Apache and Chihuahua pines, Douglas-firs, silverleaf and emery oaks, velvet ash trees, madrones, bigtooth maples, and some magnificent, thick-trunked specimens of Arizona cypress.

Just beyond the trailhead you may encounter a sign asking that birdwatchers register their names and addresses and take a card on which to report any unusual sightings—particularly of the eared trogon or the coppery-tailed trogon, two richly plumed relatives of the legendary Mexican quetzal bird that fly northward each spring to nest in this verdant canyon. Birders come from all over the nation to catch a glimpse of these exotic species, which do not generally appear elsewhere in the country. The trogon may be easily identified by its raucous call and its iridescent green and red plumage. Should you see one, please obey the posted request and do not approach too closely or otherwise disturb it.

After crossing South Fork Cave Creek a few times we pass through a fence at the wilderness boundary via a hikers gate. Soon the canyon bottom grows rougher, though no less beautiful, and the trail makes a few gentle ups and downs as it weaves along the line of least resistance. By late summer/early fall the creek may be dry up to this point, but there is always enough of a surface flow beyond here to support a few water ouzels, or dippers—small, semiaquatic birds that forage the bottoms of flowing streams for insects and crustaceans. The ouzel is readily identified by its habit of flying just inches above the surface of the water, and tracing every twist and turn of the streamcourse in its flight.

Presently we reach the signed junction of the South Fork Trail with the Burro Trail (1.6; 5600), an optional return route of Trip 60. Maple Camp, a good campsite, is just off to the right. Other fine campsites can be found ¼ mile or so upstream. Keep in mind that birdwatchers get up very early and some of them are ambitious hikers. If your privacy is valuable, go as far as you can. A worthwhile side trip can be made up the Burro Trail: walk up the Burro Trail about 0.5 mile to a rocky saddle between two branches of the South Fork, then leave the trail and scramble northeast 0.3 miles to an airy peaklet, where you will be treated to a spectacular overlook of the canyon and a high cliff looming beyond it. Visible behind the cliff is the long, forested skyline of Snowshed Ridge, which culminates in 9640-foot Snowshed Peak, at the head of the South Fork. An additional 2.4 miles along the Burro Trail takes us to Horseshoe Pass/Burro Saddle with a breathtaking view of the Cave Creek area.

Return the way you came. Or, if you have an abundance of energy, make the long, rewarding loop trip up to Sentinel Peak and Horseshoe Pass (see Trip 60).

TRIP 60
SOUTH FORK PICNIC AREA TO MAPLE CAMP AND SENTINEL PEAK; RETURN VIA HORSESHOE RIDGE

▲ **16.7-mile semiloop trip; 3920' elevation gain**
▲ **Strenuous dayhike or backpack (3 hiking days)**
▲ **Trailhead 25, South Fork Picnic Area**

▲ **Maps**
Chiricahua Wilderness (due out in 1998) or *Portal Peak quadrangle*

▲ **Season: May to October**
Water available all season along South Fork Cave Creek (miles 0.0 to 3.4 and 15.1 to 16.7), and during early season at Burnt Stump Spring (near mile 5.2) and Log Spring (mile 12.9)

〰〰〰〰〰〰〰〰〰〰〰〰〰〰

Features

This lengthy excursion is a study in contrasts—between the antipodal worlds of canyon and crest, streambank and mountaintop. After tracing insular, sylvan South Fork Cave Creek to its headwaters, the route climbs skyward to burned, pine-topped Sentinel Peak, a high, isolated summit standing apart from the central mountain-mass of the Chiricahuas and commanding an excellent view. But the climax of this trip (for the daring and adventurous) may well be the long, ridgehugging descent to Horseshoe Pass and back to Maple Camp—a kaleidoscope of far-reaching, ever-changing vistas.

Trailhead Route

Follow the trailhead route for Trip 59.

Description

Follow the directions for Trip 59 to Maple Camp (1.6; 5600). At the junction with the Burro Trail we stay right and work our way up-canyon, passing occasional good campsites off to the left. As the trail approaches the base of the huge cliff that looms on our right, it crosses the stream, climbs steeply up a short distance and back down again, and makes several more creek crossings before climbing a short distance up the right-hand canyonside to an obscure junction. Here we ignore the faint track leading off to the right, and continue winding up-canyon under a forest cover of oak, juniper and Schott's yucca a hundred feet or so above the stream. After gaining some good views up and down the canyon we drop back down, pass an excellent campsite and make one final trip across the rocky streambed to an unsigned junction (3.4; 6160), where we turn left up a tributary of the South Fork.

The first mile up this side canyon is steep and rough, and the trail frequently disappears in the boulders of the creekbed. The track is not hard to follow, however, especially where it rises above the streambed on the left or right, and its brusque, demanding character serves well to heighten the sense of wildness and seclusion the hiker feels in this isolated, infrequently visited area. Unfortunately, we soon start seeing trees singed by the Rattlesnake Fire and the higher we go the greater the damage. About the middle of this section we spot a red rock monolith off to the right of the trail and streambed. This pinnacle would be worthy of a picture postcard were it not enclosed by densely packed, live trees.

As we gain elevation, clumps of quaking aspen begin to appear, giving rise to the hope that we are finally "getting up there" to the high country. Sure enough, the narrow confines of the canyon soon fall behind us, pine duff appears underfoot, and we find ourselves switchbacking moderately up a conifer-shaded slope. From some spots we get glimpses of peaks high above—completely burned. Presently a sign indicates a spur trail (5.2; 7640) branching left to Burnt Stump Spring (reliable water in early season only). The sign is half burned away and free standing. Look for a fallen, barkless tree to the left of the trail where it takes a right turn. The tree is across a very minor drainage-almost like a thick banister rail. The sign and junction are at the far end of the tree. Our route takes the right fork here and continues upward, passing through a grassy area where the trail temporarily grows faint, and approaches the top of the pine-clad ridge northwest of Sentinel Peak. In this area, all the trees are dead from fire, the drainages are filled with coarse sediment, and the trail disappears. While the Crest Trail can be reached by heading up to the nearest part of the ridge above (less than half a mile), this book can not recommend that route. In case the trail is restored, the following is a pre-fire description of the route from the crest.

Turn left onto the Crest Trail and traverse along the ridgetop for 0.5 mile, then climb a short distance to a junction just below the peak. Turn right here; the high point (7.3; 8999) is just beyond. On the summit you will find the remains of old Sentinel Lookout.

For the return to Maple Camp, retrace your steps a short distance to the last trail junction, then turn right and begin switchbacking (occasionally quite steeply) down Sentinel Peak's brushy southeast slope. After dropping about 400 feet we reach a poorly signed junction with the Baker Canyon Trail, where we stay left. A short distance beyond is another junction. The right branch is apparently just a variant of the Baker Canyon Trail, and we go left, easing onto the long, sinuous crest of Horseshoe Ridge.

It is possible to salvage part of the old loop—but this option should only be considered by very experienced hikers with good route finding skills, a head for heights, and ankles strong enough to negotiate partially washed out trails.

Return to the Burnt Stump Spring junction and decide whether to return to the trailhead, another 5.2 miles, or to take a very difficult return as follows.

Follow the junction sign to Burnt Stump Spring—about a quarter mile. The spring is in a drainage, the tank is nearly filled with fine silt. It is possible to scoop water from the tiny puddles with a dish from a mess kit. Continue another quarter mile to a signed junction and continue left (northeast), along Horseshoe Ridge. The route crosses a minor saddle and descends moderately down a partially burned off slope. After another saddle the trail drops a bit to the right and angles across a steep slope on its right side. In approaching the saddle, the trail is a mere trace in places, overgrown, and sometimes hard to follow. In some

Red rock monolith off South Fork Trail

places along the slope the trail is a bit washed out, necessitating the use of the edges of the boot soles to keep from sliding off the trail. After a mile-long traverse of the ridge's south side, with good views over the wide gap of Horseshoe Canyon and across the southern Chiricahuas, we arrive at Horseshoe Pass (11.9; 7240), a deep notch at the foot of hulking, 8099-foot Sulphur Peak. Here we turn left onto the signed Burro Trail, gaining breathtaking vistas across Cave Creek Canyon as we swing out onto the slopes high above the South Fork. From this point the trail is much better.

Soon the inevitable switchbacking begins again, and we descend moderately past the signed spur trail to Log Spring (water in early season only). After crossing the usually dry bed of a tributary of the South Fork, the path climbs a short distance to a saddle, where we are treated to another fine view, this time of Snowshed Ridge and the spectacular cliffs across South Fork Canyon. A final spate of switchbacks then lands us at Maple Camp (15.1; 5600), from where we retrace our steps the remaining 1.6 miles to South Fork Picnic Area (16.7; 5320). These distances are for the original loop. Taking the Burnt Stump Spring bypass option reduces the loop to 11.9 miles.

TRIP 61
CAVE CREEK TO SNOWSHED PEAK AND ANITA PARK VIA THE SNOWSHED TRAIL

▲ **17.4-19.2 miles round trip; 4300' elevation gain**
▲ **Strenuous dayhike or backpack (2 hiking days)**
▲ **Trailhead 26, Cave Creek**
▲ **Maps**
   Chiricahua Wilderness (due out in 1998) or *Portal, Portal Peak, and Chiricahua Peak quadrangles*
▲ **Season: May to October**
   Water available all season (except possibly during extremely dry years) at Deer Spring (mile 7.6) and Anita Spring (near mile 19.2)

Features
Scenic Snowshed Ridge offers a lengthy, strenuous and rewarding route up to the Chiricahua highlands, but should not be considered as a through route until fire and erosion damage is repaired. For well-conditioned dayhikers, this trip reaches its climax at lofty Snowshed Peak, which overlooks the ruggedly eroded drainage basin of Cave Creek. Backpackers, on the other hand, will find that the Snowshed Trail has brought them only to the threshold of the high country, where a wealth of enticing trails wait to be explored.

Trailhead Route/Camping
Follow the trailhead route for Trip 59 but continue on Forest Road 42 (also known as Cave Creek Road in the Portal area) an additional 1.4 miles past South Fork Road. Trailhead parking is on the left side of the road just before a cattleguard between the paved and unpaved portions of this road. There is only space for one or two vehicles. There are three national forest campgrounds on the route from Portal to the trailhead.

Description
From the trailhead on the Cave Creek Road (0.0; 5300) climb up a few yards to a sign, then turn right and strike off west through a moderate forest cover of Mexican blue oak, Chihuahua pine and alligator juniper. Early risers are shielded from the sun's rays along this often warm, scantily shaded stretch by some high bluffs that loom up in the east. After 0.5 mile we cross a dry wash, whose mud-colored walls are brightened by the fresh green leaves of a few Arizona walnuts and madrones that somehow extract a livable ration of water out

Cave Creek Canyon from the Snowshed Trail

of the gravely ravine. The trail is occasionally obscure as it winds through a rocky area just beyond here—watch for ducks.

Soon the path grows more distinct and begins switchbacking onto the toe of Snowshed Ridge. Two miles of moderate climbing now bring us to Cypress Saddle (2.9; 7080). In approaching the saddle, by looking back we gain an excellent view across the jumbled cliffs and crags of Cave Creek Canyon which made the region such an effective wartime citadel for the Chiricahua Apache. After passing to the north side of the ridge we continue ascending, and soon Gambel oaks and Douglas-firs begin to appear among the junipers and Mexican pinyons welcome evidence of our increasing elevation. Because of Snowshed Ridge's varying steepness and exposure, the various life zones of the Chiricahuas are locally compressed into an unusually narrow altitude range, and by the time we amble up to Fossil Saddle (and the steep spur trail down to unreliable Fossil Springs) a few Engelmann spruce have appeared. Unfortunately, we also start to see burned trees. Most have survived in this area.

About 0.5 mile beyond Fossil Saddle we meet the Basin Trail (4.9; 7920) coming up from Herb Martyr Dam to the north. Here, there are two trail signs, both framed in steel to protect against bears. One has been severely mauled. The other is untouched. Just beyond this signed junction we climb steeply and pass through a narrow, rocky defile to Pine Park, a pleasantly shaded flat astride the ridge. Pine Park possesses magnificent ponderosa pine which have survived, despite being singed by the Rattlesnake Fire. This is a pleasant place to camp. About 0.5 mile farther the trail rounds a steep, rocky spur ridge which offers a good view across the deep gash of South Fork

Canyon to the aspen-dotted ramparts of Sentinel Peak. This area is very brushy with many thorns. The trail begins to get washed out even before entering the burned off area after which the trail becomes hazardous.This book cannot recommend going beyond Pine Park until the trail is restored.

The following paragraphs describe the rest of the route as it existed before the Rattlesnake Fire of 1994. Consult with the rangers concerning the current trail status.

Until this point we have remained on or near the crest of Snowshed Ridge, but now the crest rises high above us as our gentle climbing-traversing is unable to keep pace. The route is well shaded through here, except at a steep, barren talus slope which we cross in one mile, and aspen and spruce soon become integral parts of the forest cover. About 2 miles beyond Pine Park the trail finally begins switchbacking in a belated effort to catch up with the runaway ridge; 0.5 mile later, after crossing a dizzying, talus-choked dropoff, we arrive at the cement tank of Deer Spring (may be stagnant). 0.4 mile beyond is a signed, 4-way trail junction in a saddle (8.1; 9320), where we are presented with a wide range of options. Backpackers may wish to continue 1.5 miles to the good campsites and almost always reliable water at Anita Park and Spring, from where the summits of Flys and Chiricahua peaks are readily accessible. (To reach Anita Park proceed straight ahead 0.5 mile, then turn right onto the Crest Trail and follow it 0.7 mile farther to Junction Saddle, just beyond which is the signed spur trail to Anita Park.) 9640-foot Snowshed Peak is 0.6 mile up the rough path which branches right from here; this is a good destination for dayhikers.

Return the way you came, or via the Crest Trail and the South Fork Trail to South Fork Picnic Area (3-mile car/shuttle required for this option; see Trips 59 and 60.)

TRIP 62
ECHO CANYON TRAILHEAD TO ECHO PARK AND UPPER RHYOLITE CANYON VIA THE ECHO CANYON TRAIL AND THE HAILSTONE TRAIL

▲ **3.4 mile loop trip; 540′ elevation gain**
▲ **Leisurely dayhike**
▲ **Trailhead 27, Echo Canyon**
▲ **Maps**
  Chiricahua National Monument or *Cochise Head and Rustler Park quadrangles*

▲ **Season: all year**
No water available along route

Features

This well-developed trail offers easy access through one of the most scenic and spectacular areas of Chiricahua National Monument. Starting from a dwarf forest, the path descends through an area of fantastic pinnacles, columns, and balanced rocks.

Trailhead Route/Camping

From Willcox drive 33 miles southeast on Highway 186 to a junction with Highway 181. Follow Highway 181 east just over 3 miles to the Chiricahua National Monument where an entrance fee will be collected. Drive 2 miles farther to the visitor center, where maps are available. At 5.5 miles past the visitor center, the Echo Canyon Trailhead parking area is on the right. Or, take the shuttle to this trailhead. Departure is 8:30 A.M. from the visitor center or 8:35 A.M. from the campground. Sign up for shuttle space the day before. There is no return shuttle. An optional return route will return shuttle riders to the visitor center.

Camping is permitted only in the established campground, 0.5 mile past the visitor center.

Description

From the Echo Canyon Trailhead parking area (0.0; 6800) the trail descends gradually through a dwarf forest of trees stunted by thin soil and rapid runoff of water. Shortly, the trail reaches a junction and we bear right, continuing our descent into the Echo Canyon area. Already we begin to see outrageous rock formations but this is only a taste of what is to come.

Rocks in this area are volcanic tuff. Volcanic ash expelled into the atmosphere fell to earth while hot enough to be heat welded in layers. Some layers were compacted while hot enough to form strong layers; other layers were less compacted and formed weak, more easily eroded layers of rock. Geological forces cracked the rock, forming vertical joints. Water flowed through the joints, enlarging them by erosion. Where this process has left thick, vertical remnants, these are called *columns*. Thinner remnants are called *pinnacles*. Where weak layers have allowed the tops of these formations to be undercut, the results are *balanced rocks*. Not all balanced rocks stayed balanced. Along the trails it is possible to see many that have toppled.

As the trail descends, the rock formations seem to close in until the experience seems more akin to spelunking than hiking. In one place the trail crosses what seems to be an unrailed balcony to a lower

Monoliths along the Echo Canyon Trail

room. Before long the trail crosses the floor of that room.

About a mile from the trailhead, the path descends into the Echo Park area, where drainage has permitted growth of large trees including Arizona cypress, Douglas fir, and Apache pine. Soon, the trail crosses a creekbed (1.3; 6320) and follows it for awhile on the left, then descends more gradually as the creek drops away. Soon, the view opens into Rhyolite Canyon. The trail bears left and rises briefly to a junction with the Hailstone Trail and the Upper Rhyolite Trail. Here, you must make a choice.

If you came by shuttle and do not have a car waiting for you at Echo Canyon Trailhead, you may wish to bear right at the junction, onto the Upper Rhyolite Trail, and return to the visitor center.

To return to the trailhead, continue straight on the Hailstone Trail. This trail is named for rock that appears to be made of hailstone-sized balls of tuff formed into bedrock. Along this route you can look up to the right and see a skyline of pinnacles, columns, and balanced rocks—the Heart of Rocks. One of the balanced rocks has partially fallen against a neighbor, as if for support. The south-facing slope has vegetation more typical of a lower elevation than the luxurious vegetation of the opposite, north-facing slope. Stop at the visitor center and examine their display that explains this phenomenon.

After 0.8 mile, the Hailstone Trail reaches a junction. A right turn would take us into the Heart of Rocks route (Trip 63). We reach the Echo Canyon Trailhead by going left 0.75 mile, gradually climbing a forested drainage until we reach the turnoff to the parking area (shortly after passing the 0.3 mile turnoff to Massai Point).

TRIP 63
MASSAI POINT TO HEART OF ROCKS LOOP

- ▲ **4.1 miles one-way (including the 0.9 mile loop section), 8.8 mile loop options, or 7.3 mile one-way option; elevation gain depends on option selected; maximum change: 1470 feet**
- ▲ **Moderate to strenuous dayhike**
- ▲ **Trailhead 28, Massai Point**
- ▲ **Maps**
  Chiricahua National Monument or *Cochise Head and Rustler Park quadrangles*
- ▲ **Season: all year**
  No water available along route

Features

This well-developed route offers access to some of the most picturesque and well-known rock formations to be found in Chiricahua National Monument.

Trailhead Route

Follow the trailhead route for Trip 62 but continue 0.5 mile past Echo Canyon Trailhead to Massai Point.

Description

At Massai Point (0.0; 6860) you may wish to visit the interpretive stations of the nature trail before starting out for Heart of Rocks. Then proceed along the trail 0.3 mile, starting through a dwarf forest, to a junction where drainage has permitted large trees to grow. Here, turn left, descending down the drainage. We start to see large pinnacles and columns above and to the left. Soon we come to a junction (1.0; 6420) and bear left, climbing into Upper Rhyolite Canyon with a view of more pinnacles and columns to the upper right. After a short distance we come to a sign pointing up and to the right with the caption MUSHROOM ROCK. While there is a better view of this feature both before and after the sign, this is the point where it looks most like a mushroom.

From here the trail rises first with one tributary drainage, then another until it reaches a saddle (2.2; 6950) where we have the option of a one-mile, fairly level, round trip hike to a good view at Inspiration Point, where Sugarloaf Mountain dominates the skyline topping out at 7310 feet. While this may not be the highest point at Chiricahua National Monument, it is the highest easily reached point, requiring a hike of less than a mile. To the right, and a lot closer, we can see cars parked at Echo Canyon Trailhead and at Massai Point—seemingly, a mere stone's throw away in spite of all the hiking to this point.

Continuing past the Inspiration Point turnoff, the trail drops at first, rises briefly to 7040 feet, then begins dropping gradually with a great view to the west. Within 0.75 mile we come to Big Balanced Rock (1,000 tons, 22 feet in diameter). Shortly, we come to the turnoff for the 0.9 mile Heart of Rocks Loop. The loop trail rises and falls, sometimes up stairways, of which at least one is natural. Here are most of the picture post card features: Pinnacle Balanced Rock, Punch and Judy, Duck on a Rock, and the Kissing Rocks.

Returning to the main trail, we have two options. We can return the way we came in 3.2 miles. Or, we can continue 1.6 miles to the junction with the Rhyolite Canyon Trail and Upper Rhyolite Trail. Rhyolite Canyon Trail will take us back to the visitor center. Or, we can turn right at the junction, onto the Upper Rhyolite Trail. This trail soon drops to a crossing of two drainages, then rises to the Hailstone / Echo Canyon Trail junction where a right turn brings us to Massai Point by following the second half of Trip 62—except that we take the turnoff to Massai Point. We can also reverse the first leg of Trip 62, continuing past the Echo Canyon Trailhead turnoff to the Massai Point turnoff.

Duck on a Rock

Area 3—The Eastern Highlands

The eastern highlands region takes in the high, heavily forested, mostly rolling country of the White Mountains and the Blue Range, in east-central Arizona near the New Mexico border. Two separate areas, encompassing much of the region's best hiking, have been officially set aside for nonmotorized use—the Blue Range Primitive Area and the Mount Baldy Wilderness.

Elevations in the 173,000-acre Blue Range Primitive Area range from above 9000 feet, near Hannagan Meadow, to well below 5000 feet along the Lower Blue River. Dense Canadian-zone forests of Engelmann spruce, white fir and Douglas-fir, and some quaking aspen blanket the very highest areas. Below this, a transition-zone mixture of ponderosa pine, Gambel oak, alligator juniper and silverleaf oak prevails, giving way to a sparse, Upper Sonoran-zone cover of one-seed juniper and pinyon pine below about 6000 feet. A number of small but perennial streams within the wilderness are lined with magnificent forests of riparian hardwoods such as sycamore, walnut, bigtooth maple, box elder and velvet ash. The canyon of the Blue River, swept frequently by flash floods, is considerably more barren than its tributaries; its bouldery banks support only isolated stands of mesquite, cottonwood and sycamore.

The two greatest determinants of the Blue Range's topography are the Blue River, which flows from north to south and whose deep canyon divides the primitive area neatly in two, and the Mogollon Rim, which bisects the area from west to east. Elevations are therefore greater along the eastern and western fringes than in the center, and greater in the north than in the south. The zones of discontinuity between high and low areas—known locally as the Blue River "breaks"—tend to be heavily eroded, with numerous small cliffs and outcroppings cut out of the red conglomerates and lighter volcanic rocks that cover the area.

With its wide elevation range, the primitive area includes habitats amenable to a variety of wildlife. Javelina, bobcat and mountain lion inhabit its lower reaches, while Rocky Mountain elk, Coues white-tailed deer and mule deer are fairly common in the higher forests. A number of rare and endangered species find sanctuary here, including the spotted owl, peregrine falcon, Arizona woodpecker, kit fox and southern bald eagle. The Blue River and its perennial tributaries are home to a limited number of brook, brown and rainbow trout.

As of 1980 a proposal to reclassify the Blue Range Primitive Area as the Blue Range Wilderness had been sent to Congress. It has not yet been acted upon, but interested parties still hope for approval. Some small-scale cattle grazing is unfortunately currently allowed within the primitive area boundaries, and will likely continue for some time following a wilderness designation. Some of the trailheads have information kiosks on which are posted grazing schedules. This makes it possible to avoid sharing trail areas by going where the cattle are not grazing at the time of your hike.

The 6975-acre Mount Baldy Wilderness, in the White Mountains, is one of the smallest but most pristine areas included in the federal wilderness system. Elevations range from 9200 feet, at Sheep Crossing, to 11,403 feet atop Mount Baldy. It is one of the few places in Arizona where one can hike in the Hudsonian (or subalpine) life zone. Except for a few wildflower-sprinkled meadows and the Baldy summit area, the entire region is heavily forested with Colorado blue spruce, white fir, corkbark fir, ponderosa pine, white pine and quaking aspen. Several major streams have their headwaters on Baldy's gently rising slopes, including the East Fork White River, the West Fork Black River, and the East and West Forks of the Little Colorado River.

Mount Baldy itself is an extinct volcano, a remnant of a broad lava dome formed by a series of eruptions that ceased some 8 or 9 million years ago. Most of this ancient dome has since been eroded away, both by water and by the glaciers that, during the so-called ice ages of the Pleistocene era, bulldozed their way down the slopes of the mountain. Erosion by glaciers tends to widen the valleys that contain them, forming broad-bottomed, U-shaped troughs rather than the narrow-bottomed, V-shaped canyons formed by stream erosion. This is one reason why the drainages in the Mount Baldy Wilderness are so much more open and parklike than those at lower elevations. (Compare, for example, the stretch of the West Fork Little Colorado River Canyon above Sheep Crossing to the stretch below.) Rocks picked up by these rivers of ice were carried slowly downhill; at the end of a glacier, where the ice constantly melted, the rocks were deposited loosely in wide arcs called terminal moraines. With the advent of the warmer weather of the modern era the glaciers receded and disappeared, spreading morainal material irregularly along the length of the occupied canyons. Stream water later pooled up behind some of the moraines, creating small ponds; these gradually filled with silt, eventually forming the beautiful meadowed flats which now grace the area.

A variety of animal species prosper in the lower reaches of the wilderness, including Rocky Mountain elk, black bear, mule deer, porcupine, wild turkey and blue grouse. A few beaver colonies are active along the forks of the Little Colorado.

Severe thunderstorms are common over the White Mountains during July and August, and hikers are advised to vacate exposed areas by early afternoon during those months.

The actual summit of Mount Baldy is on the Fort Apache Indian Reservation. Since the first printing of this book, this area has been closed by the tribe to public entry. This book's trail descriptions continue to describe the routes all the way to the top, in hopes that Forest Service efforts to have the area reopened will eventually prove successful. But until they are, hikers will have to obtain special permission from the tribe (see address below) to travel past the reservation boundary. When interviewed in spring, 1997, rangers claimed they knew of no one who had obtained a permit in recent years.

Managing Agencies

SOUTHERN BLUE RANGE PRIMITIVE AREA

Clifton Ranger District
HC1, Box 733
Duncan, AZ 85534
(520) 687-1301

NORTHERN BLUE RANGE PRIMITIVE AREA

Alpine Ranger District
P.O. Box 469
Alpine, AZ 85920
(520) 339-4384

MOUNT BALDY WILDERNESS

Springerville Ranger District
P.O. Box 760
Springerville, AZ 85938
(520) 333-4372

MOUNT BALDY SUMMIT AREA

White Mountain Apache Enterprise
Fort Apache Indian Reservation
P.O. Box 26
Whiteriver, AZ 85941
(520) 338-4967

The Blue Range

Since much of the Blue Range between peaks is as high as 9000 feet in elevation and peaks are generally just a few hundred feet higher, they seem like mere hilltops, except when seen across deep drainages, such as that of the Blue River. Elevations of trailheads and destinations covered in this section range from 5,320 feet at the Blue River to 9,346 feet at Blue Lookout.

TRIP 64
BLUE LOOKOUT ROADEND TO BLUE LOOKOUT

- ▲ **2.8 miles round trip; 500' elevation gain**
- ▲ **Leisurely dayhike**
- ▲ **Trailhead 29, Blue Lookout Roadend**
- ▲ **Maps**
  Blue Range Wilderness (due out in 1998) or *Strayhorse quadrangle* or *free photocopied maps available from nearby trailhead information kiosks. There is no kiosk at this trailhead. Try KP Cienega or Hannagan.*
- ▲ **Season: June to October**
  No water available along route

Features
Offering a maximum of view for a minimum of effort, this trip to Blue Lookout is an excellent introduction to the Blue Range high country. Hikers seeking refuge from the sweltering midsummer lowlands will find this to be delightfully cool sweater country, even in August, while those willing to brave the midautumn chill will find the slopes aflame with frost-yellowed aspen leaves.

Trailhead Route/Camping
From Clifton, drive north about 65 miles on U.S. 191. Just after the road has climbed switchbacks to the Colorado Plateau and passed the Blue Vista turnoff, a forest road signed "Blue L.O. Trails" leads 4.5 miles east to a grassy parking area just below the crest of a saddle. The McKittrick Trail is the continuation of the blocked road and leads to the vicinity of the Blue Lookout. The parking area offers excellent camping. Passenger cars have made it to the trailhead when the road is at its best but the road is rarely at its best. Often, there are fallen trees with off-road detours around them. Also, when the road is wet, 4WD may be necessary.

Description

From the end of the Blue Lookout Road (0.0; 8840) we follow the trail east as it traverses the north side of the ridge leading to the lookout. The forest cover of spruce, fir and aspen is so dense along the way that we will not be treated to an open view until reaching the very top, but the immediate feeling of wildness and isolation which that density fosters more than makes up for the lack. During the summer these woods are home to small herds of Rocky Mountain mule deer and Coues white-tailed deer. Blue grouse and wild turkeys are also fairly common in the area, and with luck you might hear some of these large, ground-dwelling fowl clucking and gobbling off in the trees, or even come upon them strutting unconcernedly along the trail.

Leaving the parking area, the trail rounds a hill, then follows a ridge that is fairly level until it drops into a saddle, then winds left around another high point. After passing just below another saddle we pass a defunct sign-in register and the old road declines to a mere trail. We soon reach a signed junction with a branch of the KP Creek trail (0.9; 8920), where we stay right. A short distance later the path begins climbing more steeply, and makes one long switchback before arriving at the base of Blue Lookout (1.4: 9346). About 100 yards before reaching the lookout tower the McKittrick Trail follows a left turn at a signed junction and descends to KP Creek, arriving one mile downstream of our last KP turnoff option. Continue straight to the peak. Because of the trees that crowd the mountaintop, the clearest views are obtained from the top of the lookout tower. Those who wish to ascend the steep stairway to the "cage" may do so, but please honor the request posted at its base, and go up in groups of no more than four at a time. Usually, you will find the trapdoor leading into the observation room locked, but you may still climb to the top of the stairs for a better view. Although the tower was once occupied seasonally it is now used only in emergency situations.

This summit offers a more extensive vista than perhaps any other point in the Blue Range. This is so because it is perched on the edge of the Mogollon Rim, the 300-mile-long escarpment that separates the Sonoran Lowlands from the Colorado Plateau. To the north we look out across the high, spruce- and aspen-forested tops of the Blues; to the south the mountains fall away abruptly to the oak and ponderosa country beyond Strayhorse Divide, making a final resurgence at 8786-foot Rose Peak. Beyond that the view is likely to be obscured by the haze contributed by Phoenix, Tucson, and even Los Angeles, but on a rare clear day one can barely make out the faint blue outline of the Chiricahua Mountains, just north of the Mexican border some 120 miles distant. To the west and east it is instructive to trace the irregular scarp of the Mogollon Rim as it winds out of central Arizona, breaks down at the deep gap cut by the Blue River to the east, and then rises again to continue into New Mexico.

Return the way you came.

TRIP 65
LOWER BLUE RIVER TO HU BAR BOX AND UPPER BLUE RIVER TRAILHEAD

▲ **16.2-20 miles; 420'-750' elevation gain**
▲ **Strenuous dayhike or moderate backpack (2 hiking days)**
▲ **Trailhead 30, Lower Blue River**
▲ **Maps**
   Pipestem Mountain (approach), Fritz Canyon, and Dutch Blue Creek quadrangles
▲ **Season: all year; hot in summer**
   Water available all year along entire route

Features

The Blue River is dogged by roads for much of its entire length, with the exception of the 10-mile segment above HU Bar Ranch, which is protected against motorized intrusion by its inclusion within the Blue Range Primitive Area. Even this unroaded stretch is not completely "primitive," for you are likely to see some quite domesticated cattle grazing along its banks at all-too-frequent intervals. Though no longer passable to motor vehicles, faint remnants of the old 7.6 mile road from the trailhead to HU Bar Ranch can be seen in places. It is peaceful country, sycamore- forested and automobile-free, well worth a visit by anyone who would know all the varied facets of the Blue Range.

Trailhead Route/Camping

From Clifton, drive north along U.S. 191 about 30 miles, then turn right (east) on Forest Road 475. Drive nearly 12 miles to Forest Road 475C. Turn left and drive north 3 miles to the trailhead, just past the old ranch buildings. Both forest roads have signs warning they are unmaintained and hazardous. This is true at times. Under the best conditions, passenger cars could make the route if the occupants are willing to get out and move rocks—repeatedly. There are several rocky stream crossings. High clearance would help. Camping is permitted at the trailhead, and two Juan Miller campgrounds are along the route close to U.S. 191.

Description

From the gate at the "end" of Forest Road 475C (0.0: 4320), walk northeast along the bulldozed track that parallels the Blue River. Though designated "Forest Trail 101" beyond the trailhead / primitive area boundary, this track was a road open to the public until a few years ago. You will see traces of the road in places—usually a sandy stretch through bushes or parallel lines of larger rocks about 20 feet apart filled with smaller rocks washed in by the flooding and shifting Blue River. In most cases, the walking is no easier on the old road.

Vegetation along the Blue River's alternately sandy and gravelly floodplain is sparse, though there are some tall cottonwoods and sycamores scattered about. Mesquite trees grow along the dry margins of the canyon, and pinyon pines and scrub oaks dot the surrounding hillsides. Anglers may wish to stop and cast for some of the skittish brown and rainbow trout that inhabit the river.

Hiking this route is a matter of just seeking the easiest footing. Repeatedly, your selected route will be interrupted by the necessity of crossing the creek. You will undoubtedly meander more than did the old road for which the distances are given. Wearing boots in which you do not mind wading will save the time and effort involved in repeatedly taking off the boots to wade the stream. After a distance that seems twice as far (due to the difficulty of energy-consuming boulder hopping) we reach Little Blue Creek (4.1; 4500), at a nice grove of sycamores. After crossing the Little Blue (which is sometimes dry at this point), the route continues gently up-canyon, passing

Lower Blue River trailhead

beneath small cliffs and crossing and recrossing the main river at frequent intervals. Beyond the confluence of perennial Thomas Creek (5.5; 4560) the canyon grows narrower and, for a while, somewhat shadier. About a mile after the country begins to open up again we arrive at HU Bar Ranch (7.6; 4660), where you may find a few corrals and small outbuildings.

From here we walk a short distance to a pull gate, where all traces of the former road disappear. Beyond the gate, our route follows a cattle track northward until it fades out in the rocky, jumbled debris of the Blue River's floodplain, and for the remainder of our trip we again alternate boulder-hopping with slogging through soft sand. At a second fence, 0.5 mile beyond the ranch area, the canyon sides close in abruptly, and we enter the deep, vertical-walled slot known as HU Bar Box (8.1; 4670). To get through this narrows, we must cross and recross the river as it winds from cliff to cliff. After heavy rains and during the spring runoff this part of the route may be impassable. Backpackers will find excellent campsites on grassy, cottonwood- and sycamore-shaded flats both immediately above and immediately below the Box. Those with enough time to linger can sample the limited fishing in the river, go exploring up a side canyon, or simply relax and meditate beneath the rustling leaves of a sycamore. In this area you will reach posted private property. The U.S. Forest Service hopes to restore a route through or (more likely) around this property. Call the rangers to check current status before making any plans for a through hike. If such travel is permitted during your visit you can continue upstream; it is about 5.4 miles (cross country all the way) to the confluence of perennial Strayhorse Creek (13.5; 4940), from where it is a mile farther (along a faint trail) to the southern terminus of Forest Road 281 at the former Upper Blue River Trailhead. But HU Bar Box is by far the most interesting feature of this roadless stretch of river, and most parties will want to turn around here. Often during high-water periods the river is not blue, but muddy and brown. This is a perfectly natural occurrence, the result of heavy erosion of the myriad thinly vegetated slopes which drain into the Blue River.

TRIP 66
LOWER BLUE RIVER TO HANNAH HOT SPRING, LITTLE BLUE BOX, AND DUTCH BLUE CREEK VIA LITTLE BLUE CREEK

▲ **17.2 miles round trip; 930' elevation gain**
▲ **Strenuous dayhike or moderate backpack (2 hiking days)**
▲ **Trailhead 30, Lower Blue River**

▲ **Maps**
Blue Range Wilderness (due out in 1998) or *Fritz Canyon and Dutch Blue Creek quadrangles*
▲ **Season: all year; hot in summer**
Water available intermittently along entire route

〰〰〰〰〰〰〰〰〰〰〰〰〰〰〰〰〰〰〰

Features

Crystalline Hannah Springs Creek and its narrow, rock-ribbed gorge are the highlights of this fascinating trip. Those who venture farther, beyond Little Blue Box, will also want to explore the wild, exceedingly remote country along Dutch Blue Creek and the upper Little Blue, with its abundant wildlife and strangely eroded canyons.

Most of the route along Little Blue Creek is cross-country, and the one short section of trail is tricky in spots, making this a trip for skilled hikers only.

Trailhead Route

Follow the trailhead route for Trip 65.

Description

From the gate at the end of Forest Road 475C (0.0; 4320), follow the route of Trip 65 to the point where Forest Trail 101 (such as it is) crosses Little Blue Creek (4.1; 4500). From here, walk cross-country east through a sycamore grove, then pass a drift fence and continue up the trailless canyon of the Little Blue, alternately rockhopping and bushwacking up the creek banks. The stream is sometimes dry through here, but soon it should begin to show at least intermittent signs of life. After the first 0.5 mile the brush thins out considerably, and the generally barren aspect of the watercourse is relieved by a riparian growth of walnut, sycamore and alder. Mesquite trees grow in the drier parts of the canyon floor, while a heavy pinyon-juniper forest dominates the sun-baked hillsides.

Some 3 miles upstream Hannah Springs Creek (7.2; 4700) branches off to the right and disappears up its narrow canyon. To reach Hannah Hot Spring, scramble up the slotlike gorge for about 0.4 mile, circumventing a troublesome pool of water by climbing up a 10 foot rock wall to its left. The spring itself is an anticlimactic seep a few feet to the left of the creek. At the time of my visit, this spring was quite hot, but it did not flow strongly enough to take the chill off of the water downstream. Hot springs such as this can be notoriously capricious; perhaps in the future it will be vigorous enough to allow hikers to soak their tired bones amid curling wisps of steam, or perhaps it will dry up completely. Perhaps the real attraction here is Hannah Springs Canyon—twisting, steep-walled, overhung with trees growing out of the cliffs high overhead, and threaded from end to end by sparkling Hannah Springs Creek. Continuing upstream another few hundred yards will reward the hiker with more spectacular narrows, and some bracing swimming in a series of clear, rockbound pools.

After you return to Little Blue Creek it is another 0.4 mile upstream to Little Blue Box, a cliffy, "boxed in" narrows. Direct passage through the Box is quite difficult; to continue up-canyon it is best to backtrack a few hundred yards to where a faint path can be seen scrabbling up the west canyonside. (This point is just upstream from where Hannah Springs Creek joins the Little Blue.) Follow this track as it winds steeply upward, then begins traversing northward high above the Box. In about 0.6 mile the narrow trail passes a steep section where a slip could be hazardous—watch your step. Approximately ¾ mile after leaving the creek we reach the crest of a ridge which forms the south wall of a well-defined ravine; here our route drops steeply back down to Little Blue Creek. We are now upstream from the Box, and it is a short, easy walk the rest of the way to Dutch Blue Creek (8.6; 4820). This is a good base for further explorations up the oddly sculptured canyons of Little Blue, Dutch Blue and Ash creeks. You may see some javelinas in this area and, during the cooler months of the year, some Coues white-tailed deer as well. Camping is where you find it; look for flat spots among the trees away from the water (flash floods occur here), but don't be too picky.

Return the way you came.

TRIP 67
BLUE CAMP TO LANPHIER CREEK AND INDIAN CANYON

- 5.8 miles round trip; 800' elevation gain
- Leisurely dayhike or backpack (2 hiking days)
- Trailhead 31, Blue Camp
- Maps

   Blue Range Wilderness (due out in 1998) or *Bear Mountain and Blue quadrangles,* or *the free photocopied map from the trailhead information kiosk*

- Season: all year; best spring and fall

   Water available all year from mile 0.7 to end of route

Features

Tiny, murmuring Lanphier Creek and its pleasantly shaded canyon are both the means and the end of this short trip, which offers a maximum of seclusion and wilderness "feel" for a minimum of effort. You will likely find nothing spectacular or awe-inspiring along this quiet route—just the gurgling creek, the grapevine-laced trees, and plenty of peace and contentment.

Trailhead Route/Camping

From Clifton drive north on U.S. 191 about 85 miles and turn right (east) at Beaverhead on Forest Road 567 (Red Hill Road). Forest Road 567 is poorly signed at U.S. 191 so look for Forest Road 26, well signed, on the other side of the highway. Follow Forest Road 567 nearly 13 miles to just past the Blue River, and then turn right on Forest Road 281 (Blue River Road). This point can also be reached by driving three miles east of Alpine, then going south on Forest Road 281 for about 17 miles. Advantages of this route include better winter access and fewer unrailed dropoffs. From the junction, follow Forest Road 281, crossing the river several times (no bridges, but good solid, rocky creekbeds) for just over 3 miles to a parking area adjacent to "Blue Administrative Site," otherwise known as Blue Camp. Here, you will find a trail information kiosk and a gate. Walk through the gate, toward the river and follow the road that first parallels the river, and then crosses it. The trailhead is to the left of the corral. Camping is allowed in the parking area but there is a campground with facilities off Forest Road 567 just before it crosses Blue River.

Description

Immediately after passing the Blue Camp horse corral through a wire gate (0.0; 5640) the trail begins climbing away from briefly glimpsed Lanphier Creek. Fortunately, before we can quite get out of breath, the route levels off and begins a rocky, winding, shadeless traverse in and out of ravines a hundred feet or so above the stream. 0.5 mile later we stay right at an unsigned junction (which merely rejoins the trail a bit farther) and descend back toward the creek. A short distance farther is a signed fork (0.7; 5720), where we go left and then climb gently up-canyon through a riparian forest of box elder, Arizona walnut, New Mexican locust, maple, and an occasional Douglas-fir or ponderosa pine. The route crosses and recrosses Lanphier Creek, and it is rather easy to lose the trail in the boulders near the water. If lost, however, it can easily be picked up again by scouting around on the other side of the stream. An impressive variety of birdlife congregates in this leafy canyon, particularly in the spring, and birdwatchers may be able to spot and identify such rare species as the olive warbler and the Arizona woodpecker. A host of mammals inhabit this area as well; squirrels frolic in the trees, deer are common, and cougars and bears are at least occasional visitors.

Hikers who are abroad in the predawn hours may come upon a family of skunks parading along the trail, or surprise a raccoon in the process of washing up in the creek—or divesting a carelessly unguarded backpack of its food stores.

After two miles of alternate trail-walking and boulderhopping, the creek turns to the south and enters Indian Canyon (2.9; 6300). Backpackers will find good campsites in the vicinity, especially on the benches above the stream. This is the end of our route, though you may wish to scramble up trailless Indian Canyon a short distance. The path we have been following continues up Lanphier Canyon into the ponderosa country (see Trip 69), but beyond here it is steep and ill maintained.

Return the way you came.

TRIP 68
BLUE CAMP TO LARGO CANYON AND BEAR MOUNTAIN LOOKOUT; RETURN VIA TELEPHONE RIDGE

- ▲ **12.8 mile semiloop trip; 3150′ elevation gain**
- ▲ **Strenuous dayhike**
- ▲ **Trailhead 31, Blue Camp**
- ▲ **Maps**
  Blue Range Wilderness (due out in 1998) or *Bear Mountain and Blue quadrangles,* or *the free photocopied map from the trailhead information kiosk*
- ▲ **Season: May to October**
  Water available all season at Lanphier Creek (miles 0.7 and 12. 1) and Dutch Oven Spring (miles 3.2 and 9.6)

Features

After crossing leafy Lanphier Creek, this route takes the hiker through stately forests of oak and ponderosa to broad-backed Bear Mountain, whose strategically located summit affords unsurpassed vistas across the rugged canyon of the Blue River.

Trailhead Route

Follow the trailhead route for Trip 67.

Description

Immediately after passing the Blue Camp horse corral (0.0; 5640) the trail begins climbing away from briefly glimpsed Lanphier Creek. Fortunately, before we can quite get out of breath, the route levels off and begins a rocky, winding, shadeless traverse in and out of ravines a hundred feet or so above the stream. About 0.5 mile later we stay right at an unsigned junction (merely a short spur that rejoins the trail) and descend back toward the creek. A short distance farther is a signed fork (0.7; 5720), where we continue straight ahead, cross the stream, and climb steeply up to the crest of a low divide (1.5; 6120) separating Largo and Lanphier canyons. Beyond here we pass through a fire singed ponderosa-forested flat, then descend into Largo Canyon. The route now turns up-canyon, weaving back and forth across the bouldery creekbed (often dry) and occasionally rising and dipping steeply. This section is moderately shaded by a mixture of Gambel oak, bigtooth maple and ponderosa pine.

One mile after entering Largo Canyon we come to Dutch Oven Spring (3.2; 6600), at a round cement tank. This is the highest reliable water on our route, so you may wish to replenish your supply here though the water can be very scummy with many tiny swimming creatures. A filter will not last long with this water. The water actually seeps out at the trail, adjacent to the tank and is clean in shallow puddles along the trail except for contributions from cattle and horses.

From here the trail continues up-canyon to a signed fork several hundred yards beyond Dutch Oven Spring. The path coming down from the right here is part of our return route, the Telephone Ridge Trail. Again we continue straight up-canyon, ignoring the occasional faint spur trails that branch off to the left. After 1.5 miles of moderate climbing we arrive at a signed junction (5.1; 7480) with the trail to Bear Valley and Campbell Flat (see Trip 69). This time we go right, wind our way up a low ridgelet between two branches of Largo Canyon, and enter a burned-over ponderosa forest. In about a mile you may notice a faint, signed spur to the left. The hulking back of Bear Mountain is now visible through the blackened trees to our right. Shortly after exiting the burn area the path suddenly grows steeper, and soon we make the first of many switchbacks that climb the brushy, scantily shaded east shoulder of the peak. At the top of this occasionally steep ascent we meet the signed Telephone Ridge Trail coming up from the north; here we turn left and complete the final ¼-mile climb to Bear Mountain (6.5; 8550).

Atop the peak you will find two cabins, a corral, and an outhouse—all ancillary to the maintenance of the lookout. Since Bear Mountain's entire crown is heavily forested with ponderosa pine (despite the near approach of a fire), it is necessary to climb the series of steep ladders to the cage atop the tower to obtain an unobstructed view. Visitors are advised by a sign at the bottom that, though welcome, they climb at their own risk. The observation room will nearly always be locked, except during emergencies (when you shouldn't be here anyway) but you can still get a good view from the platform immediately below.

Among the landmarks visible from the tower are Sawed Off Mountain, Blue Peak and Rose Peak, rising above the rough-cut Blue River "breaks" to the west. The high point to the east is 8827-foot Whiterocks Mountain, situated just across the border in New Mexico. Since Bear Mountain stands on the Mogollon Rim, it is interesting to note the difference between the views to the north and to the south: to the north, rising and swelling in waves above the deep gap cut by the Blue River, is the densely forested high country surrounding Alpine, while to the southwest the mountains fall away steadily toward the sere lowlands beyond Clifton and Morenci.

When saturated with vistas, retrace your steps ¼-mile to the top of the Telephone Ridge Trail, turn left, and begin descending Telephone Ridge, passing occasional good views to the left and right as the initially gradual descent steepens. About 2 miles later we reach a signed junction, where we double back to the right and plunge down steep switchbacks to the Largo Canyon Trail just above Dutch Oven Spring (9.6; 6600). From here, retrace the morning's route the remaining distance to Blue Camp (12.8; 5640).

TRIP 69
BLUE CAMP TO LARGO CANYON, BEAR VALLEY, AND LANPHIER CANYON

- ▲ **18.l-mile semiloop trip; 3440' elevation gain**
- ▲ **Moderate to strenuous backpack (2-4 hiking days)**
- ▲ **Trailhead 31, Blue Camp**
- ▲ **Maps**
  Blue Range Wilderness (due out in 1998), or *Bear Mountain and Blue quadrangles*, or *the free photocopied map from the trailhead information kiosk*
- ▲ **Season: May to October**
  Water available all season at Lanphier Creek (mile 0.7), Maple Spring (mile 3.2), and Lanphier Canyon (miles 15.2 to 17.4); Little Blue Creek (mile 8.8) may be dry

Features

After passing within side-tripping distance of lofty Bear Mountain, this lengthy loop route descends into remote, infrequently visited Bear Valley, which sees as much of its namesake the black bear as it does of humans. An added highlight is the return trip through Lanphier Canyon, with its spectacular hardwood forests and tiny, burbling creek.

Much of this route is along trails that are unmaintained and difficult to follow (especially, where severely burned) and it is recommended only for experienced wilderness hikers.

Trailhead Route

Follow the trailhead route for Trip 67.

Description

Follow the directions for Trip 68 to the signed trail junction at the head of Largo Canyon (5.1; 7480). Those who wish to make the side trip to Bear Mountain (highly recommended) should turn right here and follow the route of Trip 68 to the summit (1.4 miles one way). Others will stay left and continue climbing gently through ponderosa to a poorly signed junction in a saddle (6.0; 7720). The trail is rather indistinct in this area—look for blazes and sawn-through logs to stay on the right track. At the saddle we turn neither right nor left, but descend straight ahead down a hot, brushy slope to the head of Little Blue Creek in Bear Valley. The creek is often dry at this point, but as we veer left and walk gently down-canyon it should begin showing signs of life. By the time we arrive at a corral and a signed trail junction (8.8; 6840) there is generally enough surface flow to support a tiny green meadow and good camping. (During dry years, and late in the season, it is advisable to check with the Alpine Ranger District about the water supply here.)

On the hillsides south and west of Bear Valley you may see signs of a wildfire—partially the legacy of the 1979 Horse Fire, which was allowed by the Forest Service to burn for several weeks before being suppressed. This action, or nonaction, was part of a new fire policy adopted in light of a greater understanding of wildfire's vitalizing role in certain natural ecosystems. Close inspection of the burned hillsides above the trail will reveal that not all of the adult trees were killed by the flames; the net effect of the fire was simply to clear away the dense, brushy understory which was competing with ponderosa seedlings, thus clearing the way for the germination and growth of a whole new generation of pines. A more recent fire has also impacted the areas crossed by this hiking route. There are some areas where the trail virtually ceases to exist. Experienced hikers, with the aid of good maps, have gotten through to where the trail resumes.

To complete the loop back to Blue Camp, proceed north from the trail junction, following a faint path that climbs gently along a streamcourse. After a mile this trail veers left and switchbacks up a brushy, shadeless slope to a saddle, just beyond which is a poorly signed junction in wooded Campbell Flat (10.6; 7560). We go straight ahead at this 4-way crossroads, rising and falling gently as the trail traverses an area devoid of landmarks. At length, when we appear to be approaching a dropoff of sorts, the trail swings right, cuts across a low, oak-forested ridge, and then descends into a minor, northward-trending drainage. Our route stays left at an unsigned fork here, then continues gently downhill to a signed junction (13.0; 7320). Here we go left again, past the remnants of an old cattle camp, and then drop steeply down to Cashier Spring, a muddy, unreliable seep in the hill-side next to a solitary carved aspen.

Below Cashier Spring the route is confused by a plethora of use trails; the correct path crosses to the right of Lanphier Canyon Creek (often dry here), heads straight down-canyon for 0.5 mile, then ascends to a bench on the right-hand canyonside. After traversing a dry, rocky slope high above the creekbed, we drop steeply back down and rejoin the creek just upstream from Indian Canyon (15.2; 6280). Here there is excellent camping and perennial water.

To complete this semiloop trip, retrace the steps of Trip 67 the remaining 2.9 miles to Blue Camp (18.l; 5640).

TRIP 70
BLUE CAMP TO FOOTE CREEK

- ▲ **5.8 miles round trip; 1040' elevation gain**
- ▲ **Moderate dayhike or leisurely backpack (2 hiking days)**
- ▲ **Trailhead 31, Blue Camp**
- ▲ **Maps**
  Blue Range Wilderness (due out in 1998) or *Bear Mountain quad-rangle*, or *the free photocopied map from the trailhead information kiosk*
- ▲ **Season: all year; best spring and fall**
  Water available all year at Cedar Springs (mile 1.2) and Foote Creek (mile 2.9)

Features

Enroute to delightful Foote Creek, this trip passes through two distinctive ecological communities—a dry, sunny, Upper Sonoran woodland, where pinyons and junipers grow against a backdrop of distant mountains, and a lush, shady riparian forest, where the sunlight is more congenial, the views more intimate. Hikers who are new to the lower Blue Range will find this route a good introduction to the contrasting moods of this little known, infrequently visited country.

Trailhead Route

Follow the trailhead route for Trip 67 to the parking area at Blue Camp. The trail starts across the road from Blue Camp.

Description

The most strenuous part of this trip comes at the very beginning, in the form of a steep, switchbacking ascent up the shadeless, cactus-studded canyonside across the road from Blue Camp (0.0; 5640). After gaining some 500 feet in the first 0.5 mile we suddenly break out onto a rolling, savannahlike mesa, and winded hikers can relax with the knowledge that the worst is behind them. The trail is occasionally faint through here, but it maintains a straight course as it descends gently westward, and is not hard to follow. Views to the south are pleasant, reaching out across pinyons, junipers and waving grasses to distant ridges receding into the haze that hangs above the San Francisco River country. Mule deer, Coues white-tailed deer and Rocky Mountain elk are occasionally seen in this area, particularly in winter and early spring, when the high-country meadows are still buried in snow.

Presently the trail drops into a shallow ravine that contains the trickling runoff from Cedar Springs (1.2; 5920). After crossing this tiny freshet and climbing back out of its channel, we pass through a pull gate, then descend into another branch of the springs' effluence. Beyond here the trail rises and falls over short distances as it begins the long traverse toward Foote Creek, which is slowly rising to meet us on the left. Soon we round a bend, where we get our first glimpse of Foote Creek canyon heading north toward the high mountains. Here the trail runs up alongside a barbed-wire fence, an unwelcome intrusion from civilization which continues to dog us as we drop into a ravine, climb out again, and resume our traverse. Finally we leave the fence behind us at another gate, then descend moderately to shaded Foote Creek (2.9; 5840). Several fair to good campsites can be found nearby, in sylvan groves of sycamore, walnut, Arizona cypress and maple. Fishing in the creek is fair for rainbow, brown and brook trout.

Down-canyon the stream quickly dries up into a series of disconnected pools (except during the spring runoff), but those who wish to
camp further up-canyon will find reliable water at all seasons for the
next two miles or so; beyond that the creek is often intermittent.
Return the way you came.

TRIP 71
HANNAGAN MEADOW TO THE BLUE RIVER VIA
MUD SPRING AND STEEPLE MESA

- ▲ 13.3 miles one way (45-mile car shuttle required); 4100' eleva-
  tion loss, 500' gain
- ▲ Moderate dayhike or backpack (2 hiking days)
- ▲ Trailhead 32, Hannagan Meadow (start)
- ▲ Trailhead 34, Blue River South (finish)
- ▲ Maps
  Blue Range Wilderness (due out in 1998) or *Hannagan Meadow,
  Strayhorse, and Bear Mountain quadrangles,* or *the free photocopied
  map from the trailhead information kiosk*
- ▲ Season: June to October
  *Water available all season at Willow Spring (mile 2.1); Mud Spring
  (mile 7.5) generally reliable throughout the summer rainy season*

Features

The "breaks" of the Blue River country—the broken, choppy
ridges that drop abruptly from the alpine high country to the river-
ine lowlands—transect three major life zones. The descending
Steeple Mesa Trail takes the hiker through each in orderly succession,
starting with the Canadian zone, where thick forests of aspen, spruce
and fir enclose bright green meadows; then through the oaks and
ponderosa pines of the Transition zone; and finally through the cactus-studded, wildflower-carpeted, pinyon-and-juniper country that
touches on the Upper Sonoran zone. The trail also provides backpackers with access to the delightful camping along KP and Grant
creeks.

Infrequently maintained and sometimes difficult to follow, this
route is recommended only for experienced hikers.

Trailhead Route/Camping

Start: follow U.S. 191 either 22 miles south of Alpine or 75 miles
north of Clifton to Hannagan Meadow Lodge. Just south of the lodge,
restaurant, and store is Hannagan Meadow Campground. Across the

street from the campground, turn east and drive a short distance to the trailhead. Car camping is allowed here but there are better facilities at the campground. Finish: to leave a car at the end of the trail, follow the trailhead route for Trip 67 but continue on Forest Road 281 an additional 8 miles beyond Blue Camp.

Description

From the trailhead information kiosk (0.0; 9120) walk east a short distance along an old dirt road to a signed junction, then turn right onto the Steeple Mesa Trail. The path is rather faint at first beneath the dense, ferny undergrowth, but it soon grows more distinct as it proceeds through a thick forest of Engelmann spruce and Douglas-fir. After walking another ¼ mile due south we meet a faint unsigned trail branching right; ignore this fork and go left (east). For the next mile we follow a shallow, gently descending valley as it leads us east, then south, to a meadow at the head of Grant Creek (water in early season). After crossing this leafy, grassy swale, passing a signed junction with the Upper Grant Trail, we re-enter the trees and continue south, topping a gentle rise and then dropping to a second meadow, which contains perennial Willow Spring (2.1; 8840). Rocky Mountain elk can occasionally be seen grazing in this meadow.

Beyond the spring, the trail is temporarily obscure, but it quickly becomes clearer as it proceeds south into the forest. After a short, steep climb we reach the top of a wooded ridge, then drop down into another cienega, where the trail again grows faint. This time the track can be found again where it re-enters the trees a short distance to the east. Now we rise and fall gently for the next mile or so, passing through a lovely grove of tall aspens before beginning the steep descent into Steeple Creek canyon. Here the forest cover changes

Near KP Mesa

rapidly. Before, the prevailing trees were the spruce and fir of the Canadian life zone, with only an occasional ponderosa pine growing in some particularly dry and sunny spot; now the ponderosas become dominant, and it is the spruces and firs that look out of place. Gambel oak and bigtooth maple soon appear along the banks of the mostly dry creek, and some three miles after beginning this descent we arrive at a signed junction. To reach water continue straight on the trail (down the drainage) 0.2 mile to Mud Spring (7.5; 6840) (may be dry before August 1). Mud Spring is the largest of several puddles in the drainage.

At the signed trail junction 0.2 mile above the spring, the Grant Creek/Paradise Park trail branches left. Hikers who are impatient for a clear view can walk out on it a few hundred yards to an overlook of the Blue River country to the east. There is excellent camping another 2.2 miles out on this trail, at Grant Creek where water is usually available. Otherwise, stay right and continue down-canyon 0.5 mile to an old corral. When Mud Spring has water available one can camp just above or below the corral. To continue our hike, we cross to the right side of the creekbed and begin climbing the south canyon wall. After gaining about 300 feet we encounter a barbed-wire fence. Walk along the fence 50 yards to the left, then pass through a pull gate (8.0; 7000). Here the KP Creek Trail comes in from the right; we continue the other way, paralleling the fence on its south side, rising and falling along the ridge that leads out to KP and Steeple mesas, and gaining good views across the canyon of KP Creek toward aptly named Sawed Off Mountain. About 1.5 miles beyond the gate, the country levels off and we begin the trek across the two mesas. Steeple comes first; then, marked only by a subtle dip and rise in the trail a mile later, comes the transition to KP Mesa. The forest cover on these dry plateaus becomes increasingly dominated by alligator juniper, a tree whose coarse, scaly bark leaves no doubt as to the origin of its name. There are no open views along this stretch, but during late summer and early fall spectacular displays of bright yellow snakeweed blossoms blanket the interstices between the trees, making up for the lack of broad vistas.

At length, just when it may begin to seem that the flat, viewless expanse of mesa must go on forever, we pass through a gate and ease off the edge of the plateau. A few broad switchbacks bring us to a small saddle, where we have a good view across KP Canyon. As we continue steeply down a ravine and onto the backbone of a ridge the forest cover metamorphoses once again: cholla, prickly pear and pincushion cacti appear, and Colorado pinyons begin to supplant the long-reigning alligator junipers. After passing through yet another gate, the trail reaches a sign at the junction with the MM Ranch Trail (12.9; 5480), where we continue straight past a large cairn indicating the continuation of our route to the Blue River. One more gate, a set of switchbacks, and we arrive behind a trailhead information kiosk at a graveled parking area just off Forest Road 281 (13.3; 5320).

TRIP 72
KP Cienega to KP Creek

- ▲ **5.8-10.0 miles round trip; 1280'-2120' elevation gain**
- ▲ **Moderate dayhike or backpack (2 hiking days)**
- ▲ **Trailhead 35, KP Cienega**
- ▲ **Maps**
  Blue Range Wilderness (due out in 1998) or *Strayhorse quadrangle,* or *the free photocopied map from the trailhead information kiosk*
- ▲ **Season: May to October**
  Water available all season along entire route

Features
KP Creek has its headwaters in the coniferous high country, but for most of its length it drops steadily through leafy midmountain hardwood forests on its way to the sun-drenched lowlands along the Blue River. It is an in-between country, tucked away in a hidden fold between desert and sierra, cactus thorn and pine needle. Here leaves rustle softly in the wind, rather than moan or sigh, and their shadows dance in soothing patterns on the ground. A profound sense of remoteness and intimacy prevails throughout this trip, out of all proportion to the modest distances involved, and even the most city-weary pilgrim will quickly find the sort of refreshment and rejuvenation that only the wilderness can provide.

Trailhead Route/Camping
Drive 67 miles north of Clifton on U.S. 191 to just past well-signed Forest Road 25 and start looking for the turnoff to KP Cienega Campground on the right. Drive 1.1 miles east to the trailhead parking area. The trail starts behind a trailhead information kiosk. The campground is a few hundred yards down the road from the trailhead; water is available there when the campground is open.

Description
From the trailhead (0.0; 8920) we set off east and gradually descend into the nascent canyon of KP Creek. The trail, though easy to follow,

Tributary of KP Creek

is occasionally overgrown with New Mexican locust—a plant which looks innocuous enough from a distance, but which in reality harbors a wicked armory of thorns beneath its tender green leaves. As the canyon grows deeper and narrower, we cross and recross the fledgling creek, and the progress of our descent may be gauged by the gradual disappearance of the spruces and firs and their replacement by increasing numbers of riparian, deciduous trees such as Arizona walnut and bigtooth maple. Peace and quiet reign in these groves, though the silence may be interrupted now and then by the exuberant cackling of a Steller's jay or the obstinate hammering of an Arizona woodpecker, a rare species that has found a refuge from possible extinction in the wild country of the Blue Range. Both the long-eared Rocky Mountain mule deer and the smaller, more graceful Coues white-tailed deer frequent this area, particularly early and late in the season. Blue lupine and yellow columbine are among the flowers that bloom in isolated pockets of the bouldery canyon floor.

After dropping nearly 1300 feet we meet a tributary of KP Creek (2.9; 7640) spilling down from a miniature waterfall and cascade on the left. The creek has by now grown to respectable proportions, and skilled anglers may be tempted to try deceiving some of the extremely skittish brook, brown and rainbow trout that inhabit its deeper pools. There are occasional good campsites downstream, but most are small—just happenstance flats here and there amid the jumble of roots and boulders which covers the canyon floor; large parties will not be able to bed down all their members in one spot except in one area just above the creek, a few hundred yards down the trail. Do not camp here if the weather could cause the creek to rise.

Those whose legs are not yet fully stretched out, and who wish to continue down-canyon from the waterfall should cross the creek and follow the trail a short distance up its north bank to a signed trail junction. Here a left-branching trail climbs back up to U.S. 191 in two miles; we turn right and resume our trail, which stays above the creek passing a waterfall in KP Creek just above the junction with the tributary creek—which also descends as a waterfall. Shortly, the trail descends to the creek and we continue a rock-hopping, creek-crossing descent, passing through more delightful groves of maple, walnut, Douglas-fir and Gambel oak. In places, the water has carved channels in basalt similar to waterslides. This effect becomes even more pronounced where the water cuts down to a redrock conglomerate. Two miles after the last junction, where a small but perennial tributary flows in from the right, we arrive at a signed junction (5.0; 6800) which marks the extremity of our excursion. Returning a few hundred yards upstream, backpackers will find a good campsite at a quietly soothing, delightfully isolated spot, and anglers will find challenging fishing for small trout along the sun-dappled creek.

Return the way you came.

TRIP 73
KP CIENEGA TO KP CREEK AND BLUE LOOKOUT ROADEND

- ▲ **10.1 miles one way (7 mile car shuttle required); 2540' elevation gain**
- ▲ **Strenuous dayhike or backpack (2-3 hiking days)**
- ▲ **Trailhead 35, KP Cienega (start)**
- ▲ **Trailhead 29, Blue Lookout Roadend (finish)**
- ▲ **Maps**
  Blue Range Wilderness (due out in 1998) or *Strayhorse quadrangle,* or *the free photocopied map from the trailhead information kiosk*
- ▲ **Season: June to October**
  Water available all season along first 6.8 miles of route only

Features

This trip partakes of the best of two worlds. After traveling down the lovely, forested canyon of KP Creek, we explore an infrequently visited, densely wooded tributary stream, where the sun is just a remote twinkling somewhere far above the filtering treetops. After a stiff climb the trip suddenly reaches its climax at lofty Blue Lookout; there we burst into the light, a vast panorama falls away at our feet, and the intimacy and closeness of the canyon world are traded for the expansive vistas of the mountaintop.

Trailhead Route

Start: follow the trailhead route for Trip 72. Finish: follow the trail-head route for Trip 64.

Description

Follow the directions for Trip 72 to the signed trail junction beside KP Creek (5.0; 6800). Here we turn right, hop across a tributary stream to its east side, and begin climbing. Almost immediately the trail forks; ignore the left branch and head for a duck and a blaze visible ahead. Soon we veer right, cross the tributary again, and come to another unsigned junction. This time the route goes left, and then begins climbing very steeply up the crest of a low ridge. After a few hundred yards of strenuous scrambling the angle of ascent eases somewhat, and we soon find ourselves cloistered in a delightful canyon that shelters an incredibly rich and varied forest of maple, walnut, box elder, towering Douglas-fir, New Mexican locust, Gambel oak and quaking aspen. At times the sky is lost entirely behind the leafy, overarching canopy, and the hiker may get the feeling of passing through an immense, steeply canted tunnel. But even while marveling at the lush forest cover, one is tempted to curse the poorly maintained trail, which is steep and rough all the way, and frequently blocked by fallen trees.

After working our way up-canyon for a little less than 2 miles we reach the ruins of a cabin which dated back to 1925 and was used to quarter firefighters who manned Blue Lookout. Here there is a signed junction (6.8; 8160), offering a choice of routes. The right-hand trail leads in three quarters of a mile to Blue Lookout Roadend in a grassy flat just below a saddle, 4.5 miles east of U.S. 191. See the trailhead route for Trip 64. Those who wish to continue directly to Blue Lookout, without intercepting the road, should follow the left branch as it crosses the creekbed and winds up the hillside east of the waning stream. After a mile of moderate climbing along the latter path we meet the Blue Lookout Trail at a signed junction (8.1; 8920). Here we turn left and continue up a single long switchback past the McKittrick Trail junction an additional 100 yards to the base of the lookout tower (8.6; 9346).

For a description of the view from the top, see Trip 64. To reach Blue Lookout Roadend, retrace your steps 0.5 mile to the KP Creek trail junction, turn left, and walk gently downhill another 0.9 mile to the trailhead (10.1; 8840).

TRIP 74
KP CIENEGA TO THE BLUE RIVER VIA KP CREEK, MUD SPRING, AND GRANT CREEK

- ▲ **19.1 miles one way (45-mile car shuttle required); 1620' elevation gain**
- ▲ **Moderate backpack (3 hiking days)**
- ▲ **Trailhead 35, KP Cienega (start)**
- ▲ **Trailhead 33, Blue River (finish)**
- ▲ **Maps**
  Blue Range Wilderness (due out in 1998) or *Strayhorse, Hannagan Meadow, Beaverhead, and Bear Mountain quadrangles,* or *the free photocopied map from the trailhead information kiosk*
- ▲ **Season: May to October**
  Water available all season along first 5.8 miles of route, and at two points on Grant Creek (miles 11.4 and 16.0); Mud Spring (mile 9.2) generally reliable throughout the summer rainy season

Features

Shady canyons alternate with open, sunny forests of oak and ponderosa along this lengthy route. Inviting campsites can be found 5, 11, and 16 miles from the trailhead, providing the backpacker with a good opportunity to make a long trip at an enjoyable, leisurely pace. Anglers can sample the fishing in two separate drainages, and all hikers will enjoy the pleasant vistas across the muted contours of the Blue River bottomlands.

The trails along this trek are occasionally difficult to follow, and the route is recommended only for experienced wilderness travelers.

Trailhead Route

Start: follow the trailhead route for Trip 72. Finish: to place a shuttle at the end of the trail, follow the trailhead route for Trip 67 driving 4 miles beyond Blue Camp.

Description

Follow the directions for Trip 72 to the signed trail junction on KP Creek (5.0; 6800). At the junction we turn left and continue downcanyon, passing occasional fair campsites, until we reach a fairly open sloped area covered with ponderosa (5.7; 6560). As the canyon begins to close in a good campsite is visible just above the creek. Shortly, we pass a junction with the McKittrick Trail, which descends 4 miles from a junction close to Blue Lookout Tower. At this point we are on the right-hand side of the stream, but approximately ¼ mile down-canyon we cross to the left and begin winding up a gentle, ponderosa-covered slope, gradually leaving the creek behind. (It is rather easy to miss this crucial crossing, as the trail is faint through here and there are fallen trees across what used to be the main trail, resulting in several use-trails; if you come to a series of 50-foot-high clifflets rising directly above the south side of the creek, you've gone 0.3 mile too far.) The trail stays fairly level after leaving the creek which descends fast in a series of falls and cascades-during high water you can hear the falls from the trail.

As we meander along the slopes north of KP Creek, we gain some fine views of Sawed Off Mountain—an abruptly terminating ridgeline whose continuation was "sawed off" by the tremendous erosive action of the Blue River. The dry, sunny spaces between the pines along this stretch are occasionally brightened by the yellow blossoms of bladderpod and snakeweed. After two miles of rising and falling, the occasionally rocky path sidles up against a barbed-wire fence atop the divide between KP and Steeple creeks. A short distance east is a pull gate (8.5; 7000), where we meet the Steeple Mesa Trail. Continuing east would take us to Steeple Mesa; our route, however, passes through the gate, doubles back west a short distance along the north side of the fence, and then begins descending into the canyon of normally dry Steeple Creek. After "hitting bottom" at a corral 0.4 mile later, we cross the creekbed and begin climbing up-canyon. Soon a few wet spots may appear in the watercourse, presaging our arrival at Mud Spring (9.2; 6840) (may be dry by August 1). The spring is down in the streambed. When Mud Spring has water, tired hikers may wish to stay at campsites located just above and below the recently passed corral. Otherwise, backpackers should plan on spending the night at far more congenial Grant Creek. Continue up the trail 0.2 mile past Mud Spring to a signed junction.

At the trail fork here, the left branch is the continuation of the Steeple Mesa Trail, which climbs up to the high country at Hannagan Meadow. We take the right fork, cutting back above Steeple Creek, and begin another long, winding traverse, this time around the ridge that divides Steeple and Grant creeks. Route finding through here is made difficult at times by the presence of numerous intertwining cowpaths, which are often indistinguishable from the infrequently maintained Forest Service trail. The exasperated backpacker will likely form their own opinion at this point of the Forest Service Multiple Use policy, which allows cattle grazing within primitive and wilderness areas where it historically has occurred. Perhaps someday the Wilderness Act will be amended to alter this situation, but until then travelers in the Blue Range will have to put up with bellowing cows, needlessly spooked wildlife, and ruined trails, all of which detract from the area's wilderness atmosphere. Anyway, look for ducks and old sawn-through logs to stay on the right track here. Most of the cow paths lead from the trail to descend to Grant Creek. The proper trail stays fairly level.

A mile beyond Mud Spring, after gaining some nice views across the Blue River lowlands, we reach the top of the Steeple Creek-Grant Creek divide (10.4; 6880). The forest cover here consists mainly of silverleaf oak and some robust alligator junipers, but as the trail doubles back left (west) and begins descending gently toward Grant Creek, ponderosa pine and Douglas-fir become dominant. At Grant Creek (11.4; 6740) there is delightful camping in a riparian forest of box elder, bigtooth maple and Arizona walnut, and fair fishing for small brook, brown and rainbow trout.

To continue to the Blue River we cross Grant Creek, turn right where a signed side trail branches upstream, and wind our way uphill northward 1.5 miles to Paradise Park, a gently rolling, nearly pure expanse of ponderosa pine. Many of the young trees here can be seen to be of almost exactly the same age, a sign that they all germinated at the same time-most likely after a wildfire had cleared away the underbrush that normally chokes off aspiring ponderosa seedlings.

Cattle graze in and around the Park, and again we must rely on log cuts and blazes to locate a signed junction (13.0; 7640) in the midst of the pines, where we turn right. As we proceed, Gambel oaks begin to appear, breaking up the uniformity of the forest cover, and presently we emerge from the forest onto an ill-defined ridgetop offering a good vista across the gaping canyon of the Blue River. Hikers armed with a pair of binoculars should be able to pick out a few golden eagles from this point, and watch them as they wheel and soar against the vast backdrop of mountains and canyons beyond. A few specimens of that shamefully rare and endangered species, the southern bald eagle, make their nests along the Blue, but they are rarely sighted; count yourself lucky to see one.

From here the trail switchbacks steeply down barren, rocky slopes some 1400 feet back to Grant Creek (16.0; 6040). On the way down, a glance at the precipitous "breaks" through which the creek flows will explain why the trail did not proceed directly down-canyon from the last crossing. For those who wish to spend one last night within the healing sway of the wilderness, there is an excellent campsite where the trail first rejoins the stream, at the confluence of an intermittently flowing tributary. The remainder of the trip is an easy, if occasionally brushy, 3-mile walk out to the Blue River. A wide variety of trees flourish along this stretch, including sycamore, walnut, maple, alligator juniper, ponderosa pine and Arizona cypress. Many of the trunks and branches are gaily festooned with wild grapevines, whose seedy but tasty fruits ripen in the fall and compensate the late-season traveler for the imminent loss of wildness at the trailhead.

After a mile or two Grant Creek may grow intermittent. All too soon we reach a barbed-wire fence indicating the primitive area boundary; the Blue River is just beyond. To reach Forest Road 281 we turn left on a path that starts faint and walk a few hundred yards upstream to the point where the path swings into near contact with the river (19.1; 5440). Cross the river. A short path comes out behind a trailhead information kiosk just off the road.

Mount Baldy of the White Mountains

Although the Mount Baldy Wilderness is the second highest range of peaks in Arizona, it does not tower over surrounding terrain, which varies from 8-9000 feet in elevation. Both hikes to the vicinity of the summit are fairly gentle.

TRIP 75
SHEEP CROSSING TO BALDY PEAK

- ▲ **13.8 miles round trip; 2180' elevation gain**
- ▲ **Moderate dayhike or backpack (2-3 hiking days)**
- ▲ **Trailhead 36, Sheep Crossing**
- ▲ **Maps**
  Mount Baldy Wilderness or *Mount Baldy quadrangle,* or *the free photocopy map from the trailhead information kiosk*
- ▲ **Season: June to September**
  Water available all season along first 3.2 miles of trail only

Features
Lush meadows, magnificent forests of spruce and fir, and a sparkling stream all lend their charms to this delightful alpine route. Views from the summit of 11,403-foot Baldy Peak are superlative, and the West Fork Little Colorado River offers good fishing for rainbow, brook and cutthroat trout.

Note: Since February 1985, the Baldy summit area has been closed to public entry. The summit is sacred to the Apache, who go there on pilgrimage. Tribal police have arrested trespassers and confiscated hiking gear. Hikers wishing to travel to the summit may seek permission from the Fort Apache Reservation to travel beyond the reservation boundary at mile 6.3 (see address on page 153). The tribe is not known to have granted any permits since the summit was placed off limits but one can try.

Trailhead Route/Camping

From Eagar/Springerville, drive 18 miles west on Highway 260 to Highway 273. Drive south on Highway 273 past Sunrise Lake and the Sunrise Ski Resort turnoff. The highway becomes Forest Road 113—well graded and suitable for passenger cars. When the road makes a sharp right bend as it dips into the West Fork Little Colorado River drainage, look for a spur to the right—Forest Road 113J. Follow this spur 0.5 mile to the trailhead. On the way in you'll see some shallow pools that offer excellent fishing opportunities. The trailhead is at a gate next to an information kiosk. This area is closed to camping but Winn Campground is a short distance beyond the Forest Road 113J turnoff. Dispersed camping is permitted in all areas except those designated as recreation areas.

Description

From the trailhead at the Mount Baldy Wilderness boundary (0.0; 9220), our trail climbs gently beside the right bank of the West Fork Little Colorado. Anglers will find this as good a place as any to unpack their rods and reels, for the trail soon moves off to the right and maintains a rather inconvenient distance from the water. Along the fringes of this meadowed stretch the dominant tree is Colorado blue spruce, a lovely "frosted" conifer whose Arizona range is restricted to the White Mountains region and the area north of the main Colorado River near the Utah border. (A spruce may be distinguished from other evergreens by the square cross section of its needles, which makes them difficult to roll between one's thumb and forefinger. The Colorado blue may be told from the more common

Baldy summit

Engelmann spruce by squeezing a sprig of needles: if you say "Ouch!"
you are holding a blue.)

The trail continues to climb gently away from the stream, but several small creeklets (water until early fall) provide refreshment along
the mostly sunny, grassy canyonside. You may see some mule deer or
elk grazing in the verdant greensward below, though you are more
likely to see just a few head of cattle, members of the herds that are
unfortunately still allowed to graze within the wilderness. The large
boulders strewn about the canyon floor are glacial "erratics"—
chunks of mountain debris that rode the ancient glaciers down from
the Baldy summit area and were subsequently left stranded here
when the icefields receded. Among the many wildflowers that flourish along this stretch are scarlet penstemon, meadow cinquefoil,
leafybract aster and aspen fleabane.

About 2.5 miles from the trailhead, after gaining some fine views
of Baldy Peak's densely forested flanks, we curve to the right and
begin a wide, 180-degree circuit of a lush, inviting meadow.
Immediately following the last glaciation of this area, this meadow
was probably a small pond, its waters dammed up behind a
"moraine," or wall of boulders which accumulated during a tempo-
rary halt in the glacier's retreat. (What is left of this moraine is now
visible as the low, forested ridge adjoining the southeast edge of the
meadow.) Over the millennia the pond filled with streamborne silt,
becoming the meadow it is today; several centuries hence this natural succession may well culminate with the grasses being wholly
replaced by the trees which are already invading the fringes of the
meadow.

Soon the trail crosses a tributary of the West Fork (3.2; 9820). The
two culvert "bridge" is a bit washed out. It may be necessary to cross
the creek on a fallen log when the water is unusually high. This is the
highest point along this trail where water is convenient to good
camping areas. The forest cover here is less homogeneous than
below; mixed in with the spruce you will find corkbark fir (an aptly
named local variant of subalpine fir) and an occasional southwestern
white pine. Here and there your eye may be caught by a showy yellow columbine blossoming in some moist, shady nook.

Beyond the meadow our route rounds a hillside, climbing steeply
at times, until it once again parallels the West Fork Little Colorado
southwestward. The canyon walls steepen as we enter a stand of
Engelmann spruce, and the trail is soon forced to make a few switchbacks beneath some rocky bluffs. A short climb from here brings us
to a notch atop a ridge (5.3; 10,860), where we are presented with a
pleasant vista toward White Mountain Reservoir and the rolling

country to the north. From this point on, the trail stays on top of or just below the crest of the ridge leading to the Baldy summit area, and it is not advisable to proceed farther if a thunderstorm seems imminent.

Continuing our moderate ascent, we soon meet the signed East Fork Little Colorado River Trail coming up from the east (6.1; 11,180). A few poor, exposed campsites can be found here, but the nearest water is 0.4 mile away, at a tiny spring down on the East Fork Trail. From the junction we continue south across a gentle rise, then drop slightly into a shallow saddle before finally scrambling onto the rocky summit of Baldy Peak (6.9; 11,403). (Just beneath the top a faint trail branches off to the left. This is the old East Fork Trail, which is no longer maintained and not recommended for travel.)

On the summit you will find extensive views in every direction. A mile to the northwest is 11,036-foot Mount Warren, easily recognizable by the light green "hanging meadow" which contrasts so sharply with the dark forests on its southeast flank. Due west is 11,150-foot Paradise Butte, rising abruptly above the deep gash of the East Fork White River canyon. Beyond the Butte, ridge after forested ridge falls away toward the horizon; on a clear day one can see nearly halfway across the state in this direction.

After taking in the view, return the way you came, or via the East Fork Trail to Phelps Cabin (4-mile car shuttle required; reverse the steps of Trip 76.)

TRIP 76
PHELPS CABIN TO BALDY PEAK

▲ **13.4 miles round trip; 2000' elevation gain**
▲ **Moderate dayhike or backpack (2-3 hiking days)**
▲ **Trailhead 37, Phelps Cabin**
▲ **Maps**
   Mount Baldy Wilderness or *Big Lake and Mount Baldy quadrangles,* or *the free photocopied map at the trailhead information kiosk*
▲ **Season: June to September**
   Water available all season along first 0.8 mile and at mile 5.5

Features

Spectacular cliffs and pinnacles contrast with bright green meadows along the lower part of this varied excursion, while far-reaching vistas await the hiker who continues on to the wind-whipped summit of Baldy Peak. The sparkling East Fork Colorado River provides Arizona anglers with a rare opportunity to sharpen their skills in a pristine alpine environment.

Note: As of February 1985, the Baldy summit area has been closed to public entry. Hikers wishing to travel to the summit must obtain a special permit from the Fort Apache Reservation to travel beyond the reservation boundary at mile 3.5 (see address on page 153). No one is known to have received such permits since closure of the summit area but it doesn't hurt to try.

Trailhead Route/Camping

Follow the trailhead route for Trip 75 but continue on Forest Road 113 an additional 2.7 miles past Forest Road 113J to a turnoff on the right signed GABALDON CAMPGROUND. Follow this access road 0.2 mile right to the trailhead. While this road is not suitable for all passenger cars, the distance is short and can be walked. Gabaldon Campground is for horse camping only. On the way in you passed Winn Campground, and Big Lake has a campground only a few miles beyond the Gabaldon turnoff.

Description

From the end of the road at Gabaldon Campground (0.0; 9400) you pass through a gate next to a trailhead information kiosk, then walk west a few hundred yards through a fenced pasture to a second gate. Still heading west, paralleling the East Fork Little Colorado River, we soon come to what apparently was once a small earth-fill dam, then to a sign announcing the wilderness boundary. Fishing in the small stream is fair-to-good for brook, rainbow, and an occasional native cutthroat trout. One mile from the trailhead, after passing through a spacious meadow sprinkled with aster and fleabane (and often a few of the cattle which are unfortunately still allowed to graze within the wilderness), the trail veers right, away from the creek, and begins a moderate, switchbacking ascent up the north canyon wall. Almost immediately we reach the base of the first of a series of dramatically shaped basalt pinnacles which stand like tirelessly attentive sentinels along the next 1.5 miles of our route. These outcroppings are the exposed remnants of lava flows that oozed out of the Baldy volcano between 8 and 15 million years ago. After this volcanic activity ended, a series of glaciers moved down the East Fork canyon, undercutting the base of the basalt canyonside and rendering it particularly vulnerable to the frost wedging and water erosion which have since sculpted the rock into its present form.

About 0.5 mile beyond the first of the outcrops, we attain a ridgetop, where the switchbacks cease and we resume traveling due west. The East Fork is now out of sight some 500 feet below us, but the loss of that delightful stream is compensated for by the good views we have gained of the dense aspen and fir forests across the canyon—views picturesquely framed by the craggy tops of the rock towers, which are also below us now. This stretch of trail is only lightly shaded, but soon after passing the last of the pinnacles we cross an indistinct saddle to the north side of the ridge, which is generously wooded with a mixture of ponderosa pine, southwestern white pine, Douglas-fir and a few aspen. Just beyond the saddle is a sign informing us that we are entering the Fort Apache Indian Reservation (3.5; 10,460). After another mile of gentle climbing we switchback moderately up a shady slope, then traverse westward to a perennial spring (5.5; 10,990), the only water along our route above the east Fork Little Colorado. Here you will find a few fair campsites in a dense spruce-fir forest, and the wrecked carcass of an Air Force jet that crashed into the mountainside above the spring in the late Forties or early Fifties.

From the spring, the trail continues gently uphill 0.4 mile to the crest of Baldy Peak's summit ridge, where, after passing a few poor, exposed campsites, it meets the signed West Fork Trail coming up from the north (5.9; 11,180). Now we join that route, turning sharply left, and follow the exposed ridgetop trail ¾ mile south to the summit (6.7; 11,403). This last stretch of trail should not be attempted if a thunderstorm appears to be brewing. (For an account of the view from the top, see Trip 75.)

Return the way you came, or via the West Fork Trail to Sheep Crossing (4-mile car shuttle required; reverse the steps of Trip 75).

coppery-tailed trogon (m.)

AREA 4—The Mazatzal Wilderness

E ncompassing over 250,000 acres, the Mazatzal Wilderness is the largest of the wild areas covered in this guide. The name Mazatzal (locally mispronounced Ma-ta-ZEL) is a Paiute Indian term; when accompanied by the gesture of pointing between spread fingers it meant "empty-place-in-between." This is an appropriate description of the Mazatzal, even today, for this wide-open expanse of mountains, plains and mesas which sprawls between the Verde River and the Tonto Basin remains one of the least-visited areas of the state.

The Mazatzal Mountains run along the east side of the wilderness, rearing up in a precipitous escarpment above the Tonto Basin to the east, falling away more gently toward the flat-bottomed Verde River Valley to the west. With elevations ranging from 2100 feet, at Sheep Bridge, to over 7000 feet along parts of the Mazatzal Divide Trail, reasonably comfortable hiking may be enjoyed in every season. Summer hikers should be prepared for hot weather, even at fairly high elevations, and for the possibility of heavy thunderstorms and local flash flooding. Winter travel is quite chancy in the Mazatzal Divide area, as snowstorms here are heavier, longer-lasting, colder, and more violent than in the southern ranges. Those who venture into the western half of the wilderness should remember that it is still very lonely country, far from help and with plenty of space in which to get lost and never be found. Of course, if you are prepared to handle it, this may be precisely the sort of country you are looking for.

Geologically, the Mazatzal Mountains consist of a melange of such rocks as quartzite, shale and rhyolite, locally uplifted and tilted by massive faulting. The latter two rocks are particularly resistant to erosion, and are primarily responsible for the spectacular cliffs you will see along the eastern scarp of the range, on the west face of Mazatzal Peak, and on the forks of Deadman Creek. In large areas at lower elevations, these older rocks are covered with newer volcanic deposits, evidence of some comparatively recent volcanic activity.

The Mazatzal's biota typifies that of the rest of central Arizona, with the fortunate exception that it remains more completely intact ecologically. The low flats bordering the Verde River feature a rich Lower-Sonoran-zone plant cover of saguaro, prickly pear, ocotillo, hedgehog cactus, paloverde, creosote bush and a variety of chollas. In the foothills a grassland community predominates, with agave, sotol, gramagrass and nolina replacing the lower-elevation species. Higher up you will see lots of manzanita and shrub live oak, with pinyon pine, Utah juniper and one-seed juniper appearing in sheltered areas. Higher still are dense forests of alligator juniper, ponderosa pine, and a smattering of Gambel oak and Douglas-fir. The larger watercourses are frequently lined with nice stands of cottonwood, sycamore and, at higher elevations, Arizona cypress.

Wildlife populations in the Mazatzal remain healthy, if not quite up to primal standard. Coyotes, collared peccaries and mule deer are all common, and there are still enough cougars and black bears prowling around to keep the local ranchers in a continual uproar over their depredations. (Limited cattle grazing is unfortunately still allowed within the wilderness area boundaries.) Golden eagles can often be seen here, soaring and wheeling high above the mesas and canyons; with luck, you might see a rare-and-endangered southern bald eagle as well. The usual crew of nocturnal prowlers—ringtails, skunks, woodrats and porcupines—are also up and about every night, as you may discover if you leave your camp provisions in a vulnerable place.

The ruins of several ancient Native American dwellings are scattered throughout the Mazatzal. Some of these are thought to date back as far as 2500 BC, but most are more recent than that, being remnants of the Sinagua people, who occupied the region from approximately 700 to 1300 AD. (Trip 84 passes the ruins of one such dwelling.) Considerably more recent evidence remains of white use of the area—in the form of old cabins, abandoned mines, and the overgrown, dilapidated camps of cowboys and sheepmen.

During the prolonged Indian wars of the late 1800s, some of the most feared of the "renegade" Apaches—the Tonto bands—operated out the Mazatzal region, which was then *terra incognita* to the whites. After several bloody battles most of the Tontos were either killed or forced to surrender, but one band, under the leadership of Chief Delshay, refused to submit. At least two stories exist concerning Delshay's eventual demise, either or both of which may be apocryphal. According to one account, he and his followers roamed and raided at will until 1890, when they were invited to negotiate a peace treaty at Fort Reno in the Mazatzal foothills. Delshay accepted, but upon entering the fort he was "mistaken" for a thief and killed. The other tale has it that he remained at large until George Crook, the famed Indian fighter, offered amnesty to any captive Apache who could produce the chieftain's head. Two heads were promptly brought in, one to the Fort Verde reservation, the other to the San Carlos. Supposedly Crook later wrote, "Being satisfied that both parties were earnest in their beliefs, and the bringing in of an extra head was not amiss, I paid both parties."

One way or another Delshay met his demise, but that did not mark the end of violence in the area. Almost as deadly as the local "Indian troubles" was the internecine warfare that broke out between cattlemen and sheepmen in Pleasant Valley, east of the Mazatzals. The infamous Tewksbury-Graham Feud, immortalized by Zane Grey in his novel *To the Last Man,* broke out in 1887, when the Tewksbury clan moved their sheep onto what had previously been exclusive cattle range. The beef-running Grahams didn't think their steers needed the competition, and the shooting that ensued lasted for five years, during which time every male member of the Graham family died, as did all but one of the Tewksburys. Ironically, when the bottom dropped out of the beef market a few years later, cattlemen began to see the hated "woollies" in a rosier light; today in the Tonto Basin, cattle and sheep often graze side by side in perfect harmony, mirroring the calm that reigns in the wild, undisturbed mountains towering above them.

Managing Agencies

Forest Supervisor's Office
Tonto National Forest
2324 East McDowell Road
P.O. Box 5348
Phoenix, AZ 85010
(602) 225-5200

Cave Creek Ranger District
7171 Cave Creek Road
P.O. Box 5068
Carefree, AZ 85377
(602) 488-3441

Payson Ranger Station
1009 E. Highway 260
Payson, AZ 85541
(520) 474-7900

Further Reading

To The Last Man, by Zane Grey (Harper and Row, New York, New York 1922) (about the Graham-Tewksbury feud)

A Little War of our Own; the Pleasant Valley Feud Revisited, by Don Dedera (Northland Press, Flagstaff, Arizona, 1987)

Arizona's Mazatzal, by Francois Leydet (*National Geographic Magazine,* February, 1974)

Mazatzal Wilderness Management Plan, available for review at local Forest Service offices

TRIP 77
BARNHARDT TRAILHEAD TO Y BAR BASIN

▲ **14.4 miles round trip; 3240' elevation gain**
▲ **Strenuous dayhike or backpack (2 hiking days)**
▲ **Trailhead 38, Barnhardt**
▲ **Maps**
  Mazatzal Wilderness or *Mazatzal Peak quadrangle*
▲ **Season: March through November**
  Water may be available below Windsor Seep (mile 7.2) after wet weather or during spring runoff

Features

Cradled high on the eastern shoulder of the Mazatzal Mountains, Y Bar Basin makes a fine destination for the dayhiker or weekend backpacker. The basin itself is secluded and prettily forested, and the trail leading up to it affords panoramic vistas across Tonto Basin and the rugged Sierra Ancha.

Trailhead Route/Camping

From Mesa, drive northeast on State Highway 87 for approximately 65 miles, then turn left onto signed Barnhardt Road (Forest Road 419). (One can also reach this turnoff by driving south from Payson for 14 miles along State 87.) Follow this good dirt road (O.K. for passenger cars) 4.7 miles, as it gradually rises up a ridge (known as Barnhardt Mesa), to the parking area at its terminus. Car camping is possible at the trailhead parking area where water from a spring fills a horse trough. Since this area is sloped it might be more comfortable to backtrack to one of the lower pulloffs for a more level campsite that offers breathtaking views—especially at sunrise.

Description

From Barnhardt Trailhead (0.0; 4220), follow the signed Y Bar Basin/Shake Tree Trail as it proceeds gently southward up a rocky, juniper-dotted slope. The trail is very worn and rocky for nearly a mile but improves just after the Mazatzal Wilderness Boundary sign. This sign was very mutilated—just a post with ragged remnants, so it could be missed. As the hillside gradually steepens, we negotiate a few moderate switchbacks, then cut to the left and traverse across the ravine-furrowed face of Suicide Ridge. After winding in and out of 5 small drainages, the trail rounds a minor ridgelet affording a good view down a rocky bottleneck in Shake Tree Canyon, a considerably larger drainage which has opened up below. A moderately dense forest cover of ponderosa pine and pinyon pine develops as we climb along the right-hand wall of this glorified ravine. Just right of the first switchback on this ridge is the first really nice campsite. There are more campsites above—some cairns lead off the trail to camping areas. If continuing up the trail, ignore the most well cairned and inviting of these side routes and go up the worn and rocky path. A few Douglas-firs—Canadian-zone trees that are not at all common in the arid Mazatzal Mountains—grow in sheltered pockets along this stretch.

After following Shake Tree Canyon to its head, the trail crosses an unnamed saddle (5.4; 6300), then drops with moderate steepness into Y Bar Basin without reaching the very bottom where there are some Y Bar cattle tanks. At one point the trail will seem to go straight ahead but is crossed with a line of rocks. Here we stay right, and continue climbing beneath the rocky southern shoulder of 7903-foot Mazatzal Peak. After a few hundred yards there are occasional good campsites along this stretch; in early spring and during spells of rainy weather, water is available from a small streamlet that parallels the trail. As we gain elevation, breathtaking vistas open up through the pines, across the rumpled lowlands of Tonto Basin to the broad, arching backbone of the Sierra Ancha. This view can be especially pleasing at sunset, when the jagged shadow line of the Mazatzal peaks creeps silently up the flanks of the distant ranges.

The trail climbs less steeply as it approaches the head of Y Bar Basin. At Windsor Seep (7.2; 6500) there are good, ponderosa-shaded campsites, with water sometimes available from the nearby creek except during dry weather spells. Do not depend on the spring itself. Just beyond is a saddle atop the Mazatzal Divide, which affords an excellent view of Mazatzal Peak's sheer, 900-foot-high west face, and a more limited view across the rugged, rarely visited fastnesses of the western Mazatzal Wilderness.

Return the way you came.

TRIP 78
BARNHARDT TRAILHEAD TO MAZATZAL DIVIDE VIA THE BARNHARDT TRAIL

▲ **12.2 miles round trip; 1960' elevation gain**
▲ **Moderate dayhike or backpack (2 hiking days)**
▲ **Trailhead 38, Barnhardt**
▲ **Maps**
  Mazatzal Wilderness or *Mazatzal Peak quadrangle*
▲ **Season: March through November**
  Water generally available, in early spring and following rainy peri-
  ods, in Barnhardt Canyon (near mile 1.4), and along unnamed
  brooks at miles 3.1 and 4.9

Features

En route to a scenic saddle high atop the Mazatzal Divide, this route winds beneath rugged cliffs and spurs, through forests of oak and ponderosa, and past pretty copses of ash and sycamore. Short sidetrips provide access to other interesting features—a spectacular "narrows" in Barnhardt Canyon and, in season, a graceful waterfall tucked away on a tributary stream. The Barnhardt Trail is one of the best-maintained pathways in the Mazatzal, making this trip a logical choice for the hiker seeking an introduction to these rough mountains.

Trailhead Route

See the trailhead route for Trip 77.

Description

From the parking area at the end of Barnhardt Road (0.0; 4220), follow the signed Barnhardt Trail westward, through a rather sparse vegetative cover of nolina, sharp-spined sotol and agave, Emory oak, Arizona white oak, alligator juniper and one-seed juniper. The trail is rocky and quite wide at first, but its dimensions quickly narrow to those of a footpath as it works its way onto the south wall of Barnhardt Canyon. In 0.5 mile we pass a Mazatzal Wilderness boundary sign, and soon start to climb a bit more steeply, staying well above the creek. Where a major tributary drainage branches off to the left (1.4; 4640), it is possible to leave the trail and scramble cross country a half mile or so west up the main canyon to the mouth of the spectacular narrows, visible ahead, from which Barnhardt Creek emerges. There is usually water here, and backpackers can find fair-to-good campsites nearby.

To continue on to the Mazatzal Divide, follow the main trail as it switchbacks, steeply at times, up the left-hand wall of the tributary

canyon. Velvet ash, Arizona walnut and sycamore grow in shady
nooks along with watercourse.
After gaining 600 vertical feet the
trail swings to the right, past an
inviting but dry campsite atop a
ridgelet with a good view, then
winds past two branches of the
tributary stream. The second of
these small creeks (3.3; 5720)
flows out of a narrow, rocky cleft;
when the water is running high,
you will find a spectacular, roaring cataract a few yards up in
this gorge. This fall makes a
worthwhile destination for dayhikers who find themselves running short of time and/or energy.

Identifying a Pine

Beyond here we climb around
a protruding ridge to a signed
junction with the right-branching Sandy Saddle Trail (4.2; 5960). (Just
0.8 miles down the latter path, in the bottom of Barnhardt Canyon, is
Castersen Seep, which may have water when the other sources along
this route are dry.) Staying left at this junction, we next wind across a
manzanita-covered slope into a shallow drainage featuring some nice
copses of ponderosa pine. A tiny creeklet here has water in early
spring and following rainy periods; camping at such times would be
delightful. Castersen Seep is a 0.7-mile scramble down the drainage
course.

From here the trail continues gently uphill for about 0.5 mile, then
drops across a brushy slope to a signed junction in a saddle atop the
Mazatzal Divide (6.1; 6020). Views are excellent from this high pass:
eastward, the Sierra Ancha swells up beyond the basin of Tonto
Creek, while to the west the vista stretches across the rugged
Mazatzal backcountry to the Verde River Valley.

Return the way you came.

TRIP 79
MAZATZAL PEAK LOOP (BARNHARDT TRAILHEAD TO MAZATZAL DIVIDE, Y BAR BASIN, AND RETURN)

▲ 16.7-mile loop trip; 2860′ elevation gain
▲ Strenuous dayhike or moderate backpack (3 hiking days)
▲ Trailhead 38, Barnhardt
▲ Maps
   Mazatzal Wilderness or *Mazatzal Peak quadrangle*
▲ Season: March through November
   Water is seasonally available in Barnhardt Canyon (near mile 1.4) and along unnamed brooks at miles 3.1 and 4.9; the drainage below Windsor Seep (mile 9.5) often has water during snow meltoff and following rainy periods

Features
Topping out at 7903 feet, flanked by steeply eroded cliffs, Mazatzal Peak is both the highest and one of the most prominent landmarks in the wilderness that shares its name. This route circles completely around the magnificent mountain, first climbing up to the head of rugged Barnhardt Canyon, the following a portion of the Mazatzal Divide Trail past the peak's sheer west face before dropping eastward into beautiful Y Bar Basin. Strong hikers can complete (and enjoy) this route in a single day, but most will find it ideal for a three-day backpack.

Trailhead Route
Follow the trailhead route for Trip 77.

Description
From Barnhardt Trailhead (0.0; 4220), follow the Barnhardt Trail to the signed junction atop the Mazatzal Divide (6.1; 6020) (see Trip 78). Here we turn left, onto the Mazatzal Divide Trail, and traverse southward across a series of brushy, thinly forested slopes. This section of the trail is somewhat overgrown in spots, but is not hard to follow. There are occasional good views eastward, across the barren Mazatzal foothills to Pine Mountain and East Cedar Mountain, rising in the distance beyond the Verde River.

At a saddle (7.6; 6060) the signed Brody Seep Trail branches off to the right. (It is 0.9 mile down to the seep, which generally has water in winter and early spring only.) The sheer, 900-foot high western cliffs of Mazatzal Peak loom directly ahead as we continue our traverse. After winding in and out of a pair of small ravines, the trail passes beneath these cliffs, then switchbacks moderately uphill to a wooded saddle containing a signed fork. Now we turn left, onto the Y Bar Basin/Shake Tree Trail, and drop a short distance downhill to Windsor Seep (9.5; 6500), where there is good camping beneath tall ponderosa pines (water is available in the nearby drainage after wet spells or during snow meltoff). To complete your loop from here, reverse the steps of Trip 77 the remaining 7.2 miles back to Barnhardt Trailhead (16.7; 4220).

TRIP 80
BARNHARDT TRAILHEAD TO Y BAR BASIN, DAVENPORT WASH, DEADMAN CREEK, MOUNTAIN SPRING, SANDY SADDLE

▲ **43.2-mile loop trip; 8900′ elevation gain**
▲ **Strenuous backpack (allow at least 5 hiking days)**
▲ **Trailhead 38, Barnhardt**
▲ **Maps**
  Mazatzal Wilderness or *Mazatzal Peak, Table Mountain, Cypress Butte, and North Peak quadrangles*
▲ **Season: November to May, except after snowstorms**
  Drainage below Windsor Seep (mile 7.2) only during snow meltoff or rainy periods; Club Spring (near mile 16.0) and Mountain Spring (mile 23.7) usually have water all year; water also available at Davenport Wash (mile 17.1), Deadman Creek (mile 20.0), and other points (see text)

Features
After climbing up to pretty, forested Y Bar Basin, this lengthy route crosses the Mazatzal Divide and samples a healthy chunk of the rarely visited western Mazatzal Wilderness before looping back to the trailhead via Barnhardt Canyon. Along the way it passes through some of the roughest, most pristine country left in Arizona, where one is as likely to encounter a bald eagle or black bear as another human.

Because many of the trails on this route can be hard to follow, it is recommended only for skilled and experienced hikers.

Trailhead Route
Follow the trailhead route for Trip 77.

Description
From the parking area at the end of Barnhardt Road (0.0; 4220), follow the Y Bar Basin/Shake Tree Trail to Windsor Seep (7.2; 6500) (see Trip 77). At a signed junction in a saddle 200 yards beyond the spring

continue straight ahead, on the northbound Mazatzal Divide Trail now, then drop down a few switchbacks and traverse northward beneath spectacular, 900-foot-high cliffs of Mazatzal Peak. At a second saddle (9.1; 6060) there is another junction; here we turn left and follow the signed Brody Seep Trail down into the minor drainage that contains Brody Seep (water available in winter and early spring only). (According to the U.S. Forest Service, Brody Seep is no longer a system trail and is not maintained. If the sign is removed and the turnoff is missed, it is not necessary to return and seek the turnoff. Continue on the Mazatzal Divide Trail to the next junction, then turn left and proceed to the next junction with the Davenport Wash Trail. This route will add approximately 2 miles.) The trail now traverses 0.4 mile across a brushy slope to a fork, where we turn left onto the unmaintained, old Davenport Wash Trail, which drops abruptly downhill (west). After following the Brody Seep drainage channel for a short distance, the trail climbs around a sunny, south-facing hillside covered with yucca, agave and some massive alligator junipers and meets the new Davenport Wash Trail coming from Chilson Camp. It then switchbacks steeply down into a narrow canyon and crosses South Fork Deadman Creek (12.5; 4320). There are a few fair campsites in this area, shaded by a riparian growth of sycamore and ash. The creek generally flows until midspring or so, and briefly during summer rainy spells. During very wet periods, it is worthwhile to walk a few hundred yards downstream to view a high, lacy waterfall.

Immediately after crossing South Fork Deadman Creek we climb, occasionally quite steeply, out of the canyon to the west. The trail levels off temporarily to cross a small, usually dry streamcourse, then climbs moderately to a broad ridgetop forested with pinyon pine and some large shrub oaks. Here we pass through a gate in a stock fence, then descend gradually, leaving the trees behind and passing into more open country. After dipping in and out of a series of shallow drainages, we drop steeply onto a low, grassy ridgetop. Here the trail bends left, cuts over another ridgetop, then drops across a minor streamcourse and contours south into a small but comparatively lush, oak- and sycamore-shaded canyon. During wet weather spells, when running water is present, camping would be delightful here.

An unsigned sidepath branches to the right in this canyon, just before the Club Trail crosses the streambed; we stay left and proceed 0.4 mile farther to the site of Club Cabin (16.0; 3780), which now consists of little more than some old corrals and a pair of leaking cabins. The buildings are still used from time to time by local ranchers—please do not disturb any supplies which may be found inside. Club Spring (water available year-round) is about 200 yards up a signed spur trail to the left.

From Club Cabin the trail descends gradually to Davenport Wash (17.1; 3520), where there is another corral, good (but shadeless) camping, and a wet-season-only creek. After crossing (or fording, in wet season) the bouldery, barren wash we climb up to a trail sign, visible from below, where we turn right, onto the Deadman Trail. This path soon sidles up alongside a long, shallow ravine, which we follow, steeply at times, to its head at a saddle (18.4; 4340). Here we are treated to some fine, extensive views—both northward, across the oak-dotted Mazatzal foothills, and southward, to the distant, forested tops of Mount Peeley and Sheep Mountain.

From this gap we drop, gently for the most part, into the canyon of Deadman Creek. Near the bottom of this descent the trail passes through a pull gate, then switchbacks downhill a short distance farther to a corral near the canyon bottom. The route now swings left and runs parallel to a fence for 100 yards, after which we turn right, pass through a gate, and ford Deadman Creek (20.0; 3090) to a cairn visible on the far side. Several excellent campsites, shaded by an occasional tall sycamore, can be found in this area. The creek, one of the largest in the Mazatzals, generally flows well into the spring months.

The beginning of the ascent out of Deadman Canyon is quite steep. At the crest of a small, protruding ridge partway up, the trail levels off for awhile, cuts northward across a succession of gullies, then resumes climbing steeply. At length, after passing yet another stock fence, we reach a saddle (21.6; 4460) which overlooks Willow Spring Basin to the north. Rather than dropping down from this gap, as one might hope for after such a steep ascent, the trail turns to the right and switchbacks moderately up a ridgeline. As we gain elevation the view southwestward opens up to include Horseshoe Reservoir, on

Mushrooms

the Verde River beyond the Mazatzal foothills. Presently the trail levels off, then descends to a signed junction (23.7; 4840) with the Willow Spring Trail coming from Sheep Bridge. A few fair campsites are to be found in the area, in a sparse forest of oak and juniper.

Our route turns right at the junction here and proceeds east a short distance to another fork. The trail that branches right leads to nearby Mountain Spring, which flows year-round. The main trail switchbacks some 600 vertical feet up to a saddle, and then follows a series of ridgelines and shallow ravines past a stock fence to the base of Midnight Mesa. After completing a rollercoastering traverse of this mesa's steep eastern face, we drop onto the divide that separates Wet Bottom Creek from Deadman Creek, negotiating a few minor ups and downs before descending a short distance to cross a usually dry tributary of Wet Bottom Creek (27.2; 5210).

A steep, 1000-foot climb now brings us to a high point overlooking Maverick Basin, from where we follow a ridgeline northeastward past several ups and downs. After about a mile the trail veers off this ridge to the left, then proceeds across relatively gentle terrain to a signed junction (30.5; 5860) in The Park, a ponderosa-pine and alligator-juniper-forested basin at the head of Wet Bottom Creek. There are several excellent campsites in this beautiful area, with water available at Pete's Pond in a nearby ravine (in early spring and following rainy periods only).

At the junction in The Park we turn right, and follow the Mazatzal Divide as it switchbacks moderately up onto a ridgetop, then traverses southward to a saddle overlooking the gently sloping headwaters of North Fork Deadman Creek. After dropping slightly across a rocky, sunny hillside, we pass the signed, left-branching spur to Hopi Spring (which flows during rainy periods only). About 1 mile beyond here, a sidetrail (35.1; 6080) branches right a short distance to Horse Camp Seep (usually reliable until late spring).

Continuing south along the Mazatzal Divide Trail, we next descent slightly, then cross a small creeklet just upstream from a steep drop-off. At a junction just across this creekbed we turn left, onto the signed Sandy Saddle Trail, and follow the dwindling watercourse to its head at Sandy Saddle (36.4; 6420). After taking in the rather limited views from this pass we traverse southward a bit, then drop steeply some 700 feet down a brushy ridge. After crossing a minor drainage, the trail climbs a bit before finally descending to the floor of Barnhardt Canyon at Castersen Seep (38.1; 5620). Camping is fair here, with water available in winter and early spring only. For an interesting side trip, scramble downstream about ¾ mile to the upper end of the steep-walled narrows of Barnhardt Canyon.

To complete your long loop trek, follow the trail as it climbs up a ravine, crosses a minor saddle, and then ascends to a signed junction with the Barnhardt Trail (39.0; 5960). Turn left here, and reverse the steps of Trip 78 the remaining 4.2 miles to Barnhardt Trailhead (43.2; 4220), just across the parking area from where the trip began.

TRIP 81
CITY CREEK TRAILHEAD TO FULLER SEEP

▲ **20.2 miles round trip; 4500' elevation gain**
▲ **Strenuous backpack (2-4 hiking days)**
▲ **Trailhead 39, City Creek**
▲ **Maps**
   Mazatzal Wilderness or *North Peak and Cypress Butte quadrangles*
▲ **Season: all year, except after snowstorms**
   Fuller Seep (mile 10.1) has water only during snow meltoff and following rainy periods; water also generally available along unnamed brooks (mile 6.2 to mile 7.0)

Features

This route climbs stiffly up from the lowlands near the East Verde River, past the soaring, heavily timbered ramparts of North Peak, then winds for miles through the pleasant shade of the dense, mature stands of ponderosa pine and alligator juniper which cloak the northern Mazatzal high country. Fuller Seep provides delightful camping, as do a number of other forested nooks along the trail.

The second half of this route is rough, can be difficult to follow, and is recommended only for experienced hikers.

Trailhead Route/Camping

From Payson, drive west on Main Street/East Verde River Road (Forest Road 406). This road is steep in places but is mostly suitable for passenger cars when graded. Call the Payson Ranger District office for current status. About ten miles beyond Payson the road descends steeply as it approaches the trailhead. This short section is so steep that 4-wheel-drive vehicles towing horse trailers sometimes have trouble coming back up when the surface is wet and muddy. This is the section most likely to be hazardous for passenger cars; drivers should stop and walk the section before driving it even when it is dry. At this point there are only a few hundred yards to the trailhead, on the left side of the road. Trailhead parking is about another 50 feet ahead on the right. The small parking area is often filled and not very pleasant for car camping. By driving about a mile beyond the trailhead parking area one reaches a section of the road with a nice selection of car camping areas. The best sites are just before a locked gate, 1.5 miles past the trailhead. Watch for a gate with a broken cattleguard. If it has not been repaired, take the bypass cattle gate to the left. Low-clearance vehicles may have trouble here.

Description

At the signed trailhead on East Verde Road (0.0; 3440), pass through a hikers bypass gate and cross City Creek (which may be dry during the summer months) and follow the trail which is (mostly) well defined. This path slowly diverges from City Creek as it rises toward a ridgecrest, then swings to the right to avoid a wash and climbs more steeply to the ridgecrest. There is much catclaw in this area, as well as a few small shrub oaks.

After following the ridgecrest briefly, the trail goes through a wire gate (1.1, 3920) then veers right to parallel the fence. A few hundred yards after passing a Mazatzal Wilderness boundary sign (1.4, 3920) we ascend moderately uphill to a ridge, whose crest we then parallel to a saddle (2.6; 4540). The approach to the saddle overlooks the East Verde River drainage to the north. Rising from the saddle, we get good views of the City Creek drainage. After twisting up another set of switchbacks, the trail circles around the head of a tiny drainage planted with manzanita, mountain mahogany, and a variety of scrubby oaks. There may be a trickle of water here during rainy periods. After leaving this drainage via a small saddle we resume switchbacking moderately uphill. Many switchbacks later, a thicket of Gambel oaks heralds the end of this long, nearly shadeless climb; just beyond, the trail rounds a high ridge and traverses westward. This section affords an excellent view across Hell's Hole and the deep gash of City Creek to the massive, densely forested crown of 7449-foot North Peak.

Soon we exit the Hell's Hole drainage via an unnamed gap, just beyond which, in a shady forest of tall ponderosa pines and stout alligator junipers, is a signed junction with the right-branching Red Hills Trail (5.5; 6080). Here we turn right, drop slightly to another saddle, then bend left and switchback down into a canyon on the west side of the Mazatzal Divide. Once on the floor of this drainage, the trail follows a creeklet gently downhill to a beautifully forested area where three small streams come together. In early spring and during rainy periods when the creeks run, camping is excellent here.

After crossing the third streamlet, we switchback steeply a short distance up to a minor gap, then climb more moderately along a canyonside to a signed junction (8.3; 6080) atop the flat, ponderosa-pine- and alligator-juniper-crowned mesa known as Knob Mountain. Our route goes left here, striking off southward across the plateau. About 0.4 mile later, where the mesa breaks off sharply, we swing to the right and switchback very steeply some 700 feet down to the floor of a basin. Once on the bottom of this basin we proceed a few hundred yards down its gently sloping floor, cross a creek (one of the tributaries of Wet Bottom Creek; water in early spring and during rainy periods) to its left side, and then meet a sign announcing that we have arrived at Fuller Seep)(10.1; 5280) (the actual seep, with its year-round water, is apparently a few hundred feet downstream, at the confluence of a tributary drainage). Several excellent campsites, shaded by a sparse-to-moderate forest cover of ponderosa pine, pinyon pine and alligator juniper, can be found in this area. Worthwhile side trips can be made up- or downstream. Return the way you came.

Note: According to a Payson Ranger District trail patrol ranger, City Creek Trail now approaches Jones Spring. This change is so new that the current Mazatzal Wilderness map does not show the new route. Looking at the City Creek Trail route on this map, about two thirds of the way from City Creek Trailhead to the Red Hills Trail junction, right where the trail veers left above the 4,400 foot elevation designation, the trail now goes straight to Jones Spring, then veers left to rejoin the old route. Call the Payson Ranger District for the status of this spring.

TRIP 82
CITY CREEK TRAILHEAD TO BARNHARDT TRAILHEAD VIA THE MAZATZAL DIVIDE AND Y BAR BASIN/SHAKE TREE TRAILS

⌃ **27.5 miles one way (30-mile car shuttle required); 4860' elevation gain**

⌃ **Strenuous backpack (3-5 hiking days)**

⌃ **Trailhead 39, City Creek (start)**

⌃ **Trailhead 38, Barnhardt (finish)**

⌃ **Maps**
  Mazatzal Wilderness or *North Peak, Cypress Butte, and Mazatzal Peak quadrangles*

⌃ **Season: March through November**
  Water is available at the Park (near mile 9.0), Horse Camp Seep (near mile 13.6), and Chilson Spring (near mile 16.0). Water can be found in the drainage below Windsor Seep (mile 20.3) during snow meltoff and following rainy periods

Features

Utilizing a lengthy section of the Mazatzal Divide Trail, this fine route parallels the high crest of the northern Mazatzal range, from North Peak to Mazatzal Peak. Except at the trek's beginning and ending, elevations are well above 5000 feet, making this an excellent choice for backpackers seeking a measure of relief from the heat of lowland summers.

Trailhead Route

Start: follow the trailhead route for Trip 81. Finish: follow the trailhead route for Trip 77.

Description

From the City Creek Trailhead (0.0; 3440), follow the Mazatzal Divide Trail to the signed junction with the Red Hills Trail (5.5; 6080) (see Trip 81). Bear left here, and continue along the Mazatzal Divide Trail as it ascends a gently rising ridgecrest to a broad saddle atop Knob Mountain. After dropping steeply back down this hill's southern flank, the trail climbs again for a short distance, then dips into one of the diminutive headwaters of City Creek, which may contain some running water during early spring and following heavy rains. We next climb around a low ridge and enter a beautiful, nicely forested area, known as The Park, at the head of Deadman Creek. Where the signed North Peak Trail branches left, we go straight ahead and continue south a few hundred yards to another junction (9.0; 5860), also signed, where the Willow Spring Trail goes right. There are several excellent campsites in this area, shaded by tall ponderosa pines and some magnificent, thick-trunked specimens of alligator juniper. Water is generally available in a nearby ravine (called Pete's Pond) following rainy periods and on the heels of the spring snowmelt.

At the second junction in The Park we turn left and follow the Mazatzal Divide Trail as it switchbacks moderately up onto a ridgetop, then traverses southward to a saddle overlooking the gently sloping headwaters of North Fork Deadman Creek. (It may strike one as odd that, while traveling southward, one should intercept a creek's north fork *after* crossing its main branch, but such is indeed the case here.) After descending gently across a rocky, sunny area where manzanita and agave temporarily replace the trees, we pass the signed, left-branching spur trail to Hopi Spring (which may be dry during the summer). One mile later, a second spur (13.6; 6080) branches right to Horse Camp Seep (usually reliable until late spring).

Continuing south along the Mazatzal Divide Trail, we next descend slightly, then cross a small creeklet just upstream from a steep dropoff. The signed Sandy Saddle Trail branches left here; this path provides a shortcut for hikers who are in a hurry to get to Barnhardt Trailhead (see Trip 80). Our route goes straight ahead, then winds in and out of two small drainages before climbing a short distance to a saddle (15.5; 5690). About 0.5 mile beyond this gap, a signed trail branches right to Chilson Camp and Chilson Spring. Chilson Camp, in a forest of massive alligator junipers 0.2 miles down this trail, has good campsites and a few ruins. The spring generally flows year round, except possibly during very dry weather spells.

Staying left at the Chilson Camp cutoff, we contour eastward into a minor drainage channel, which we then follow to its head atop the Mazatzal Divide (16.9; 6020), where the Barnhardt Trail branches left at a signed junction. To complete your journey from here, turn right and follow the Mazatzal Divide and Y Bar Basin/Shake Tree trails past Windsor Seep (20.3; 6500) to Barnhardt Trailhead (27.5; 4220) (follow the directions for the second half of Trip 79).

TRIP 83
SHEEP BRIDGE TO DEADMAN CREEK

⌃ **27.8 miles round trip; 5900' elevation gain**
⌃ **Strenuous backpack (4 hiking days)**
⌃ **Trailhead 40, Sheep Bridge**
⌃ **Maps**
   Mazatzal Wilderness or *Chalk Mountain and Table Mountain quadrangles*
⌃ **Season: November through April, except after snowstorms**
   Willow Spring (near mile 7.2) and Mountain Spring (mile 9.8) have water all year; water also generally available at Deadman Creek (mile 13.9) in winter and early spring

Features

Remote Deadman Creek and its many forks reach into the wild heart of the Mazatzal backcountry. The creek's bouldery banks, dotted here and there with tall sycamore trees, afford delightful camping and provide challenging cross-country access to the tens of thousands of acres of pure wilderness country which flank them.

The trails used to reach Deadman Creek are for the most part in poor condition, and this trek is recommended only for experienced wilderness travelers.

Trailhead Route/Camping

From Carefree, drive east along Carefree Road (paved) for 6 miles to a junction. Continue straight ahead about 2 miles farther to a junction just beyond the end of the pavement. Continue straight again, following Forest Road 24 north past Seven Springs and Cave Creek campgrounds to signed Tangle Creek Road (Forest Road 269) (approximately 38 miles from Carefree). (One can also reach this junction from the north, without fish-hooking through Carefree, by taking the I-17 exit for Bloody Basin Road (Forest Road 269) and following it southeast for 27 miles.) Bear east on Tangle Creek Road here (a right turn coming from Carefree, straight for those coming from I-17), and follow it past the remains of Tangle Creek Administrative Site to Sheep Bridge on the Verde River (about 12 miles from the end of Forest Road 24 at Tangle Creek Road). Parts of this route will prove very troublesome for passenger cars. After rains, it may require a 4-wheel-drive vehicle. There are many car-camping opportunities along the route and at the trailhead. Adjacent to Sheep Bridge (foot traffic only) is a hot tub filled with water from a nearby hot spring.

Description

From the trailhead hear the end of Tangle Creek Road (0.0; 2100), walk across Sheep Bridge and follow the well defined trail eastward, around a big boulder, through a grove of mesquite that has the atmosphere of an orchard, across a first small drainage, ignoring a faint spur trail, then across Horse Creek (which generally has a good flow during the winter wet season) to its north bank. Just beyond is the junction of the Verde River and Willow Spring trails—marked with a cairn and posts which used to have signs. Someone has crayoned "trail #223 Willow Spring" for the right fork. Here we bear right and climb gently eastward, through a trail that is somewhat overgrown (no thorns) and rocky at first, toward the Mazatzal foothills. The ground cover hereabouts consists mostly of mesquite and creosotebush, but shortly after crossing a shallow wash we enter a more familiar, Lower-Sonoran-zone plant mix.

Just before passing between two low hillocks we reach a Mazatzal Wilderness boundary sign (2.2; 2430). Beyond here the trail continues eastward, every once in a while swinging within a stone's throw of Horse Creek. Presently we climb gently onto the crest of a low ridge that roughly parallels the watercourse, then drop back to creek level near a solitary, tall cottonwood tree (5.5; 3000). When Horse Creek has water, this spot makes a good first night's camp.

About 0.5 mile beyond here the trail bends left, away from the creek, and sneaks up a ravine to a saddle that affords a good view back across Horseshoe Reservoir and parts of the meandering Verde River. Next we wind moderately uphill, staying just beneath the crest of a ridge, to a second saddle (7.2; 3860), where a signed spur trail branches off to Willow Spring (¾ mile down the side trail to the right; water available year-round). Beyond this junction the trail continues up the ridgeline. After touching another saddle the gradient steepens considerably, and we ascend many switchbacks to a rocky prominence (8.8; 5020) with a sweeping view of the Verde River Valley and the southern Mazatzals. From this point we proceed one mile downhill to the terminus of the Willow Spring Trail near Mountain Spring (9.8; 4840). There are a few fair campsites here, in a sparse forest of one-seed juniper, Utah juniper and shrub live oak. The spring has water all year long.

At a junction here we turn right, onto the Deadman Trail, and climb steeply uphill to the south. Some 600 feet higher the trail tops out, then drops along a ridge to a saddle (12.0; 4460), between Willow Spring Basin and the canyon of Deadman Creek. From here we traverse westward a short distance, then drop steeply past a stock fence. The angle of this descent soon eases, but only for a while; after touching a minor saddle, the track abruptly plunges straight down a ridgeline to the bouldery banks of Deadman Creek (13.9; 3090). There is excellent cool-weather camping here, and for some distance up- and downstream, among mesquite trees and an occasional tall sycamore or cottonwood. The creek generally runs throughout the winter rainy season and well into spring. Hikers with a layover day (or two) may wish to scramble up-canyon and explore the stream's

Teddy-bear cholla on HK Mesa

rugged, cliffbound forks, or continue along the trail to Davenport Wash and Club Cabin (see Trip 80).

Return the way you came.

TRIP 84
SHEEP BRIDGE TO HK MESA, FULLER SEEP, CHILSON CAMP, DAVENPORT WASH, DEADMAN CREEK, AND RETURN

- ▲ **56.2-mile loop trip; 11,200′ elevation gain**
- ▲ **Strenuous backpack (allow at least 6 hiking days)**
- ▲ **Trailhead 40, Sheep Bridge**
- ▲ **Maps**
  Mazatzal Wilderness or *Chalk Mountain, Wet Bottom, Cypress Butte, North Peak, , Mazatzal Peak, and Table Mountain quadrangles*
- ▲ **Season: November to May, except after snowstorms**
  Water available all year at Dutchman Grave Spring (near mile 5.6), Fuller Seep (mile 19.1), Club Spring (near mile 39.0), Mountain Spring (mile 46.7), and Willow Spring (near mile 49.3); in early spring and following rainy periods, water also available at Wet Bottom Creek (mile 16.1), The Park (near mile 23.8), Chilson Spring (near mile 32.3), Deadman Creek (mile 42.6), and other points (see text)

Features

Experienced backpackers looking to stretch their legs and test their skills will want to try this lengthy, challenging loop trip. Good for a week or more of hiking days, this route winds through the shrubs and cacti of the desert lowlands, climbs into the pine- juniper-forested high country, fords icy, rushing creeks (in season), and visits ancient Indian ruins, abandoned mines, and dilapidated cowboy cabins.

Much of this route is obscure and hard to follow; do not attempt it until you have successfully completed easier trips in the Mazatzal. Carry a map and compass, and know how to use them.

Trailhead Route

Follow the trailhead route for Trip 83.

Description

From the trailhead walk across Sheep Bridge and follow the Willow Spring Trail eastward. Follow the directions of Trip 83 to the signed junction marked with a massive cairn. Our route turns left here, in the direction of the post marked "trail #11 for trail #22". Trail #11 is the Verde River Trail, and proceeds a short distance northward to pleasantly forested, appropriately named Sycamore Creek—larger than Horse Creek, and considerably more likely to have flowing water.

After rock-hopping Sycamore Creek we walk uphill a few hundred feet to a signed fork (0.7; 2150), where we turn right, onto the Dutchman Trail. This path now winds uphill, steeply at times, toward the flat top of HK Mesa. This area supports a nice growth of saguaro, foothill paloverde, ocotillo, prickly pear, barrel cactus and teddy bear cholla. Once on top of HK Mesa the trail levels off, and as we catch our breath we can enjoy the fine view of the forested Mazatzal peaks, still far away to the east.

Near the east end of HK Mesa we pass a Mazatzal Wilderness boundary sign, beyond which the trail drops a short distance to a low, broad saddle (3.4; 2570) overlooking a refreshingly green strip of cottonwoods that line Sycamore Creek. This riparian grove offers delightful camping, and is an easy, 0.5 mile cross-country jaunt down from the saddle. Sycamore Creek is perennial in the area of these trees.

Continuing northeast from this gap, the trail crosses a small wash and climbs past a steep, badly eroded section to another, higher saddle. Following the descent of a similarly steep and eroded trail on this saddle's far side, we work across a flat, brushy area to a creekbed, which we cross at a cairn just upstream from the influx of a tributary. There may be running water here until early spring. The trail next parallels the tributary eastward to a surprisingly lush area shaded by cottonwoods, sycamores and some large mesquites and shrub live oaks—good camping. Just beyond here, at an unsigned junction(5.6; 2900) marked with a cairn, the Dutchman Grave Trail branches right and passes Dutchman Grave Spring (water available year-round) a short distance away.

From this fork the Red Hills Trail swings north and then undulates over a pair of low gaps. The section immediately beyond the second of these saddles is potentially confusing; follow the very faint, poorly ducked track as it heads across a small creekbed, climbs past an unsigned, left-branching spur trail, then drops slightly and veers northward to a small grove of cottonwoods and sycamores near the ruins of an old prospector's camp. The way soon grows clearer, and we ascend steadily up the right-hand wall of a spacious drainage to a saddle. Here the trail contours to the right, into a small canyon, and climbs very steeply past some good views across the Verde River Valley to Horseshoe Reservoir and portions of the Verde River to the top of an ugly pile of mine tailing visible from below (8.2; 3900). Copper ore was apparently taken from this mine, which is now abandoned. Be very careful if you explore any of the horizontal mineshafts from which the tailings emerge; they may contain hidden vertical drop-offs.

A short, steep climb from this mine brings us to a saddle; here we swing to the right and ascend a rocky ridgeline to an unnamed mesa. A slight rise on this plateau affords a magnificent vista across the Mazatzal midlands to the high, forested peaks to the south and east. The trail peters out temporarily as it proceeds southeastward, and we must rely on a series of widely spaced ducks and cairns to guide us to some mystifying Indian ruins—crude (but obviously man-made) agglomerations of dark stones, apparently built by people of the ancient Sinagua culture around 1100 AD.

At the mesa's far end the trail reappears, swings left toward the edge of a drainage, and then climbs moderately through a pinyon-pine forest to a saddle (10.7; 4660). After traversing northward 0.5 mile or so we drop into an oak- and pinyon-shaded canyon and pass a good campsite near the confluence of two minor drainages (water available during rainy periods only). The trail now follows the larger of these two creeks upstream, crossing frequently from bank to bank. About 0.6 mile later, after a tributary comes in from the left, we climb abruptly up a ridgeline, pass a stock fence, and then drop gradually back to creek level. After recrossing the drainage bottom in a small basin, the trail meanders uphill through a rocky, potentially confusing area—watch for ducks. This comparatively gentle ascent soon metamorphoses into steep switchbacks, which top out at a high saddle (13.0; 5140) overlooking the rugged canyon of Wet Bottom Creek. Here we turn right and proceed first south, then east, staying on or just below the crest of a broad ridge. Shortly after passing a stock fence the trail descends moderately through a pretty, shady stand of smooth cypress, then drops more steeply down a narrow ridge. This long descent ends at Wet Bottom Creek (16.1; 4440), which generally has water throughout the winter rainy season. A few poor-to-fair tentsites, beneath a scanty riparian growth of sycamore and oak, can be found nearby; much better ones are located about 0.5 mile up- and downstream

After crossing Wet Bottom Creek the trail turns up a side canyon and, after passing a few more fair campsites, climbs along a series of ridges and hillside to a saddle. A gentle, contouring descent then brings us to signed Fuller Seep (19.1; 5280), where there is water all year long, a corral, and excellent camping amid a smattering of alligator junipers and ponderosa pines. From the seep area we walk gently uphill a short distance, then switchback steeply up an ill-defined ridgeline. Some 700 feet higher, the trail abruptly levels off and proceeds northward across pine- and juniper-crowned Knob Mountain. At a signed junction (20.9; 6080) atop this flat mountaintop we turn right, continuing on the Red Hills Trail, and drop gently into a canyon. This descent soon steepens, and a terminal flourish of steep switchbacks lands us in a cozy, forested basin where three streamlets come together. During rainy periods and in early spring, when the creeks are likely to flow, camping is excellent here.

The trail exists this basin via the easternmost of the three streams, whose course we follow to its head at a saddle, then cut right and climb a few switchbacks to the Red Hills Trail's terminus at the signed Mazatzal Divide Trail (23.8; 6080). To continue your loop trip from here, turn right and follow the Mazatzal Divide Trail as far as the signed cutoff to Chilson Camp (32.3; 5660) (see Trip 82). Then turn right and walk gently downhill 0.2 miles to Chilson Camp and Spring, where there is reliable water (except possibly during very dry weather spells) and good camping in a forest of stout alligator junipers. Next, continue downhill from Chilson Camp, cross a minor drainage, and climb a short distance to a signed junction (32.8; 5590) with the Club Trail. Turn right here, then follow the route of Trip 80 to Mountain Spring (46.7; 4840), then turn left onto the Willow Spring Trail. Follow this trail as it descends a bit, climbs westward to a rocky point affording a good view across the Verde River Valley, and then switchbacks steeply down a sparsely vegetated ridgeline to a saddle containing another junction (49.3; 3860). From here, it is three quarters of a mile to Willow Spring via a signed spur trail that branches left. The main trail swings to the right and circles the head of a small basin to a second saddle, where we catch a glimpse of Horseshoe Reservoir shimmering far away on the Verde River.

A short switchbacking descent now brings us to the floor of the shallow canyon drained by Horse Creek. A lone, tall cottonwood tree down by the watercourse is probably the best campsite in this otherwise shadeless area; the creek usually has water until early spring or so. Soon the trail climbs a short distance away from Horse Creek, then follows a low ridgecrest westward for about three quarters of a mile before dropping back down almost to creek level. Here we leave the Mazatzal Mountains behind and descend very gently onto the creosote bush-and palo verde-dotted floor of the Verde River Valley, gaining good views back toward the high country as we pull away from the foothills. Wildflowers are abundant here in the spring-look for bottlebrush, desert mallow, owl clover, golden poppy, verbena, and desert mariposa, among others.

After about a mile, Horse Creek meanders off away from the trail to the south; we continue westward, and in another mile pass a Mazatzal Wilderness boundary sign. (54.3; 2430) between two small hills. About 1.7 miles farther, where Horse Creek returns north from its meanderings, we drop down a short distance toward creekside to a semi-signed junction marked with a large cairn. Here, the Verde River Trail branches right; we stay left-as per directions scribbled on a signless post. In a short distance we come to Sheep Bridge (56.2; 2100).

Appendix

WHERE TO BUY MAPS

Tucson and Phoenix Area Outdoor Equipment and Map Sources:

Arizona Hiking Shack
11649 North Cave Creek Road
Phoenix (602) 944-7723

Audubon Nature Shop
300 East University Blvd.
Tucson (520) 629-0510

Bob's Bargain Barn
2230 North Country Club Rd.
(520) 325-3409

Desert Mountain Sports
2824 East Indian School Road
Phoenix (602) 955-2875

Popular Outfitters
(many Phoenix area locations)

Recreational Equipment, Inc.
12634 North Paradise Village
   Parkway West
Scottsdale (602) 996-5400

Recreational Equipment, Inc.
1405 West Southern Avenue
Tempe (602) 967-5494

Summit Hut
5045 East Speedway Blvd.
Tucson (520) 325-1554

Tucson Map & Flag Center
3239 North 1st Avenue
Tucson (520) 887-4234

University of Arizona
Main Library-Map Room
(520) 621-6441

Wide World of Maps
2626 W. Indian School Road
Phoenix (602) 279-2322
(800) 279-7654

Wide World of Maps
1334 South Country Club Dr.
Mesa (602) 844-1134

Southern Arizona Hiking Club
(over 2,000 members, a monthly
hiking list, and over a dozen
hikes per week)
Tucson (520) 751-4513

Pinetop/Lakeside Area Outdoor Equipment and Map Sources (convenient to Mount Baldy Wilderness):

Mountain Outfitters/
   the Skier's Edge
594 West White Mountain Blvd.
Pinetop (520) 367-6200

Springerville Area Outdoor Equipment and Map Sources (semi-convenient to Blue Range Primitive Area):

Ben Franklin/Western Drugs
106 East Main Street
Springerville (520) 333-4321

To Order Forest Service and USGS Topographic maps:

United States Forest Service
517 Gold Ave. S.W.
Albuquerque, NM 87102
(505) 842-3292

Also, maps are available at ranger station visitor centers.

Index

Your safety is your responsibility

Hiking and camping in the wilderness can be dangerous. Experience and preparation reduce risk, but will never eliminate it. The unique details of your specific situation and the decisions you make at that time will determine the outcome. This book is not a substitute for common sense or sound judgment. If you doubt your ability to negotiate mountain terrain, respond to wild animals, or handle sudden, extreme weather changes, hike only in a group led by a competent guide. The authors and the publisher of this book disclaim liability for any loss or injury incurred by anyone using information in this book.